DATE DUE

DEMCO 38-297

Teaching Troubled Children

A Case Study in Effective Classroom Practice

Teaching Troubled Children

A Case Study in Effective Classroom Practice

Joseph Cambone

TEACHERS
COLLEGE
PRESS

Teachers College, Columbia University
New York and London

Published by Teachers College Press, 1234 Amsterdam Avenue
New York, NY 10027

Library of Congress Cataloging-in-Publication Data

Cambone, Joseph.
    Teaching troubled children : a case study in effective classroom practice / Joseph
Cambone.
    p.   cm.
    Includes bibliographical references and index.
    ISBN 0-8077-3304-0.—ISBN 0-8077-3302 (pbk.)
    1. Problem children—Education—United States—Case studies.   2. Socially handicapped
children—Education—United States—Case studies.   3. Teachers of problem children—
United States—Case studies.   4. Teachers of socially handicapped children—United
States—Case studies.   5. Classroom management—United States—Case studies.
    I. Title.
LC4802.C36   1994
371.93—dc20   93-33594

ISBN 0-8077-3304-0
ISBN 0-8077-3303-2 (pbk.)

Printed on acid-free paper

Manufactured in the United States of America

98 97 96 95 94   8 7 6 5 4 3 2 1

CONTENTS

FOREWORD

Teaching Troubled Children addresses the central educational crisis in America today. Are we really willing to educate all of our children? Are we ready to make the investment in human and material resources that will ensure that all children will be successful in school? Too many children are at risk for failure in America's educational system. As we examine the groups of children at risk—children of color, children requiring special services, troubled and troubling children, poor children, children placed in the low "track," homeless children, children whose first language is not English—we realize that children so categorized are becoming the majority. The dominant approaches to teaching these sometimes overlapping groups has been to isolate them (formally or informally), simplify their curriculum, and lower expectations for their academic success. These approaches have not served the children or our democracy.

This book describes a teacher and an educational institution that seek a better way for educating even the most troubling children; that is, those whom the public schools have determined they cannot educate. The staff at "Brighton" share a commitment to restoring these children to normal lives. Attention to the strengths, needs, and interests of the "whole child" and high academic expectations are essential components of the culture. They have created a web of services and support that sustain the children, families, and staff. To a great extent, as we learn in this book, the children gain grade-level academic skills, insight into their emotional struggles, skills in working with others, and control over their troubling behaviors.

The focus of the book is "Anne," teacher of the five youngest children in the school. The author develops a portrait of Anne's students and her pedagogy based on monthly videotaped observations of the class. He transforms observation into analysis by discussing these tapes with her, interviewing her about her goals and reactions, and adding to her "voice" his own assessment of themes and patterns. Dr. Cambone's hope is to share with us what he has learned about how a fine teacher thinks. The emphasis is on revealing the teacher as an intellect. That is, the author seeks to reconstruct for us how Anne diagnoses and evaluates what is happening with the children in the classroom. He carefully explains how this evaluation leads to the evolution of a curriculum, instructional strategies, and a learning community that are at once responsive to the needs and strengths of the children and cognizant of the steps that are required for them to succeed as students.

As the chapters unfold, we become increasingly aware of the number of variables that Anne considers in making moment-by-moment decisions in the classroom: her knowledge of the subject matter of early childhood education and psychological and sociological theory; her understanding of how children learn to read and understand mathematical principles; her ability to assess and respond to the "tone" of the class; her knowledge of how to structure the day and her own interventions to support safety and "groupishness"; her insight into the individual strengths and struggles of the children and of how they are transformed by the dynamics of the group; her recognition of her own goals, biases, strengths, and needs; and her patience and belief that over time, the combination of dedicated teaching and student strengths will lead to healing and academic success.

The emphasis on teacher as intellect is not incidental but deliberate and corrective. The pervasive underestimation of the skills required to become and remain a fine teacher, so common in American culture, is directly challenged by this portrait. For those who are learning to "think like a teacher" and those teachers who have shared Anne's dedication over many years, this analysis should be revealing, stimulating, and confirming. The possibility that fine teaching in the context of institutional support can sustain such growth in these children, and that these successes are and have been multiplied with other children and other teachers at "Brighton," is profoundly hopeful.

In his analysis, Dr. Cambone rejects the particular kind of behaviorist approach to teaching troubled and troubling children which he considers to have dominated the field of special education. He believes that the characteristic emphases on control and management of behavior, correcting deficits, and isolating children from their peers has proven to be ineffective in teaching children to think critically, develop socially and emotionally, and achieve academic success. He asks instead for the creation of a common understanding among teachers of regular and special education that merges psychological, philosophical, and sociological knowledge with developmentally appropriate and rigorous academic curricula and pedagogy.

Cambone's observations should help enliven the debate about the utility of our theoretical models in helping us teach the most troubled children. What we need is a model that will help us to analyze individual children's potential paths to academic success, regardless of the starting point. We need a model that supports teachers in their efforts to teach all the children. The words are simple, but the challenge is not, as this portrait of five children's paths to learning amply demonstrates. Dr. Cambone's book is an important starting point for helping educators review and rethink the foundations of our practice.

Susan McAllister Swap

PREFACE

"You must be a very special person to work with those kinds of children." I have heard this comment often throughout my teaching career, and many of my colleagues have said they've been told the same thing. I suppose people have had good intentions when they've said it. Yet, when I was a young teacher of emotionally disturbed students the comment invariably caused me to bristle, coming as it usually did in response to my talk about a particularly interesting or difficult child, lesson, or incident. I remember resenting what I felt were the implications of the comment, especially when I considered the safe distance the comment put between the speaker on one side and me and the children I taught on the other: "Those kinds of children" were clearly not the kind of children the speaker had experience with, or cared to learn more about. They were troubled and sick, placed away from the other kids, beyond the scope of the regular schools and teachers; moreover, they were outside the realm of the person's comprehension, and it seemed to my young idealistic mind that most people were glad of that fact. As for me and my colleagues, we were "special kinds of persons" not like the rest of the persons who were mostly regular folks doing regular work. Our work was outside of regular understanding as well; at best it was complex and incomprehensible, and at worst it was merely idealistic and futile.

Over my 15 years of work with troubled children and their teachers, I have come to understand that the children and their lives are, indeed, hard to comprehend. My young teacher's belief that I could heal the psychically wounded has given way to humility at the thought of the task of teaching anything at all to these children. I have learned that even for those of us who have worked with the children every day, it is often difficult to take into our minds the stories of their lives, tragic and frightening, and find some way to help them. The children I have known, and whose lives I have tried to understand, walk through my memory: There was streetwise Teria, who ran away from the group care facility and returned 3 weeks later covered with cigarette burns on her inner thighs and mumbling about the men who "did nasty things"; there was lumbering, frightened Yvette, who had a white discharge that turned out to be from a tube of toothpaste some other girls had shoved into her vagina because she flirted with another girl's boyfriend. It had lodged there, and she had been afraid to tell what happened for fear of reprisal; there was devilishly handsome José, "Prez" of the Young Skulls, who at 14 had already killed another boy; and there was Eric, nervous and hyper-verbal, who set his mother's bed afire while she slept with the newest of her many boy-friends; there was brilliant Steven, who whenever he was asked to learn a new concept in math class would fall to the floor like a rag doll and stare into space, refusing to move or to talk, sometimes for an hour or more; there was Jason, born in prison, who at age 5 had already been in nine foster homes and was so violent and wild that no family would have him for any amount of money. Sadly, there have been hundreds more children who have touched my life alone; I can only guess how many more there are that I have never met, with difficulties that I could not easily comprehend.

These days, I find it mostly understandable why some people might say that it takes a special kind of person to work with these kinds of children. In fact, I have made it my goal to understand exactly *what* is special about the kinds of teachers who can work with these children; for there are teachers who can take in the stories of troubled children, make some sense of those children, and find ways to teach them. Most of us have met or heard of at least one such teacher. I have met some of those teachers, and they are indeed special—not in any romanticized way in which they work miracles and reverse the course of tragic lives. But they are special in their ability to perceive a means for teaching in the midst of the emotional, behavioral, intellectual, and sociological miasma that surrounds troubled children. They are special mostly because they are able to do the daily work—work that is difficult in the ex-treme and unquestionably unromantic. They are able to make small changes in the lives of children when no one else could; they are teachers who con-tinue to come to work every day and do what must be done.

It isn't surprising that their work is not often discussed in the research literature or reflected in the policy decisions that are made regarding the edu-cation of troubled children. Perhaps this is because the lives of these children and the work of their teachers are simply too hard to look at without feeling hopeless; perhaps the careful study of the classroom lives of troubled children is so complex that it quickly exhausts the research methods we currently use; or maybe what we find too easily confounds our theoretical explanations; per-haps the phenomena are simply too resistive to treatment and change. What-ever the reason, there is little careful examination of the work of teachers in classes for disturbed children.

I think it is important that we turn our gaze to the work of these teachers and try to penetrate its meaning. They are teaching at one place where the fabric of our collective life is torn. And where the fabric of our life tears, the many threads that compose it are most evident. Examining those threads and carefully tracing them back into the weave of our lives may help us to understand the whole; examining the threads, we may even find a way to mend the tear.

In what follows, the names of the children, teachers, and the school itself are all pseudonyms because I have promised these people complete anonymity in telling their story.

ACKNOWLEDGMENTS

I am indebted to my many teachers who, with good cheer and infinite patience, have shepherded me and my work along the long road from idea to book: Catherine Krupnick shared her remarkable insights and her methods for analyzing videotaped data, and Barbara Neufeld made clear to me exactly what the quality was in qualitative data analysis. Courtney Cazden challenged me to write a narrative that was also an analysis. And Sara Lawrence Lightfoot listened to me and helped me find my voice, for which I am truly thankful.

I am indebted to "Anne," who has been my teacher, as well. She willingly invited me into her classroom so that I might learn about her profoundly important work. I am grateful for the unharried hours of interviews she gave to this project over the years, cheerfully adding more work in her already overburdened day.

I thank Tom Latus, Rick Small, and Ken Kunin for their assistance and encouragement with the book. I thank them especially for having taught me so much about troubled children, and the power that good teaching and schools can have in changing the course of their lives.

Pam Rollins has my deepest gratitude for her careful, repeated reading of the manuscript, and for each insightful question, encouraging comment, and patient redirection. I could not have finished without her.

I thank Kathy Brown and Tom Cambone for the late night and Sunday morning calls that kept me focused and helped me to laugh; and I'm thankful for Steve O'Donnell and his unflagging patience with my continual whining. Thanks to Trudy Paradis for staying with me for as long as I needed her, and to the "Circle" of friends who are also my family.

Thank you to my teaching team, Ellen Davidson and Joan May Cordova, for overlooking my faults and forgetfulness as I worked to complete this book.

To Jim Haungs, I owe thanks too numerous to list, but which are profoundly felt, nevertheless.

Finally, I thank my mother and father, Kathryn and Antonio, whose commitment to social justice has continually shaped my mind and heart, and who have always believed that being a teacher was a gift from God. I dedicate this book to you.

CHAPTER 1

TEACHING TROUBLED CHILDREN

There are, and have long been, troubled and troubling children in our public schools who consistently challenge our ability to teach them. They are the children who, with the institution of compulsory education 100 years ago, earned the labels Backward, Incorrigibles, Discipline Problems. They are the ones who, as the century progressed and understanding improved somewhat, were labeled Emotionally Disturbed, or ED for short; others called them BD, Behaviorally Disordered. They are complex children who are hard to describe using a single label or description.

Since 1975, federal government regulations have referred to them as SED, or Seriously Emotionally Disturbed; but in educational regulations in the 50 states, 20 different variations in labels remain for these children. Teachers, parents, doctors, policy makers, and legislators have for years found it troublesome to find an adequate descriptor for these children, largely because the labels people use imply both a specific type of behavior and a specific cause for that behavior. But behaviors vary among the children, and there are very few causes that one can point to with certainty.

The problems we have finding labels reflects the persistent and troubling paradigmatic differences among those who live, teach, and learn with these students: Serious Emotional Disturbance (SED), the term used in the Education for All Handicapped Act (EHA) (1975) definition,[1] is widely regarded in the research literature as vague to professional educators who must deal objectively with behaviors and not emotions (Hewett & Taylor, 1980; White,

---

1. The definition reads, "The term means a condition exhibiting one or more of the following characteristics over a long period of time and to a marked degree, which adversely affects educational performance: (1) An inability to learn which cannot be explained by intellectual, sensory, or health factors; (2) An inability to build or maintain satisfactory relationships with peers and teachers; (3) Inappropriate types of behavior or feelings under normal circumstances; (4) A general pervasive mood of unhappiness or depression; or (5) A tendency to develop physical symptoms or fears associated with personal or school problems. This term includes children who are schizophrenic. The term does not include children who are socially maladjusted, unless it is determined that they are seriously emotionally disturbed" (Federal Register, 1977, Vol. 42, No. 163, August 23, 1977, p. 42478).

1

Beattie, & Rose, 1985). Most critics of the SED label advocate the use of Behaviorally Disordered to describe these children, maintaining it is behavior, and not emotions, about which teachers can do something (White et al., 1985). Still, Emotionally Disturbed remains the commonly used term and acronym among many practitioners. The labels we use appear to depend on our theoretical orientation regarding the etiology of the difficulties. In fact, we know surprisingly little about the source of the children's behavior and even less about the most effective ways to teach them.

These paradigmatic differences within the field regarding the nature of nonconforming behavior—and the public school response to it—have led, in part, to a third label for this population. *Troubled or troubling* is associated with writers such as Hobbs (1975), Apter (1984), and Kugelmass (1987), who state that neither label, ED or BD, is appropriate for this population. Such labels serve only to focus attention on the child alone and deflect attention from the complicated, often troubled, ecology of the home, school, and community of which the student is a part. In these authors' formulations of the problems of troubled youngsters, a child's behavior cannot be separated from the meaning others place on that behavior in the child's context. Kugelmass (1987) argues that BD is no more a "scientific" or objective label than ED is, as some claim, and that "a good deal of subjective judgment is used in deciding which behaviors are disordered and which are appropriate. It is not the behavior, but rather the meaning attached to it by a particular teacher, that determines whether or not it will be targeted for modification" (p. 11). Troubled and troubling are the labels that I have chosen to use in this book, because they reflect the complexities these children experience in life, as well as the complexities they engender for us at every level of our relationship with them.

Who, then, are these children? Descriptions of their troubles help to bring them into clearer focus. During the elementary years, boys are more prevalent than girls in classes for SED children (Morse, Cutler, & Fink, 1964). Mastropieri, Jenkins, and Scruggs (1985) reviewed the research on the academic and intellectual functioning of students they refer to as Behaviorally Disordered. They found that these students score, on average, in the low-average range on tests of intelligence, with Performance scores usually exceeding Verbal scores. Although these scores would predict near-average school performance, students score consistently lower than expected on tests of academic achievement. Emotions and behaviors attendant to the testing situation, such as anxiety reactions of withdrawal or outbursts of anger, often mitigate results. Reports of classroom performance for these students are varied, but students in public settings often exhibit equal difficulties in reading, arithmetic, and writing.

Students placed in classes for SED students exhibit many and disparate observable behaviors, making it difficult to use valid group descriptors beyond those just cited. Students who are perceived by teachers and school personnel as aggressive or who frighten teachers in some way are most likely to be identified as disturbed (Hewett & Taylor, 1980). The distinction between aggressive behavior and frightening behavior is important: Aggressive behaviors include the range of minor to major verbal and physical threats or actions against adults or other children, or destruction of property. But adults are often frightened by behavior they consider abnormal, bizarre, or incomprehensible. Consider these three examples. Latus (1988) describes one boy who had just begun a program in a public school after a 3-year stay in residential treatment. To the horror of his teacher, he licked and got his tongue stuck to a metal pole on an extremely cold day. He claimed he did it out of curiosity; an alternative explanation is his high level of stress at trying to succeed in public school and to manage the increasing violence of his father at home.

Kugelmass (1987) relates the story of a child psychotherapist who attempted to engage a young African-American client in play therapy. The therapist began to doubt both her effectiveness and the psychological health of the young boy, after he spent weeks sitting in stony silence, with his feet up on the desk staring at her. It was then that the child announced that he was playing "the White Man." It is deeply troubling that race plays a significant role in who is labeled ED or BD and that a disproportionate number of minority males are labeled and separated from the public schools because adults are frightened by their behavior, which is deemed disordered (Kugelmass, 1987; Lytle, 1988/1992; Office of Civil Rights, 1986; Sigmon, 1987).

In a third story, taken from my own records, quiet, handsome, well-behaved, 12-year-old Roy attempted suicide by overdosing on his mother's tranquilizers. After his year-long hospitalization, his teachers and principal were still shocked and upset and insisted that his suburban school district pay for a subsequent year in residential treatment. They worried that Roy's incomprehensible, self-destructive behavior would recur.

On closer inspection, each child's troubled and troubling behavior had probable external causes or antecedents. Yet adults' frightened or confused responses to the behavior figured heavily in how the behavior was labeled. However, certainly not all identified children's problems stem from social or other external causes, nor do the labels they are given depend exclusively on the responses of adults. Children with clear clinical syndromes are prevalent in this population, as well. For instance, Sam was a 10-year-old boy diagnosed as schizophrenic. His paranoia was pervasive: Frightened of animals, of driving in a car with another person, of any possible danger, Sam would repeatedly ask about safety, never reassured by the answers he received. In stressful times, Sam would disrobe and run from the school building, hallucinate, or become aggressive. Although many of his behaviors emanated from psychic disturbances and were not necessarily in response to the stimuli in his current environment, Sam eventually confided to a trusted adult and then testified in court that he had been repeatedly sexually abused by a former psychiatric hospital attendant. Though he remained in need of constant supervision and psychiatric attention, to those who worked with him much of his external behavior seemed more comprehensible.

Some students in this population have problems in school due, at least in part, to changing demands in the school setting. Seven-year-old Wayne had an IQ of 130 and was, by all accounts, charming. Placed in foster care as an infant and eventually freed for adoption, Wayne exhibited some behaviors associated with fetal alcohol syndrome, hyperactivity and short-term memory problems being the most prevalent. In times of significant stress, he could have long and trying tantrums. Throughout kindergarten and first grade he did well in school, although the adults in his life attributed much of his success to his strict, nurturing, and understanding teachers. In general, adults described him as "a handful," yet his occasional tantrums were predictable and mostly manageable. But by December of second grade, Wayne had been placed in a substantially separate program for disturbed children, his current teacher complaining that he was inappropriately placed in her class and in public school. Wayne perceived this as a major failure and began a long slide into troubling behaviors, which increased until his running from class, swearing and refusing to follow directions, and poor academic performance caused school officials to place him in residential treatment. There, he eventually performed above grade level academically, was adopted, and experienced a difficult reintegration to public schools. He was moved from teacher to teacher, until his parents eventually located one who was willing to manage him in her third-grade class, where he did reasonably well.

As these brief descriptions demonstrate, the children who seem to end up labeled ED or BD can display widely varying behaviors, and come from equally varying circumstances. Thoughtful professionals consider the *type, severity, and duration* of behaviors before labeling a child as disturbed, disordered, or troubled—and they weigh their own cultural, racial, class, and personal biases in relation to the child. But the fact remains that the tolerance threshold of individual adults and the local standards of behavior with which the child must contend play important roles in how children are labeled.

Teaching these children is what this book is about. They are difficult to understand and difficult to teach. They remain a puzzle for many teachers, and because so often they are separated from their mainstream peers and kept at the periphery of public education, they are often overlooked when we seek to improve the quality of public education. They are indeed troubled and troubling.

A GAP IN THE LITERATURE

Although the research literature provides numerous descriptions of individual student cases like those mentioned above, it lacks thorough descriptions of actual classroom practices used to educate them. This is true despite the fact that, although they are at the periphery of public education, they form a substantial portion of the school population. Fifteen years after EHA was passed in 1975, approximately 400,000 students, or 1%, of the school age population of the United States attended classes especially designated for SED students (OSERS, 1979, 1988). But many experts claim that emotionally disturbed students are grossly underidentified (Braaten, Kauffman, Braaten, Polsgrove, & Nelson, 1988; Morse, 1985). They estimate between 3 and 5% of the school population are in need of special services due to troubled or troubling behaviors (Viadero, 1990). Of those children who are labeled, an estimated 90% are educated apart from their cohorts for at least part of the day, and 50% are completely segregated, despite the EHA mandate to educate students in the Least Restrictive Environment (LRE) (Singer, Butler, Palfrey, & Walker, 1986). Further, these students can expect to be separated for more years than all other special education students (Walker, Singer, Palfrey, Orza, Wenger, & Butler, 1988), and recent studies show that these students are failing academically and are dropping out of school, or being expelled, at disproportionately high rates (Knitzer, Steinberg, & Fleisch, 1990). Thus, many troubled students can expect prolonged attendance—and eventual failure—in segregated classrooms. Yet, there exists scant documentation or analysis in the research literature of what transpires in those classrooms, making it hard to unravel what is contributing to student failure.

Until now, the research literature on educating emotionally disturbed students has fallen into two related categories: First, researchers and policy makers have given high priority to the behaviors students should be taught to facilitate their success in regular classrooms. Using applied behavioral theory, they have devoted massive attention to developing and investigating curricula and techniques that predict, control, and modify students' troubling behaviors (Avery, 1985; Edwards & O'Toole, 1985; Knitzer, Steinberg, & Fleisch, 1990; Petty, 1989). Second, because Special Education is an entitlement program, researchers have given priority to the organization of special education services. The literature is replete with proposals, evaluations, and counterproposals regarding optimum design, delivery, and effectiveness of service models (Braaten et al., 1988; Fuchs & Fuchs, 1988; Gartner & Lipsky, 1987; McCauley, 1984; Stainback & Stainback, 1984; Wang & Walberg, 1988; Will, 1986). Although these two issues dominate the literature, they have been discussed in the absence of descriptive, integrative data exploring curric-

ulum and pedagogy as they are actually practiced in classes for emotionally
disturbed students. Indeed, the existing literature is either theoretical or focused on quantitative studies of controlled interventions. Consequently, we
can only infer much of what we know about actual teaching and learning in
classrooms for emotionally disturbed students.

The Literature of Control and Conformity

If we consult the first category of research, that is, the literature on teaching these students, we can infer that academic learning plays a secondary role
in emotionally disturbed classes. The literature is devoted almost entirely to
teaching behavioral control and conformity. Fifty percent of all articles published since 1984 in the four journals of the Council for Children with Behavioral Disorders (CCBD) propose, describe, or measure the effects of curricula
in social competency and behavioral control. Only 10% of all articles had any
discussion of academic or intellectual pursuits, and that was usually minimal
(Cambone, 1990). After an extensive search of the literature for experimental
studies addressing the improvement of academic skills in behaviorally disordered, public school students, Ruhl and Berlinghoff (1992) found only 10
articles published between 1976 and June 1990. The literature used in
teacher preparation is equally skewed: Maddux and Candler (1986) reviewed
textbooks for training teachers of troubled children and found less than half
the textbooks had a single chapter on academic curriculum and pedagogy.
Approximately one-third mentioned academic pursuits briefly, and nearly a
quarter made no mention of them at all. Gable, Hendrickson, and Young
(1985) point out that teacher preparation programs for teachers of troubled
children emphasize coursework in behavior management, while programs
preparing teachers for classrooms for learning disabled students emphasize
academics. In their extensive study of the policies and programs designed for
troubled students, Knitzer, Steinberg, and Fleisch (1990) conclude that applied behavioral systems have actually become the entire curriculum in these
classes, and virtually no innovative practices exist within this "curriculum of
control."

Given this pervasive emphasis on behavioral control, it is not surprising
that the very few academic curricula that do exist also place heavy emphasis on
the management and control of behavior. In most of these curricula, learning
deficiency criteria are clearly delineated, scope and sequences are rigidly out-
lined, and teaching approaches are heavily scripted (see D'Alonzo, 1983;
Hewett & Taylor, 1980; Mastropieri & Scruggs, 1987; Stephens, 1977;
Wang, 1980). The expressed purpose of these, and all behaviorist curricula,
is to remediate the perceived social and academic skill deficits that prevent

students from participating in the mainstream. The proponents of these curricula have long maintained that only after classrooms are brought under control can students' academic and intellectual needs be addressed. However, I have found no comprehensive descriptive studies of teachers using these curricula that corroborate this assertion.

Recently, these long-standing behaviorist practices have come under scrutiny, and critics are calling for new and different conceptualizations for educating emotionally disturbed students that incorporate or emphasize intellectual development. Heshusius (1984, 1986a, 1986b, 1988) rejects behavioristic approaches entirely and argues that schooling based on strict adherence to social learning principles unnecessarily reduces learning to facts and rules. She argues that teaching with rigidly sequenced task analyses atomizes learning and prevents children from building the intellectual tools they need to construct and understand whole ideas. Other critics, though not rejecting behaviorist notions completely, echo this serious concern when they question whether students will be able to learn higher order thinking skills when learning is purposely kept at lower cognitive levels (Bickel & Bickel, 1986; Morsink, Soar, Soar, & Thomas, 1986). In a related argument, Knitzer and colleagues (1990) argue that behaviorist curricula place inordinate emphasis on controlling emotionally disturbed student behavior, and not enough on teaching them to manage themselves.

Compelling arguments against purely behavioral methods are offered by teachers who use constructivist curricula and pedagogy with emotionally disturbed children. Constructivist teaching is developmental in nature and grounded in the work of such developmental theorists as Vygotsky (1978) and Piaget (1966), and curriculum theorists as Bruner (1960, 1961) and Duckworth (1987). Different from behaviorist methods that are designed to remediate perceived deficiencies in the student, constructivist methods emphasize the knowledge with which children come to school, regardless of their emotional or behavioral disabilities. Constructivist teachers seek to build new knowledge using the learner's previous knowledge and skills. Teachers encourage students to initiate activities of interest to them, and emphasize student strengths instead of deficiencies.

For instance, using a constructivist approach, Latus (1988) describes troubled students initiating their own science laboratory projects and successfully carrying them out with teacher guidance; Marr (1982) describes grade school nonreaders who learn to read through stories taken from their own language using the Language Experience Approach (Ashton-Warner, 1963); Cutler and Stone (1988) relate that primary students in a class for emotionally disturbed students learned to write using Process Writing methods (Graves, 1985). Some of these accounts are descriptive, notably Latus's (1988) description of science education with a schizophrenic boy. All of them suggest alternatives to behaviorist methods of teaching and learning. I refer to these curricula as examples of a Constructivist Teaching Model, and the previously mentioned behaviorist curricula as a Behavioral Teaching Model (Cambone, 1990). Comprehensive analysis and comparison of these models raise numerous questions about what constitutes effective curriculum or pedagogy with emotionally disturbed children, as well as the role teachers and students might play in classrooms for emotionally disturbed students. However, without deeper descriptions of what is done, and how it is done in both behaviorist-oriented and constructivist-oriented classrooms, any and all questions about teaching and learning with troubled children remain abstract and hypotheses about effectiveness are merely speculative.

The Literature on Service Delivery

The second category of research literature in special education encompasses studies and critiques of the design and effectiveness of service delivery models. Throughout the 1980s and early 1990s, the entire special education service delivery system has been subjected to major criticism, most notably regarding the provision of EHA that requires all students to be educated in the LRE. Researchers and policy makers had expected positive outcomes for EHA in the form of increased mainstreaming of students. However, reintegration of students into regular classes is actually infrequent, so much so that the federal government does not keep statistics (Gartner & Lipsky, 1987). In fact, the number of students being educated in special classes almost doubled between 1977 (6%) and 1987 (11%). Although many claim that this growth is indicative of a greater commitment to serve students with special needs (Braaten et al., 1988; Singer & Butler, 1987), others insist this burgeoning, segregated population is mislabeled (Shepard, 1987), that it is stigmatized by being unnecessarily denied access to "regular" students (Stainback & Stainback, 1984), and that emotionally disturbed students do not need methods, materials, or instructional groupings that are any different from those provided to other children (Ysseldyke, 1987a, 1987b, 1987c). Furthermore, they claim, special educators are unable to point to demonstrable success for the $20 billion spent annually (OSERS, 1988). Critics have joined in what is referred to as the General Education Initiative (GEI). They are calling for Special Education services to be dismantled and for all children to be educated in regular classrooms (see Davis & McCaul, 1989, for summaries of various critiques).

Because they are without descriptive data on which to draw, advocates for emotionally disturbed children find it difficult to untangle the particular needs of these troubled children from the sweeping criticisms and claims of the GEI. They have been forced to acknowledge the inadequacies of current special education, while at the same time they have argued that calls for radical reform gloss over important issues and that a unitary educational system cannot meet the needs of many emotionally disturbed students. There are four main arguments in their rebuttals. First, advocates for emotionally disturbed students argue that the growing numbers of students in emotionally disturbed classes, and subsequent expansion of services, are justified: Various studies suggest only 10 to 30% of students in need are being identified (Viadero, 1990) and mental health services have been and continue to be inadequate for the numbers already in emotionally disturbed classes (Knitzer, 1982; Knitzer et al., 1990). Second, advocates have pointed out that students are often labeled by peers and teachers as a result of their behavioral differences long before they are stigmatized by any placement in special education services (Cole, Dodge, & Kupersmidt, 1989). Third, contrary to those who claim that special education students do not require special methods and materials, advocates argue that emotionally disturbed students, by definition, present unique learning problems. EHA describes emotionally disturbed students as those who show "an inability to learn which cannot be explained by intellectual, sensory, or health factors" (Federal Register, Vol. 42, No. 163, August 23, 1977, p. 42478). Thus, very special methods and materials are needed and used to make instruction effective (Braaten et al., 1988; Gable, Hendrickson, & Young, 1985; Gable, McConnell, & Nelson, 1985). Fourth, advocates argue that because emotionally disturbed children are unpredictable, confused and confusing in their behavior, and sometimes abusive or assaultive, teachers need to develop and maintain very particular attitudes and tolerances to teach them (Braaten et al., 1988). These students challenge teachers with the unique problem of balancing the teaching of social, emotional, and behavioral goals with teaching academic goals. Currently, teachers in "regular" classrooms are not required to manage this challenge and indeed prefer not to have the responsibility of doing so (Johnson, A., 1987; Latus, 1989). Missing from these rebuttal arguments are data drawn from microanalyses of actual classroom practice, data that might prove compelling for the maintenance of special education classrooms for emotionally disturbed children.

The Need to Investigate Teaching

It is clear from this discussion that the current literature presents two different macroanalyses and related discussions for improving the special education of these children. One macroanalysis is aimed at altering the service

delivery structure; the second is aimed at altering the curriculum and pedagogy used in emotionally disturbed classrooms. However, neither offers discussions of actual classrooms, and the absence of such micro-level data on
emotionally disturbed classroom teaching and learning leaves discussions of
service delivery, curriculum, and pedagogy impoverished. As a result of this
gap, we are left to rely only on macro-level conceptualizations—and we can
only infer what we believe to be true about the most effective practices in
classrooms for emotionally disturbed students.

The study reported here is an effort to move away from such macro-level
discussions prevalent in the research literature toward a deeply descriptive
analysis of what transpired in these classrooms. Doubtless there are changes
needed in the education of emotionally disturbed children. However, this
study was based on the rationale that ideological discussion of behaviorist
curricula versus constructivist curricula, or dismantling versus protecting current special education service delivery, are uninformed, even moot, without
knowledge of what is actually occurring among real teachers and emotionally
disturbed students. Emotionally disturbed children are educated by teachers,
and policy changes generated by researchers and policy makers ought to reflect the grounded knowledge of teachers and teaching. To do otherwise is
folly. There is ample evidence that change in schools, whether it is curricular,
pedagogical, or systemic, hinges on the ability and willingness of teachers to
implement it (Cohen, 1988; Peterson, 1988; Sarason, 1971). Therefore,
changes, especially of the type suggested in the GEI, in the education of
troubled students will succeed only if teachers think the proposed changes
reflect the difficulties and successes of their practice. Given the paucity of
knowledge that is available on effective teaching and learning with troubled
children in separate programs, there is scant help to offer teachers in mainstream programs who might have to begin educating troubled and troubling
children—should initiators of the GEI succeed in unifying the educational
system.

To inform the far-reaching decisions of policy makers, it is important to
turn to the work of expert teachers. Experience tells us that there are individual teachers or groups of teachers who have found effective ways to educate
these children; those of us who work in schools know, or know of, teachers
who can somehow "get" to these children, keep them in class *and* teach them
to read, write, and do mathematics despite their behavioral and social difficulties. They are the people who have been able to integrate their own knowledge of teaching and pedagogy with their knowledge of the psychological,
sociological, and philosophical foundations of teaching disturbed children
(Paul, 1985).

However, judging by the research literature, it is clear that those teachers
have not yet communicated their knowledge to the larger field of education.

Such neglect may be, at least in part, an artifact of what the research community has chosen to study; it may also be a result of the fact that most teachers have barely time enough to teach, and even less time to write about teaching. Whatever the cause for neglect, the time has come to penetrate the thinking of exceptional teachers and to uncover the ways of thinking that guide their effective actions.

A STUDY OF CLASSROOM PRACTICE

I undertook this study to give a voice to one such teacher and to provide a deep description and analysis of her classroom practices with one group of emotionally disturbed children. I concerned myself with the work and the thinking of "Anne," a teacher of troubled children who is regarded as an effective, even exceptional, teacher by her teacher-colleagues, the administrators of her school, and the parents of her students. I selected Anne and her classroom for study because of her acknowledged effectiveness, hypothesizing that careful, continual attention to such teachers could uncover dimensions of teaching practice that would inform the impoverished discussions of special education policy and objectives; more specifically, I hypothesized that the accrual of such case studies would reveal teaching practices that coalesce into what could be considered a "best practice" model for teaching troubled and troubling children. For these reasons, I chose to focus my investigation squarely on what was effective in Anne's practice, and why.

Anne teaches the youngest children at "Brighton," a residential treatment center for emotionally disturbed and learning disabled boys located in a suburban Massachusetts community. In the fall of 1988, she had been assigned five young boys to teach, all between the ages of 5 and 8. By all accounts they were, for their age, five of the most violent and disturbed children that had ever been enrolled at the school. For the subsequent 2 years, beginning in October 1988 and ending in June 1990, I used monthly and bimonthly videotaped observations and a series of interviews with Anne elicited from viewing those videotapes together, to trace how she developed an effective curriculum and pedagogy with these boys. During those 2 years, Anne's classroom progressed from one dominated largely by violent behavioral difficulties to one dominated by meaningful academic activity. My investigation was aimed at discerning how, over time, Anne diagnosed and maintained appropriate academic expectations for those students while adapting to their severe social and behavioral difficulties. At the same time, it focused on discovering what and how Anne thought about forming the curriculum in her classroom and how she subsequently translated that thinking into pedagogical choices.

The result is a detailed and contextual ethnography of the events of the classroom in narrative form, documenting the dynamic and shifting interplay among the boys, Anne, and the curricular content. It is an effort to reveal how the curriculum of the class unfolded over time and eventually became ordered and coherent. In the narrative, I pay particularly close attention to the severe social, behavioral, and academic learning needs of the boys, individually and as a group, as well as the aspects of the boys that are strikingly similar to "normal" boys their age. What happens and what is said in this class among the boys and between teacher and students is highly charged and structurally complex, and Anne's teaching choices can be understood only in the context of the boys' distinctive needs and behaviors.

In parallel to this description of classroom events over time, is an analysis of Anne's thinking as she tries to resolve her teaching dilemmas. Using Anne's elicited responses as she watched videotapes of her own teaching, I traced how she mediated the extreme difficulties in her class through constant observation, listening, and reflection. Thus, by parallel paths, I describe what transpires in the classroom from an observational standpoint, while attempting to understand Anne's dilemmas from her viewpoint. My analysis bridges the distance between my observation and her subjective experience so as to capture Anne's thought translated into action. Throughout, I have worked to report in fine detail what Anne thinks about and what she does, in an effort to draw the reader as close as possible toward experiencing the class as Anne did.

My findings corroborate what others have noticed about Anne. She is a teacher of considerable skill and intellect, a woman whose practice combines a unique and cohesive curriculum with a carefully considered pedagogy for the education of emotionally disturbed children. The majority of the book explicates her curriculum and pedagogy as they developed over the length of the study and provides a grounded narrative of classroom teaching with disturbed children. By no means are the findings generalizable to all classes and teachers for emotionally disturbed children, nor do they add up to the best practice to which I've just referred. However, what emerges is a story of a teacher who invokes four important and interrelated dimensions of thinking and action which enable her to be an effective teacher. The first dimension is what I call her method of thinking; the second dimension is a mature theory of curriculum and pedagogy; the third is her systematic management of shifting curricular goal structures over time; the fourth is the synergy she has found with the institution in which she works. In later chapters of the book I analyze these dimensions and show that they are substantially different from what we have come to expect in special education teachers and classrooms for emotionally disturbed students. I show further that these dimensions of teaching, thought, and practice can inform current arguments regarding special education policy, curriculum, and pedagogy.

ORGANIZATION OF THE BOOK

The central portion of the book is organized to reflect Anne's progression through three distinct, yet overlapping, stages in her curriculum and pedagogy. In Chapters 2 and 3, Brighton and Anne are introduced, providing both an historical and contemporary context for the narrative ahead. With Chapter 4, the first stage is introduced, showing that, in a period lasting roughly from September through December 1988, Anne was preoccupied largely with shaping an environment that supported learning about appropriate classroom behavior. The narrative reveals how she struggled to teach her violent and unpredictable students to be physically safe, tried to differentiate the group behavioral problems from the individual behavioral problems, and taught basic classroom routines. Chapter 5 illuminates the behavioral curriculum that grew from her increasing insights into the children and describes her efforts to establish and integrate that curriculum into the context of the academic day.

In Chapter 6, the second stage of her work emerges. During this time, roughly from November 1988 through March 1989, Anne's efforts at socializing the students accelerated and she reorganized her approach to teaching so it was more in tandem with the boys' social interests and strengths. Her use of language as a vehicle for social teaching and learning became most pronounced, as she taught the boys language that enabled them to interact socially in increasingly successful ways. Chapter 7 presents the ways in which she used the group to foster the boys' movement away from egocentric thinking, toward more sociocentric ways of interacting; and it describes how she created learning situations that taught the boys that learning can be, and should be, meaningful and enjoyable.

In the third stage of development, beginning in late January of 1989, her academic curriculum saw its full ascendency and was firmly established by June. Matching the boys' needs and interests with exceptional improvisational instruction, Anne was able to integrate the social, behavioral, and academic goals for the students into a curriculum that was devoted to academic pursuits. Chapter 8 is devoted to an explication of the academic curriculum and pedagogy and explores Anne's constructivist philosophy of academic learning, the goal structures for each academic area, and the pedagogy she employed in academic instruction. A day in the classroom is traced in an effort to show how Anne's behavioral, social, and academic curricula and pedagogy interacted to keep the academic learning focus intact. In occasional digressions, I offer a summary of learning outcomes for the 2 years.

By organizing the narrative to reflect these stages in time, matching each with the ascendency of another curricular structure and pedagogy, I do not mean to imply that each curriculum was not operating prior to the stage in which I place it. Indeed, from the first day of class, reading, writing, and mathematics were the order of the day. Rather, the stages demonstrate periods of Anne's preoccupation with refining the different curricular structures and integrating each with the others in both thought and action. They represent subtle shifts in Anne's attention over time and the subsequent shifts in the activities of the class.

Throughout this process, Anne exhibited patience: She knew that it always took time to develop a group into a functioning unit that could tolerate a full day of academic teaching without major behavioral problems. But Anne was an opportunist. Despite how slow and difficult it was to progress with this group, she cleverly bided her time, was watchful of every opportunity to get them involved in learning—and took it. The trajectory of the class was in many ways a function of Anne's ability to tolerate the time and effort it took to think the problem through, as well as the time it took to bring interventions to fruition.

Chapter 9 provides an elaboration of Anne's method of thinking and how that thinking got translated into curriculum and pedagogy. This discussion attempts to uncover the mental processes of a teacher who realizes that the same class of boys who can erupt into dangerous, wild behavior almost without warning, is also a group of boys with substantial curiosity and intellect. The discussion captures the quickness of her thought and action, her careful planning coupled with her highly improvisational teaching, and the means she employs to locate and solve problems. Anne undergoes qualitative changes in her thinking as a result of each problem solved or managed, and is herself a learner as well as a teacher.

Anne's thinking translated into action yields a normalizing academic classroom filled with developmentally appropriate, intellectual challenge in reading, literature, writing, mathematics, social studies, and science. She believes in the therapeutic power of normalizing activity, in emphasizing student strengths as the key strategy for remediating their weaknesses. The behavioral and social objectives, clearly important learning needs for these troubled children, are addressed intentionally, but within the context of a firm academic activity structure. Thus, the curriculum and pedagogy in each area are more than a set of appropriate objectives, materials, and methods; they are embodied in the learning environment itself, in its structure, composition, and expectations.

Chapter 10 discusses the implications of a paradigm shift for teaching troubled children, away from applied behavioralism, toward a cognitive-developmental orientation. The discussion focuses mostly on the implications for teachers and the ways our thoughts, skills, and attitudes must necessarily change if we are ever to realize the quality education we want for our students. The discussion acknowledges how difficult it has become to find common ground between special and general educators, struggling as we do to find shared language to speak of our work and similar values to guide our efforts. It is clear that we must engage in a deeper discussion about the educational and social needs of troubled students, but we can no longer neglect a discussion of our own needs as we struggle to teach those children.

OBJECTIVES OF THE BOOK

What emerges is a mixture of story, theory, and implication, which provides complex, useful content for substantive discussions of teaching and learning with troubled students among teachers, researchers, and policy makers. The story is a much-needed exploration of the happenings in a real classroom over a long period of time—and it is long overdue. Too often, teachers find themselves alienated from the work of the research community because they do not find their voices or their authentic dilemmas reflected in the research. Teachers are distrustful of studies that do not actively acknowledge that teaching and learning take time and are difficult, messy processes that resist classification. The story told here is an effort to invite teachers to take their rightful part in a conversation about what teaching and learning actually are in real-life classrooms. In telling the story, I make every attempt to give Anne her voice and to speak about her knowledge and experience.[2] My hope is that teachers who read the story will speak back—agree, disagree, empathize, even repudiate—all in an effort to clarify the thoughts and the actions that they take with their students.

It is not just teachers of special education that I seek to engage with this story, though. Anne's experience provides substance for the badly needed discussion among special and regular education teachers regarding ways to

---

2. In this effort to elaborate Anne's teaching and to focus tightly on her thoughts and actions regarding her work, I chose to forgo a description of her intricate interactions within the broader context of Brighton. Clearly though, Anne's—or any teacher's—effectiveness, shortcomings, and failures are always embedded in, and mediated by, a social context. However, a much longer volume would have been required to give the fullest reading of Anne's teaching, to situate it in its most complete social context, and to include the multitude of interactions that create the context of a school like Brighton. As important as these are, I have reluctantly trimmed them back in the narrative to leave enough room for a more complete description of Anne's work in the classroom.

effectively manage and teach troubled and troubling children in the mainstream classroom. As the narrative unfolds, one sees that Anne's teaching dilemmas are unique, and at times extreme. However, they are at the same time
familiar and not unlike the ones many teachers encounter. Her experience is
Anne's particularly, but in some important ways it is shared by teachers univer-
sally. In fact, it is the extreme nature of some of her experiences with her
students that, at times, is most helpful in illuminating the common dilemmas
of special and regular education teachers. It is true that the social context of
regular public classroom life is largely absent in Anne's story, swamped by the
behavioral, social, and learning difficulties of her students. However, what
remains are some of the persistent problems that many teachers experience
with their most difficult students. As Anne finds and solves those problems,
her story prompts questions about whether the knowledge and practices of
teachers such as her might be useful to elementary school teachers in their
efforts to understand and teach children who challenge the limits of teacher
experience. I think that it is, and in the final chapters I turn to this theme of
sharing knowledge among regular and special education teachers. I argue that
many teachers of troubled students have much to offer their mainstream colleagues, and that a deep discussion among practitioners is necessary to bridge
the ever-widening gaps in knowledge, experience, and attitude between these
two groups of teachers.

The story is intended for researchers and policy makers, as well, although
some tend to be less amenable to the use of stories as a means for understanding teaching. Many find qualitative research reports to be too "soft" in their
findings, and they require just-the-facts-please about teaching and learning.
But such research reporting tends to lose the subtlety of life in classrooms
and the vitality of the human relationships. These are, I believe, some of the
very qualities that are crucial to retain when one tries to understand teaching
and learning. Anne's is a story rich enough to encourage theory making about
dimensions of effective practice with troubling students. It is also strong
enough to raise important questions about existing practice, particularly because her philosophy, curriculum, and pedagogy diverge in significant ways
from those that are currently advocated by researchers and policy makers in
special education. Moreover, they are effective.

Ideally, Anne's story and my analysis will prompt among researchers and
policy makers a deeper discussion about the continued use of behaviorist
practices as our sole methods with disturbed youngsters. The field of special
education has too long resisted scrutinizing behaviorism and behaviorist
methods in educating disturbed students, ostensibly because such methods
are effective in controlling the behavior of those students. But as I have discussed previously, there is scant documentation that, beyond learning conformity, these children are learning much else of what public education promises

to teach. If the field is to remain intellectually honest, we must thoroughly re-examine our suppositions about who disturbed children are, what their learning needs are, and whether the sole use of behaviorist methods are the most effective—and humanistic—means for teaching and learning. Case studies like this one of Anne can assist us in this endeavor.

CHAPTER 2

BRIGHTON

Anne pulls her blue Nova into the school parking lot with just enough time to grab a cup of coffee before her supervision meeting with Alex at 7:45. It is a clear and crisp November morning; the campus is a New England pastoral painted in a palette of earth colors and washed in low morning light. The mist clings to the marshes down the hill, and the oak trees touch the blue sky with spidery fingers. The only sound is the whoosh of cars far in the background. But Anne doesn't seem to notice the scene as she grabs her bag and her bookbag from the car seat and heaves them over her shoulder. She hasn't slept well—Aaron and Jason, in fact all five of the boys, have marched through her dreams the past few nights, giving her little rest. These past 3 months have been the hardest she has ever spent at Brighton; the work here has always been intense, but these boys are particularly violent and unpredictable. As she walks up the hill toward her classroom door her thoughts have locked onto the day ahead and she doesn't even hear the flock of geese fly directly overhead.

Visitors to Brighton Home and School are often surprised to find the beautiful campus wedged between three affluent, well-manicured suburbs of an old New England city. Across the road from the school, a river curves gently away through the surrounding area past the landscaped yards of well-paid executives. Along the adjacent roads, the fields are crisscrossed with stone fences and dotted with horses; the venerable homes of the region's leisure class peek out from wooded copses. Behind its stone gate, the Brighton campus is orderly and peaceful, blending seamlessly into the local environs. The lawns and athletic fields are kept meticulously and lead up to a graceful Victorian mansion painted pale beige and renovated as a residence for children. A matching carriage house stands a respectful distance away. Near the entrance, a large renovated barn divided into staff offices is topped by a copper weathervane in the form of a cow, a reminder that this was a dairy farm over 30 years of ago. Close by there is a red cottage, servants quarters in bygone days and now a residence for children. Far from the road, a very modern building houses the school. Beyond the fence, horses run and the "back field" stretches out and up until it overlooks the river on one of its characteristic, sharp turnarounds.

For the visitor, as well as those who work here, this verdant backdrop is both an irony and a comfort. It is an irony because the grounds belie the activities and residents of the school. Brighton is a residential and day school for emotionally disturbed, mostly violent, latency age boys. The patient guest will eventually learn what the staff already know, that at any moment the country silence can be easily broken by Robbie, who has climbed high into a majestic oak and is hurling obscenities at the adults below, demanding that they find his mother for him or he will never come down; that the pastoral picture of geese in flight can be torn utterly by simply glancing back toward earth to see Stephen, wild with rage, held on the ground by three adults while a fourth protects the boy's head as he grinds it into the asphalt walkway. For Anne on this particular day, the beautiful November surroundings cannot hold her attention. Yesterday's revelation that 6-year-old Jason and 7-year-old Aaron have been involved in fairly extensive sexual activity with each other occupies her mind entirely.

Still, the surroundings can be, and often are, a comfort. At Brighton, there is unconcealed hope in the face of genuine despair—a paradox somehow embodied in the campus itself. Despite the chaotic lives of the children, the school is very well kept, pretty, and proper; it is a far cry from any Dickensian images of orphanages or stereotypes of asylums. There are no barred windows, no broken doors, no graffiti. Trash is in strategically placed cans, while flowers in beds and pots grow undisturbed. But the well-kept state reflects philosophy, not wealth, as the fiscal officer is quick to say. The orderly condition of the school is a legacy of its founder, a symbol to students, parents, and staff alike that healing is possible against great odds, and that each person can, as the school's mission statement says, "find a better way."

Anne is a teacher, and a good example of the young, sanguine Brighton staff. She has worked with disturbed children since she was 17, and at 25 she continues to believe she can find a better way to help children and families cope with their tumultuous lives. That belief is costly: It requires that she weather the consistently high expectations and extreme emotions and behavior of her students and their parents, as well as the even higher expectations she places on herself to help. But mostly it requires that she find ways to walk the line between hope and despair without letting cynicism overcome her. Brighton is a place of powerful paradoxes and ironies bonded one to another and hard to untangle. The work here is as invigorating as it is emotionally, intellectually, and physically brutal. Anne continues to welcome this challenging work, although it has taken a toll. Lately she has begun to wonder if she can do it for much longer.

Children, parents, social service agencies, and public schools present themselves to Brighton only in dire circumstances. Hope, disappointment, frustration, and anticipation attend each boy and his family or guardians from the first moments of contact with the school. Most boys who come here have

few choices left: They've either pushed to the limits their local school's ability
to educate them, their family's ability to support them, or both. Some are
virtually orphans: In the years since 1985, increasing numbers of boys have
been placed at Brighton because they currently have no family. Either they
have been abandoned or disowned by their parents, they have been removed
through court order from their homes for care and protection purposes, or
their parents are incarcerated. A majority come to the school following psychiatric hospitalization. On the other hand, some students do have families
that feel able to have them live at home and send them as day students. In
the fall of 1988, 52 boys aged 5 through 12 attended the school, 30 of whom
were residents. Staff make dark jokes about the deepening seriousness of the
problems these children experience, how each year seems to bring more and
worse cases of abuse, neglect, and disturbance. They joke as well about the
increasing difficulties they have in finding better ways to help the children.
Anne and her colleagues live and work in a world that is painfully askew and
absurd, and their pungent banter, sarcasm, and laughter are often unexpect-
edly soothing and a necessary pressure release.

For instance, it is absurd to the staff that, given the increased difficulties
of the school population, ever-tightening regulatory demands and the worsening financial conditions of towns and the state too often take precedence
over the treatment needs of the children. The boys at Brighton can expect to
stay for as short as 1 year and as long as 5, although most stay for about 3
years. Usually, their care and education at Brighton begins and ends through
recommendation of a Special Education evaluation at the local school level
or through the Department of Social Services (D.S.S.). The yearly cost to these
agencies for care at Brighton is high—in 1988 it was $29,000 for a day stu-
dent (not including private transportation) and $49,000 for a resident. By
1990, the yearly rate for residents had risen to $57,000, and for day students
to $32,000. Although public school and D.S.S. representatives believe that
the money is well spent, they want to make as short-term an investment as
possible. Brighton's director feels pressured to develop and employ short-term
therapies in response to the outside financial concerns—even though the
needs of the children have increased and worsened. Further, he has felt com-
pelled to open enrollment to serve some of the most difficult child welfare
cases; in some instances the school has accepted and maintained children
whose extreme violence prompted even the state hospitals to reject them for
service. To further complicate matters, the state's worsening fiscal crisis has
caused the legislature to renege on its financial commitments to the school;
this has forced the director to enroll six additional children, bringing the total
to 58.

These are bitter ironies to the director as he pushes Brighton's staff to
serve more children in worse condition over shorter periods of time. They are

bitter ironies to staff as well. Anne earned about $18,000 in 1988 teaching some of the most difficult children in the state of Massachusetts. She is angry about how devalued teachers are and hopes someday to be one who changes society's perception and willingness to pay for good teaching. Nevertheless, in one of the recurring paradoxes found among Brighton's staff, she cannot imagine taking another job just to make a lot of money. What Brighton cannot give her in dollars is made up for in intellectual stimulation, she says. The work is fulfilling. She is not angry with Brighton, but with the misaligned social values to which Brighton, and she, must bow. Although these social and economic ironies and paradoxes arouse her passion, somehow they recede into her consciousness during her still more passionate hours of work with the children.

Part of Brighton's difficulties rest in its paradoxical legal status. It is a private institution funded with public monies and it is therefore subject to local, state, and federal government regulations. Local Educational Agencies (LEA) fund the placement of children either as day students or as residents, depending on the severity of the educational need. Educational need is measured by complicated means explained in the Massachusetts special education law. Chapter 766, as it is called, is one of two state laws in the nation by which children are not labeled as having a specific handicap and subsequently awarded handicap-specific services. Rather, children receive services in an amount and of a type commensurate with their assessed needs. In section 502 of the law, more than 10 prototypical service delivery plans are listed and numbered corresponding to severity of need, but not handicapping condition. Although the original intention of the law was to avoid stigmatizing labels, ironically students are now referred to by the subsections of section 502 of Chapter 766: A child is often referred to as a 502.1, or 502.2, for instance. Brighton offers services for students whose severity of need is described in section 502.5 and 502.6 prototypes. Placement in a 502.5 prototype program means that a child's special needs are so great that he or she cannot be educated in a public program and must be placed in a specialized, private program for the full school day. Children in a 502.6 program presumably have special needs so great that they require 24-hour care and education. Children at Brighton are in either a 502.5 or a 502.6 prototype when their needs are assessed strictly from an educational perspective. Often, however, a child needs an educational day placement but not 24-hour educational treatment, yet is under the care and protection of D.S.S. In those numerous cases, D.S.S. shares with the LEA the cost and responsibility of placement in 24-hour care, setting up a complicated and often adversarial relationship between the two funding agencies. There are also children who are placed in residential treatment solely through the action of D.S.S. for care and protection purposes.

These regulatory exigencies directly influence Anne and the rest of the

Brighton staff. They are accountable to more than just the children and their parents—people who already have widely varying family, social, and economic backgrounds. Additionally, the complicated and often conflicting funding structure exposes the Brighton staff to the different accountability procedures of the different agencies, the standards and expectations of culturally and economically differing communities (at the time of the study, children from 32 different towns in Massachusetts attended the school), as well as the myriad "outside people," as Brighton staff call them, such as social workers, public school liaisons, pediatricians, psychiatrists and psychologists, adoption workers, and child advocates from watchdog agencies, whose expectations may often surpass those of the individuals or agencies they represent.

Staff are acutely aware of these expectations in part because of the school's small size and in part because it is organized specifically to increase face-to-face interactions among staff, parents, social workers, and school liaisons. Almost every major educational and treatment decision for a child is made by a "treatment team" of staff working closest with the child, in combination with parents or guardians and other outside people. As a consequence, Brighton staff members, regardless of their professional disciplines, are knowledgeable about many aspects of individual cases, and of children and families in general: Treatment team members are cognizant of not only school and on-campus residence issues, but diagnostic rationales, medications, home issues, fiscal considerations, court orders, and more. This complex, copious information is managed largely by individuals on the treatment team acting as repositories of certain portions of it. Members divide responsibility for the information on the basis of whether it is educational, clinical, or related to the "life space" (that is, all that is not school and not therapy, family, or social services related). The division of information mirrors the functional divisions of the institution.

There are three departments in the school, Educational, Clinical, and Residential, organized by function and usually by professional discipline. The Clinical department is staffed by clinical social workers who provide individual and group therapy for the children, family therapy, or counseling, and who manage cases with outside social service agencies. The Residential department is staffed by trained child-care workers who administer all recreation programs and programs for daily living. There are three residences on campus, and two family-style group homes in the village 3 miles away. The Education Department, of which Anne is a part, is more structurally complicated because it incorporates a number of professional disciplines. Each of six classrooms is staffed by three adults in a team. The teacher usually holds an advanced degree; he or she is assisted by a full-time, paid teaching intern who often is seeking a Master's degree and certification in special education from a local college; the third member of the team is a child-care worker who is responsible for planning and implementing all nonacademic portions of the school day, including crisis management. Additional staff include a reading and learning specialist, a speech and language therapist, and an art therapist/teacher.

An individual child's treatment team, then, comprises his teacher, teaching intern, classroom child-care worker, individual therapist, family worker, and residential child-care worker. The team may include other professional members, depending on the complexity of an individual case, or the ancillary services the child receives. It is this small group of people that has major responsibility for decisions about care and treatment for the child. Each nonsupervisory staff member serves on as many as 10 treatment teams and as few as five. Anne serves on each of her five students' treatment teams.

THE CONTRIBUTION OF TEACHERS AND TEACHING

At Brighton, there is a strong sense of reciprocity between staff and administration as both groups work together toward a common goal. Anne and her colleagues receive unusually large amounts of trust, responsibility, and support, and most rise to the challenge and thrive on it despite the attendant stress. Staff are exposed to, and participate in, every aspect of child treatment. This exposure informs their particular professional practice, which in turn affects the efforts of the entire team. As a teacher at Brighton, Anne's thinking is especially influenced by a handful of practices and philosophies in her department that, taken together, shape teachers' contributions to the overall child treatment effort. One such influence is the way in which teaching at Brighton is data driven and how teachers are expected to be expert analysts of cognitive, social, and behavioral data. Teachers work hard to understand how their students actually think and to design curriculum that is highly customized. But as diagnostic in nature as this sounds, teaching at Brighton does not conform to the prospective behavioral methods that are common in special education. Indeed, curriculum is aimed at increasing intellectual and academic engagement using pedagogies that are eclectic and holistic, and based on sound developmental principles of elementary education. The Education Department members try to contribute to each child's treatment what they consider to be the best of current elementary educational curriculum and methods, combined with the most effective of special education pedagogy.

Understanding How a Child Learns

Through the efforts of four principals over the years, the school program has continually refined its means for diagnosing students' academic needs:

The principals have frequently studied and revised the formal batteries and informal assessments that are used; they have hired qualified academic diagnosticians in the position of Learning Specialist; and each year, they have had the Learning Specialist, and others, devote the entire 2 months of summer to diagnostic work. But three facts mark Brighton as unique, as far as Anne and her teaching colleagues are concerned. The school makes efforts only to collect testing data that will be useful in understanding the needs of the students and thereby will be helpful in refining the curriculum and pedagogy. Very little achievement testing is done and the curriculum is not achievement driven. Second, these diagnostic data are shared with and used by teaching staff. There is no dichotomy between those who test and those who teach. Finally, qualitative data are valued highly and are sought in making curricular and pedagogical decisions. Teachers use their anecdotal records and portfolio assessments of students' work when shaping their academic programs. The diagnostic pictures that emerge for students at Brighton are thought of as Student Profiles, amalgamations of student strengths, weaknesses, preferences, and interests. These profiles provide the means by which staff set academic goals and form instructional groupings.

Every child at Brighton undergoes an individual battery of academic testing in reading, mathematics, spelling, and writing at the time of admission and every summer thereafter. The basic reading battery consists of the Durrell Analysis of Reading Difficulty (Durrell & Catterson, 1980), the Stanford Diagnostic Reading Test (Karlson, 1976), the Rosewell–Chall Reading Test (Rosewell & Chall, 1978), and three informal reading inventories, as well as the Test of Written Spelling (Larson & Hammill, 1986). Math is diagnosed using the Key Math–Revised (Connolly, 1988). Additionally, a cognitive test, usually the WISC-R, is performed at admission if it has not previously been performed. These test batteries are administered by either the Learning Specialist, the principal, or, often for continuing students, their teachers. The tests are not pro forma, but are, when added to narrative summaries of yearly progress written by teachers, used to write a rounded picture of each boy's skills, preferences in learning, interests, as well as suggested means for addressing various academic goals. During the last week of August and the first of September, teachers and interns meet with their supervisors to review and digest the information in these documents. Using them as blueprints, they begin to plan the first instructional units of the school year.

Approximately two-thirds of the students at Brighton are learning disabled as well as emotionally troubled. Thus, reading ability and achievement are the most closely scrutinized academic areas. A brief summary of how a boy's reading skills are profiled and goal structures are formed demonstrates one way that the institution shapes Anne's (and her colleagues') academic teaching.

Students are tested in their oral reading, silent reading, listening comprehension, word recognition, word analysis, sight word vocabulary, and written spelling. The profiles then elaborate a boy's need for review or instruction in 13 phonetic skills and seven structural analysis skills; narratives are provided on each boy's word analysis skills, with additional suggestions on how teachers might improve those skills. Similar profiles and suggested methods are provided regarding oral reading quality and comprehension. These are added to teachers' summaries of what materials and skills were taught the previous year, and their assessments of a student's motivation and behavior.

A profile of one of Anne's students, Brian, provides a cogent example of the formal testing. Written in the summer of 1990 after his second year of instruction, it shows that at age 7 years, 7 months Brian's word analysis skills and his oral reading were at a middle first-grade level. Interestingly, his silent reading was at a low second-grade level, and his listening comprehension was at a fourth-grade level. Two years before, he had begun instruction with only pre-primer skills in reading, and in that time he had mastered all consonant sounds and diagraphs and all short vowel sounds, and could decode and encode words that follow the consonant–vowel–consonant (CVC) pattern. Of the 200 frequently used sight words in English, he knew 136. The profile also informs us that he still was resistant to re-reading what he did not understand and self-correcting what seemed obviously wrong; the specialist suggested that his teacher consider making cloze books, where words are missing from interesting stories, in order to help Brian use context cues with alacrity. She pointed out that he had no noticeable difficulties learning to read, enjoyed reading, and loved retelling stories; he showed little need for the kind of highly sequential and ordered reading program that many learning disabled students need. She suggested a detailed reading plan that Anne might use as a model for instruction, emphasizing some materials he might enjoy. She also encouraged Anne to schedule Brian for instruction in very small groups because his penchant for being distracted into mischievousness by his peers often kept him from doing well in class.

Each teacher spends between a half and a full day in late August reading and discussing these profiles (along with information about other academic areas) while meeting with the principal and specialist. These meetings begin both the process of deepening teacher knowledge about the needs of the individual children, and also the discussion about managing the whole group of individuals—a dilemma that Anne's story will demonstrate can often feel insoluble, at least at first.

Once all the information has been collected, the principal works with the teacher to form instructional groupings for reading and math. Several factors enter into these decisions. They consider first which students have either academic or behavioral needs that warrant tutorial instruction. For instance, three more of Anne's students—Paul, Jason, and Samuel—each required tutorial instruction in reading during the first year of the study. Paul was taught in tutorial reading because of his wild and unpredictable behavior; Jason because he was (and remained) severely disabled in reading and in need of extremely specialized teaching; and Samuel because reading was his greatest strength and he was far ahead of the others, but also because he needed to have stimulation reduced in order to learn.

Second, the principal and teacher consider which students could be grouped by academic skill level and still tolerate each other behaviorally. They also consider which boys could be grouped heterogeneously by skill, and because they are compatible behaviorally, or motivated in a particular academic area, can work in groups together and still gain from instruction. Grouping decisions made on the basis of social or academic skills are not made according to a formula; each grouping requires a great deal of analysis of individuals and their interactions with others. There are times when a grouping decision is made in order to satisfy the need of a child to be with a certain adult. This was true of Samuel, who was scheduled during the second year of the study for reading with Anne, largely because he had had tutorials with others and his relationship with her needed to be more firmly established.

Each grouping decision affects the overall scheduling of the class, and considerable time is devoted to these efforts. Yet, creating small groupings for reading and math based on solid pedagogical reasoning is the cornerstone of the Brighton school program. They are made possible by the high staff–to–student ratio, the institutional commitment to in-depth analysis of student learning needs, as well as the commitment of ancillary resources to meet those needs.

ECLECTIC AND HOLISTIC ACADEMIC PHILOSOPHY

A past principal of Brighton says that the academic philosophy of the school has always been "to do what was needed to get kids to learn." He and his predecessors were pragmatic about their work and were not wedded to a single curricular model. The prevailing belief was that wholesale adoption of any one model for teaching would probably limit flexibility in addressing the myriad and ever-changing needs of the population. Moreover, it might limit creative thinking on the part of staff or close off avenues to new research. Thus, the school leadership has always supported an eclectic curriculum. The approach to reading instruction provides an excellent example: The Alphabet Phonics (Cox, 1980) reading method, a highly sequential phonetic approach to teaching decoding skills, is used in the beginning reading tutorials and groups for all learning disabled students. On the other hand, beginning readers like Brian, who exhibit no learning difficulties, receive what Anne calls a more "regular first-grade" approach that includes phonics, but not in so structured or sequenced a way as Alphabet Phonics.

In reading classes, students read from vocabulary-controlled trade books and serial readers. But the principal and teachers have never been comfortable having the reading program pivot on phonics and publisher-controlled readers alone. To provide a literate classroom, they have the children participate in a read-aloud and a literature class every day. Read-aloud is a literature-based reading program in which a wide variety of books are chosen just for the fun of reading, and the vocabulary and content are not controlled. In older classes, read-aloud is supplanted by silent reading time. Literature class in Anne's room happens through Big Books, wherein language and its written structure are investigated. In older classes, all reading instruction is literature based, and students with decoding difficulties are provided daily tutorial classes. The goal at Brighton has been to do what was needed to get children to decode, but to develop a love of reading as well.

Mathematics is also a good example of eclectic curriculum. In the curriculum guide developed at the school in the mid-1980s, the principal writes that teachers found students bored and thwarted by uninteresting and rigid test-based math. They assessed students as having little understanding of the underpinnings of mathematics, such as the concept of number, place value, or estimation. And because traditional math programs emphasized learning computation rather than understanding math, many of their students were unable to solve problems once the calculation-without-understanding approach broke down. The staff remodeled the curriculum to emphasize concrete experience with the physical world through manipulation of materials, and visual models of mathematics. However, instruction in computation was by no means eliminated, and a mixture of traditional and experiential math instruction has been the result.

Although the curriculum is eclectic, it is also holistic. Changes in the curriculum often have stressed more experiential learning. Research in the whole language approach resulted in the introduction of read-aloud and Big Books; the impetus for word time came from research in language experience (Ashton-Warner, 1963; Johnson, 1987); the math program grew from staff reading and thinking about Duckworth's (1987) and Baratta-Lorton's (1976) notions about math learning. These efforts are unique for special education dominated by behaviorist and direct teaching methods.

Although the curriculum is eclectic and holistic, there is a clear educational model at work. The Brighton Model attempts to consciously walk the line between the high level of *structure* needed to manage behaviorally and emotionally troubled and cognitively disorganized children, and the provision of rich and, for many Brighton children, compensatory *experience* that children need in order to learn. Anne's classroom efforts are reinforced by the institutional emphasis on mixing highly structured goals and objectives, and behavioral management, with well-designed opportunities for wide and enriching experience in learning. This is difficult at best, as Anne's experience will show. But it is a model that has been largely successful for students who, in public school, would have otherwise missed the intellectual challenge of schooling largely due to their serious learning disabilities, behavior, or both.

The Emphasis on Literacy and Language

The strong emphasis on language and literacy at Brighton is an important institutional foundation for Anne's work. Her academic curriculum (indeed all of the Brighton classrooms' curricula) relies heavily on the use of language to provide the content and also to serve as the mainstay of the pedagogy. It is for this reason that developmentally disabled children or those with severely impaired language abilities are rarely accepted into the program. All academic learning in Anne's class relies on promoting discourse between teacher and students, and among students. In Brighton's pedagogy, even mathematics, which in traditional instructional models relies more on visual modalities and on working alone, relies heavily on extended discourse between and among participants. Science and social studies are also group-oriented and collaborative, necessitating extended communication among participants.

The emphasis on literacy is also high. Activities and instruction specifically planned for reading, writing, spelling, and language development take 2.5 hours out of every 5.75-hour day in Anne's class. Comparable hours are spent in the other primary classes at Brighton. If one considers that Anne bases most of her science and social studies curriculum on the use of storybooks about such topics as dinosaurs and butterflies to convey information, another hour can be added to the amount of instruction that accentuates literacy goals.

Reflection Through Discourse

The role of language in the academic activities of the classroom is mirrored by the emphasis that Brighton's philosophy and organizational structure place on reflective discourse among adults. Fridays at Brighton see the children released at 12:30 p.m. to allow classroom teams and boys' treatment teams time to meet until 5:00. Anne meets with Alex, the principal, one morning a week for an hour before school to discuss her curriculum, teaching, team concerns, and the progress of her students. For her, this time has been "definitely . . . the most influential" in thinking through the problems of teaching. "I think in supervision for me, it's where I sort of wrestle out: 'Can I really expect this kid to do this or is he really too crazy?'

But supervision is used for more than just wrestling out what she can expect from the students. In one supervision session in late August just before the commencement of her second year teaching this group, Anne and Alex used their time together to discuss seven major agenda items and any number of minor ones. Both teacher and principal arrived at the meeting with written lists. Anne came concerned about reviewing the classroom schedule for its appropriateness; she wanted to brainstorm with Alex what she could do to sequence activities for the first few weeks of school, until she got a rhythm going; she and her child-care partner Karen had a new idea for a behavior management system that she wanted to elaborate for Alex and get his honest feedback on; Paul had moved up to the next classroom (his treatment team thought that he, being something of a violent bully, might learn from being the youngest and smallest in a group instead of the oldest and biggest) and had been replaced by Mark, about whom she knew very little.

Alex had on his list to talk about Anne's new assistant teacher, Tanya (assistant teachers change every year, often because they have finished an internship for certification); he wanted to discuss whether Anne's supplies arrived and were complete; he wanted to know what she was thinking about doing for the first month of the math curriculum, a school-wide unit he coordinates on estimation and numbers; he wanted to talk over some ideas he had for the science curriculum, ideas and materials he had gathered about investigating insects (science curriculum, especially using the outdoors, is Alex's area of expertise); finally, they needed to find a weekly supervision time.

The conversation that ensued for an hour and 30 minutes moved through some items quite quickly: Yes, Anne tells him, all the supplies arrived and they're great. But could he run to the supply store for a few things more that she had forgotten? Just show me what you need, he replies. Others take considerably longer: Anne is not well versed in the insect world, which does not appeal to her at all. Alex doesn't need to convince her that a focus on insects would be fun for the boys; she knows that it's a good idea. She just doesn't feel confident and will need to look to him for help. He has already assembled some books and materials for her to begin her research, and he has more should she need them. He has mail-order books ready so they can order butterfly cocoons. They agree to continue discussion of the unit during ongoing supervision.

For Anne, the success of her supervision comes from the shared philosophy she senses with her supervisor:

I think there's some basis of feeling like we're talking the same language, like at some deep down place even though I may be at differ-

ent points, know less, or be at an earlier stage of professional development, that there's some agreement philosophically; that we're sort of
working down the same road.

She finds the atmosphere of her supervision to be supportive and safe. It
is here that she can safely be angry at a boy, another staff member—or even
herself. She feels that "I can burst into tears in his office and it's okay." But it
is not just a place to vent her feelings; it is a time to think aloud, a protected
space in a very busy week to clear her congested mind, to put her perfectionistic self into perspective:

> Sometimes it's just supporting . . . when I'm being supervised I do a
> lot of my . . . I like criticize myself before anyone else can get a chance
> to do it kind of thing . . . so I tend to enumerate all the problems my-
> self and say "this and this and this is wrong and what do you think
> about this and this and this?" So some of my supervision winds up be-
> ing either agreeing or disagreeing with what I've listed as a strength or
> problems.

For a woman like Anne, a person who is harder on herself than anyone
else can be, it is important that she feel that she will be understood and not
judged too harshly for her faults.

> I think that support is making me feel like I'm okay whether or not a
> specific thing is okay. Making me feel like I'm moving in the right direc-
> tion, that I'm on a track. Making me feel like it's not horribly, devastat-
> ingly awful that I'm not—and here are some things you can do.

Supervision provides Anne and her colleagues with an unusual institutional support for their work; it is an acknowledgment that staff cannot be
expected to give intellectually, emotionally, and physically without having
some way of replenishing and refocusing their energies. Fully one-third of
Alex's time is spent supervising staff; before Brighton hired an assistant principal to share some of the load, Alex's predecessor spent one-half his time offer-
ing supervision to staff. For their part, supervisors know that they can be successful only if they remain nonjudgmental with supervisees. They put a large
emphasis on building trusting, professional relationships and basing their
comments on data taken from class observation. Because they participate in
classroom activities and observe teachers at least weekly, they have substantial
data on which to draw in their discussions with teachers. Supervisor effort is
rewarded. Supervision is one of the things staff mention as a benefit to working at Brighton when they are asked how they can work at such a difficult job

for so little money; it's one of the things that they say keeps them coming back to work every day.

Clearly, Anne could not be effective without her colleagues and without being a part of an institution that supported her efforts. Overall, there is a powerful and reciprocal relationship between staff and institution, which enables teachers to engage in the treatment and education process with remarkable vigor. Days of work with the troubled children and families at Brighton can be extraordinarily confusing and painful. The reciprocal efforts of staff and administration are geared toward building comprehension of the myriad problems that they must face together, helping each other bear the misery of the people they serve, and celebrating each small movement toward health. The synergy that staff have found with the people who lead them has created a strong culture in which "finding a better way" to live actually seems possible.

CHAPTER 3

ANNE

Anne came to her profession intentionally. She is definitely not a person who fell into a teaching career and stayed, as so many teachers are known to have done. Rather, teaching troubled children is a logical extension of an intense desire to help others that has long been Anne's way of life. Even as a young child and the oldest of three siblings, she was very mature, "helpful and responsible and looked out for everyone and took care of everybody else. . . . I was a very serious, intense, responsible little kid." She was also quite bright and did well in school, something she considered a mixed blessing at the time. She says, "I was always the kind of kid teachers love to have in their classes. I was not particularly popular, I was not particularly cool. . . . I got a certain amount of shit from other kids for doing well in school and that made me really angry. And my response to that was never that I should try to act dumb so that other kids would like me better. It made me think that those other kids were jerks." Her parents, "prim and proper," with strong old-world values, prompted and then echoed Anne's emerging sense of self by being shocked and dismayed that she would allow others to belittle her for doing well. They valued intelligence, hard work, and service, and worked to instill those values in Anne by word and example throughout her formative years.

Her family's history, culture, and religiosity figure strongly in the values they sought to convey. Her father is an architect who came to the United States with his parents in 1938, a Jewish family fleeing Austria's annexation to Nazi Germany. She describes her father as a frugal and proper man, a boy who "grew up in a very poor family who were sort of sociologically an upper middle class family who circumstances had made poor. . . . His parents had grown up as educated, cultured sorts of people who lost everything they had." Her mother had a more privileged background. Her family had emigrated from Eastern Europe a generation earlier, and her mother's father was an American success story, "sort of the poor Jewish boy in Brooklyn who worked himself up and became this very assimilated, successful lawyer." As a result of their own upbringing, her parents were people who lived somewhat paradoxically, that is, quite simply and practically but in an affluent Long Island town. Anne never realized that her family was comparatively well off until she began

filling out financial statements for college. Although there were differences in
her parents' attitudes toward the value and use of money (she laughs now
when she recalls that her father did not understand why it was important for
her mother to spend such "ridiculous amounts of money on clothes" for her
daughters to attend their socially competitive, upper middle class high
school), Anne took from her youth the belief that material gain is a by-
product of one's hard work, but that fulfillment is found through the disciplined use of one's mind and talents. Yet, as a result of her experiences as a
child, she has a strong sense of the paradoxes and contradictions of living out
those beliefs and values. She still displays a kind of ambivalence about being
intelligent, about working for material gain, about her chosen career, and
about the relationship among the three. She feels somewhat uncomfortable
when someone asks what she does, because she knows teachers and teaching
are devalued in American society.

> I want to say that I'm a teacher and I want to be proud of that answer.
> I also want that person to know that I am an intelligent, well-educated
> person. And the common assumptions don't have those two things go
> together. A lot of times, I say things and I get really mad at myself. I
> say things like I work at a residential treatment center for emotionally
> disturbed kids because for some reason that makes me feel like people
> are going to think it's more important. And then I get really mad at
> myself because if I was teaching normal first graders I would be just as
> important!! And I should be able to say that without feeling I have to
> tack something on to the end—I'm a teacher of emotionally disturbed
> children but my SAT scores were—you know.

Anne is stung by the fact that she derives intense satisfaction from something that is not valued highly by most people. Yet, that does not stop her
from doing what she loves to do: As a youngster, she took satisfaction in
learning and as an adult she takes satisfaction in teaching. She is someone
who becomes more assertive of her desires in the face of others' doubts. Beginning in her first year of high school and continuing throughout college,
Anne found satisfaction in teaching others, even when that wasn't a particularly "cool" thing to do. Her first teaching opportunity came in ninth grade
when she participated in a tutoring program for seventh graders. She remembers being drawn to work with the "losers"—kids whom she perceived to be
like herself, shy and "not part of the cool group," as well as kids who were
considered the delinquents. During that summer, she was a counselor-in-
training at the day camp she had attended as a child. She was happy leading
and teaching groups of small children, and she was much more serious and
responsible about the work than her friends who, she felt, were on a summer's

lark. It was here, also, that she encountered her first emotionally disturbed child "without knowing what I was doing and not knowing what he was called." Now she knows that he was autistic; at the time he was just a sad, weird kid whom no one else cared to work with. By the end of the summer, she had helped the 6-year-old learn to put on his bathing suit and come into the pool's deep end with her. She was enormously satisfied and pleased with her ability to help this youngster. She experienced a growing understanding of people who, like herself, were different from others, and she recognized early on that she had an ability to connect with them in helpful ways.

This recognition was compounded when, as part of her already extensive activities at her temple, she began helping in Hebrew class. She was called on to assist a teacher who was preparing a class of learning disabled boys for their Bar Mitzvahs. Anne concluded that the teacher was "a total loser and I hated her. I was a little cocky because I decided that I was better with the kids than she was. . . . She might not have been so awful. . . . But I think it's really interesting being that I was really good with these kids. Because the kids liked me better than they liked her." From a young girl who was "helpful and responsible and looked out for everyone and took care of everybody else" in her family, Anne grew to experience herself as a powerful helper of people she perceived as forsaken.

Her growing self-confidence solidified when, in tenth grade, she enrolled in her high school's alternative program. Here she experienced herself transformed from a "shy, quiet, nerdy, labeled person" into a leader. She moved from being someone teased and unsure about the value of her intellectual gifts, to someone who believed her intelligence could be used for good reasons. The alternative school was called the SWS, or school within a school, and its program and faculty had a lasting effect on Anne as a learner and as a teacher. Finally given the opportunity to be among other students who were bright and individualistic, Anne immersed herself in every aspect of what was a democratic education program. Students were given wide latitude in their choice of coursework, and an emphasis was placed on human relations and community building. Her regular teachers and some of her friends chided her for her involvement, warning her that she was squandering her formidable intelligence and would not be able to get into a prestigious college as a result.

But her parents supported her decision to enroll in SWS, believing she should do what she felt was right. As for the issue of college, they were characteristically practical, eschewing the pressure she was getting from others to apply to Ivy League schools, and instead encouraging her to use college to learn a skill that would help her find a job. Anne welcomed the opportunity to make her own choices; reflecting on SWS 10 years later, she realizes that it was a watershed experience. In that program, "you had more say, more choice in what you were doing. Teachers were real human beings. You could talk to them, you could have relationships with them." It gave form to her sense of confidence and purpose, and it has shaped her educational philosophy as well; in many respects she has adopted the SWS philosophy into her own.

One of the important tenets of that philosophy is choice in learning. She faced the biggest choice of her young life when at age 17, she announced her intentions to become a teacher of special needs children. Reactions were mixed. Her parents thought it was a noble profession and a practical, economical choice. Her SWS teachers thought that she should investigate this option, but keep in mind that her desire might change in the future. However, her guidance counselor and regular teachers were not supportive at all, Anne says, first because they believed it was impossible for a girl so young to know what she wanted and second because they did not value teaching as a profession for a smart girl. She went to a high school "where they wanted to have statistics of how many kids they had going to Ivy League schools," and she was told that she was too intelligent to become a teacher and that she should wait to make a decision about career until after she had a four-year, liberal arts education.

This dichotomous reaction from her parents and important school adults renewed her long-standing confusion over the value of her intelligence, over the ways in which people perceive intelligent people and the things expected of them. Flattered by the perception that she was gifted, but convinced that she wanted to teach, she attempted to resolve the dilemma by finding an Ivy League school that had a certification program. She found none. However, she did find Tufts, a competitive school, respected by the adults in her life, that offered certification. It was a self-satisfying decision to apply and be accepted as an early admission.

Determined to get on with what she believed would be her life's work, in the summer before college she applied for and accepted a job at a well-known special needs summer camp. In what was probably her single most important formative experience as a teacher, Anne spent the next eight summers working 7 days a week, 24 hours a day with disturbed children. The work was thrilling and challenging—and extremely intense. To some extent, the intensity was what she thrived on, and continues to thrive on. But she also was happy to work in a community of people who shared the same values and to see the small changes that could happen in a child.

> I found people who were as intense as I was and loved doing what I was [doing] and were there spending their summers working with these crazy kids 24 hours a day, 7 days a week with no days off and not a whole lot of money 'cause they loved it! And that was really great to be working with people who shared that feeling. . . . The intensity of it is partly what I loved. It was very intense and was very hard. But you saw

things happen, you saw changes and you saw really neat things happen and you discovered these really neat hidden, inner parts of these kids who on the outside looked really crazy. And I also saw that I was good at it and I was successful with working with these kids. That was a sort of reconfirmation of . . . something I was really good at and it was something that I really liked.

She continued working at the camp summers throughout her years at Tufts, excited when her coursework presented theoretical constructs that gave a name to what she had already been doing at camp. In retrospect, she also believes she absorbed much of the developmentally oriented philosophy of Tufts, that it gave reason to her strong desire to make learning fun and challenging, even for emotionally disturbed students. But it was not until she began her practicum at Brighton that she was able to express what had already taken seed through her experience with troubled children. At Brighton, she says, the explicit philosophy was that learning could be "creative, fun, exciting, developmental . . . that you can focus on strength and health rather than on pathology. And that you can teach skills and competencies and that can be the most therapeutic thing of all." This philosophy resonated strongly in Anne, echoed back to what her parents, and her own experiences as a child and teenager, had taught her.

At the end of her practicum she was offered a job, which she accepted immediately. At Brighton, she has felt that she is part of an institution where a premium is placed on the intelligence of employees and on their ability to meet the incredible demands of the work with flexibility and originality. It is a place that she believes expects the children to learn to be more than their past predicts, where school and learning are a central focus for helping students "find a better way" to solve their problems. As she says, "There are people here who are smart enough to be doing anything in the world, but choose to be doing this work." Anne relishes the intellectual challenges of teaching troubled children.

The fall of 1988 presented Anne with a prime teaching problem, the complexity of which challenged her completely: Teach five boys, each troubled in unique ways, each with certain strengths and capabilities on which a skilled teacher might capitalize, but who are, as Anne once described, "five little orbits sort of separately going their own ways." The metaphor was apt. They were five boys in constant motion, whose violent behavior and unpredictable patterns created a chaotic and often scary climate as they brushed against one another and sometimes collided outright. In the early stages, the class left Anne feeling like she had insufficient experience and skill to draw upon. Yet, by the end of 2 years, she had brought about remarkable changes in the classroom learning environment, moved from a class preoccupied with behavioral problems to one preoccupied with academic activity. She moved the class from a group of individual students who were in "five little orbits" into an organized system.

Donald Schön (1983) has written that effective practitioners are those who can find meaningful problems as well as solve them. Anne exemplified this kind of effectiveness as she sorted out the important quandaries from the ongoing chaos in her class. She found the key problems to be addressed, and she shaped her encounters with this group of students into increasingly flexible ways of thinking and acting. Of course, this ability did not suddenly spring forth in response to this group of boys; Anne is adamant when she says that her ability to find and solve problems is a natural outgrowth of her experiences, her disciplined study of child development, and her overall attitude toward her work. When she finally looked back over the 2 years of work with these students, she was able to explain where her responses to the challenges fit into the continuum of her professional and intellectual life. When we place Anne's experience with these children in the context of her growth as a teacher, we can see that she is oriented, both intellectually and by temperament, to manage the kinds of challenges these children presented.

AN EXPLICIT MIND SET

Anne engages with her work using a particular mind set. There are some for whom the phrase "mind set" holds a connotation of inflexibility of thought; this is not what I mean to imply in the case of this teacher. Rather, I intend the phrase to encapsulate the group of intellectual, philosophical, and emotional orientations Anne holds toward her work. That set of orientations is distinct and plays a key role in what problems she chooses to think about—to find or to solve. I would venture to say that the same is true for most teachers (and others, of course). Understanding teachers' mind sets is important for understanding what they perceive as salient in their classrooms and what they will tend to overlook, as well. Given the vicissitudes of her work with the children, it is Anne's mind set that provides the necessary ballast for her to continue teaching them. Five recurring thoughts, or clusters of thought, orient and equilibrate her in the sometimes overwhelming flux of information that rushes toward her during any given classroom episode and amasses as the day progresses.

To begin, Anne focuses her energy and effort on the students' strengths. One cannot underestimate this ability, particularly when one considers how strongly the children present their aberrant behaviors. More important, though, one cannot overlook how this ability runs counter to common behaviorist practices in special education, where practitioners are exhorted to locate and remediate student behavioral and learning deficits, but where little encouragement is given to locate and exploit student strengths (this subject is discussed in greater detail in Chapter 10). For instance, at one point in this study, when she was at the nadir of hope about finding a way to keep her class safe, and particularly and Jason's ability to reduce his violent and sexualized behavior, she noticed him actively participating in a lesson. She immediately commented on his strengths. "I was just thinking," she said, "about how cute and polite and intelligent Jason is being in contrast to what I just said about feeling hopeless about him . . . he's starting to show some of his strengths again." And then, with a laugh and a sly glance toward me as if to reveal a secret, she said, "Maybe we can fix him after all!" Because she sees her students' strengths, she is always willing to re-engage, to push them to use those strengths, even at the risk of creating more short-term problems. She sees the boys as more than their problematic behaviors, and that vision propels her back into the work.

There are times when other workers at Brighton, usually therapists and child-care workers, think she pushes the boys in her class too hard to engage in school work. For instance, she related that during the first year of the study Paul's residence workers and therapists were concerned that her expectations were too high for him. No, she insisted, Paul has strengths that he needs to exercise if he is to begin to believe in himself: "I think that Paul is capable of a higher level of functioning than what they're expecting from him in the residence. And I'm pushing him harder, and he's having more behavioral problems, but in the long run, it's gonna be better for him 'cause he's going to learn that he can meet those expectations." There is a reason, a driving force to this decision to push them harder.

> In terms of high standards and pushing the kids . . . maybe [I'm] caus-
> ing more behavioral problems cause I'm gonna push them to do
> things. It wouldn't be worth doing that if they were always going to be
> at a place like Brighton for their whole lives. Like *who cares,* you know,
> how much socially appropriate behavior they learn, and if they learn
> how to read and do math and those kinds of things. I think that there
> is always in the back of my head the thought and the hope that at some
> point down the road they're gonna go to some more normal setting.
> Whether they're gonna be adopted and stop living at Brighton, or they
> go back to a public school at some point. Or that they stay at a place
> like Brighton and are more successful there. You know or whatever.
> That there is a goal that each one of these kids is capable of more, [of]
> higher functioning.

Anne is of the mind that her students are more than their past, or their circumstances, predict. There is hope for students because they have strengths, and that's a good enough reason for her to do the necessary work.

The second component of Anne's mind set is her focus on teaching the whole child. She chose her career because within that discipline she could address more than just academics in her teaching.

> In choosing to work with these kinds of kids, clearly I'm not just inter-
> ested in academic teaching. I'm interested in the social [and] emotional
> growth of kids. So I expect that some proportion of my time is gonna
> be spent dealing with social, emotional, [and] behavioral issues with
> kids and not just with teaching [academics].

Even though she believes that intellectual stimulation is crucial for troubled children, Anne makes choices in her classroom that reach beyond academic considerations. She puts substantial effort into planning "neat curriculum" ideas, but "the neat curriculum isn't as important to me as how the kids are doing altogether." Thus, for instance, when Brian had just heard that his social worker was coming for a visit to tell him some news about his mother, whom he had not seen in some time, he became increasingly impulsive and bizarre in his behavior. Anne went out of her way to keep him in class. She didn't want to "boot him off" to someone else so she could return to the academic task at hand. Seeing that the remainder of the group was in relatively good control, she kept him with her in an effort to both support and prepare him for the difficult meeting ahead, and she saw that emotional support and preparation as part of the job she loves to do.

While Anne is interested in the whole child, at the same time she is interested in academic production. She wants the children to have the experience of finishing their work, writing stories, doing science projects, and the like. She knows that the experience will enhance their sense of intelligence and power. She is oriented toward students producing products—she worries that she is too much so. Yet, it is her product orientation that provides the necessary balance to her process-oriented view of the whole child.

> You know, all my preschool education training says don't be product
> oriented, the experience is what is important . . . [and] the last thing
> I want to be is the traditional old-fashioned first-grade teacher. . . .
> That's not what I want. But at the same time, I . . . want them to have
> products. I knew they would like the products and feel proud.

Without her product orientation, she knows she runs the risk of making excuses for the children to not finish their work, to not do normalizing activities. She has seen other teachers at other schools and institutions who, in their compassion for troubled children, mistakenly expect less from them.

It is Anne's opinion that such lowered expectations foster the helplessness troubled children feel. On the other hand, she knows that being too product oriented might result in her being brittle, unable to understand why her "neat curriculum" needs to be pre-empted by the emotional baggage the children bring to school. She has seen teachers whose tolerance for anything but academic schoolwork is exceedingly low. Anne knows that it is in those classrooms that her students would inevitably fail.

One important benefit derived from her willingness to deal with the whole child, troubles and all, is that it predisposes her to accept and work with a wider field of explanations for their behavior. Hence, nothing really ever comes "out of the blue" for Anne. She is never thrown off her stride for long with the children if, for example, they present antisocial behaviors when they ought to be doing mathematics. Each is her concern, math as well as pro-social learning, and she is able to move fluidly from one to the other and back again. One would never hear Anne claim that it is not her job to deal with the troubles children bring from home, for instance. As far as she is concerned, that is her job exactly.

It is not uncommon today to hear many elementary teachers say that they are trying to teach the whole child. Anne is an elementary teacher who has made that phrase operational; it means very specific things that she can delineate in her mind and point to in her practice. Teaching the whole child requires a detailed understanding and tolerance for the behavioral, social-emotional, and academic aspects of student learning—and considerable skill at balancing the three.

The third component is closely related to the previous two: The best therapy for any of the children is to learn skills and competencies. A student's self-esteem can be founded only on an accurate self-assessment of his abilities. To help students reach that point, Anne insists that she must focus the largest share of her attention on her students' health and not on their pathology—and that she must find ways to make learning fun. This requires that she discover at what developmental level each boy functions in social, academic, and emotional domains. That knowledge helps her plan for each, as well as for the group as a whole; it gives her the ability to check when she has gone astray or expected too much or too little from an individual boy.

Anne maintains that, to a large extent, she was trained to focus on student health and individual children's development throughout her years of summer camp work and through the studies in early childhood education that she received at Tufts University. She combined the practice of camp and the theory of the university into her current attitude toward working with disturbed children. Her preservice training was truly formative of Anne's thinking, comprising as it did a mixture of practice, theory, and strong supervision.

A companion to her expectations of students, and the fourth component of her mind set, is her very high expectations for herself. She strives to be "perfect" as a teacher, is unflappable in the face of chaos and violence. She possesses knowledge of herself that allows her to be highly self-critical without being self-deprecating, and to laugh at herself and her faults without caving in under the weight of her controlling tendencies. Anne is emphatic that, although this group of boys is the hardest she has taught to date, she can and will make a difference, but only through considerable effort on her part.

> I guess I have incredibly high expectations for myself as well as for what is going to happen with the group. And so it's . . . not good enough for me to say that this is a hard group and that everyone says it's a hard group and it's just going to take some time. That helps because I know it's true. But at the same time I feel like there have got to be things I can be actively doing better to make it better. It's still gonna be a hard group; they're still gonna be crazy kids; it's still going to take a long time. But there have gotta be things I can be actively doing better to make it better.

To actively make things better means that she is continually critical of her lessons, of her approach, of her language. She picks lessons apart both when they are successful and when they fail, paying particular attention to the impact of her own actions and her own expectations on the lesson. If a lesson fails, or a period is disrupted, Anne rarely places responsibility anywhere but on herself: "I was some of the problem . . . my expectations were wrong," she told me after an early, disastrous lesson intended to teach about things being the same and different, using four different types of apples and the five senses as tools. She had done the lesson with students in former years and previous classes and it had always been a resounding success. But with this class, she concluded, she had misread their abilities, planned a lesson that was too advanced, "was a little stupid in saying, 'Well, this is a great lesson that I'd done before and I don't really need to think about it very much.'" She laughed at herself, as she often does when she is struck by the irony of being perfectionistic yet imperfect.

Anne believes that her work and her effort are important catalysts for growth. She smiles when she says, "I don't think I can 'fix' them." But her expression becomes earnest when she says, "I think I can be part of making them healthier people . . . I'd like to think that all the time and effort and energy that's going into everything that I'm doing and that others are doing with [them] is going to mean that 10 years from now [they] can lead some sort of productive, normal life." She believes that success or failure in helping the children is directly connected to her efforts. This aspect of her thinking is important if we are to understand what and how she teaches. Her propensity for taking responsibility for what happens in her classroom is remarkable; she is not the kind of teacher who blames television for her students' lack of attention, for instance, or parents for students' lack of school readiness. Her nature is not self-deprecating; rather, she is like a strategist who replays every move she's made, searching for the false ones. Her attributions of success or failure are, in large measure, what propel her to use her considerable natural intelligence in increasingly flexible ways as she tries to cope with the whole child as he presents himself.

Doubtless, there are some who will read parts of Anne's story and wonder if she wasn't preoccupied with controlling her students to the point of rigidity. Certainly, in the early stages of working with her students her main concern was finding some way to control their dangerous behaviors, either through control and manipulation of environmental variables or by physical control of their behavior. But throughout my observations and analyses of her work, I did not perceive Anne as self-serving in exercising her power and control in the class. Rather, I found her to be uncommonly reflective of the power differential between herself and her students, and committed to using that power constructively to shape a safe, structured learning environment.

Investigating questions about how, why, or when teacher control is appropriate in classrooms is crucial to the improvement of classroom practice with troubled children, as well as their mainstream peers. As events unfold in Anne's story, some of her thoughts and actions raise these important questions, and in the final chapters of the book I shall engage those questions. For now, it suffices to say that Anne attributes her students' success in large part to her own efforts; that she can be perfectionistic with herself; but that she has a strong ability to reflect on these propensities that tempers her behavior and orients her positively toward her work and her students.

Finally, Anne loves her work and she is satisfied with it, even though it is difficult, even discouraging. In the times when her energy is low and she feels defeated, she consciously reminds herself of that fact.

> I remind myself of the times when I feel hopeful or of the good things that can happen, and of my real belief that things will get better . . . I say to people "Well, it's a good thing that I love this kind of work, because it would be easier to forget this week!!"

This capacity to love her work in the face of intense and persistent challenges binds her core values together and helps to shape her sense of vocation as a teacher. Throughout her working life with children, it is this set of attitudes and values to which she returns when she needs to re-calibrate her plans, her decisions, and her emotional responses. These values run deep, back through her life to her youth, her family, and the beliefs they first instilled in her. Anne knows herself well; her history, her present work, and her direction in life seem to her to be unified. To watch Anne teach is to witness a teacher who is confident, insightful, decisive, and, more often than not, effective.

CHAPTER 4

CHAOS AND QUANDARIES

Once Aaron had finally divulged to his residence worker that he and Jason had been having sex with each other on the weekend, Anne felt an odd mix of things. A small part of her was relieved to know that there was a cause for the two boys' recent intense, regressive behaviors. Anne didn't feel she was in the dark any longer; she knew that ". . . at least there was a reason for it. . . . It wasn't me, it wasn't the classroom, it wasn't just out of the blue!!" It was a comfort to know that each boy's treatment team had responded immediately and decisively to the crisis. The residence staff had rearranged bedrooms and free play time, and were keeping the boys within an arm's distance at all times; the boys' clinical workers had immediately begun the difficult process of therapeutic intervention with Jason, Aaron, the other boys in the residence, and their families. But the knowledge was small comfort when she mixed it with her increasingly strong feelings of disappointment and frustration. It was November, and during her years at Brighton she had come to expect significant improvement in her class' behavior by this time of year. "Things always improve by Thanksgiving," is a truism on which the entire Brighton teaching staff relies. She had to admit that, this year more than any in the past, she had banked her hopes on improvement by Thanksgiving.

Thus far, fall 1988 had been a time of unprecedented violence, disruption, and emotional chaos in her class. She had struggled through the first months of the school year with the behaviors of each of the five boys in her class and the behavior of the boys as a group; and the boys had struggled with each other. They were some of the youngest children ever at the school. Between 5½ and 8 years old, their extreme youth and their profound disturbance shocked even the most senior members of the Brighton staff. The group was so difficult, and presented Anne with such challenges, that sometimes she felt like a first-year teacher all over again; she just wasn't as sure of herself or whether the old rules applied to this group. Even this far into the year her mind was working overtime—as she drove to and from work, over dinner with friends, while she slept—trying to grasp the extent of the behavioral problems plaguing the group, trying to find some way to bring them under control. Things were already hard enough without the problems of two boys involved in sex!

She couldn't help feeling a little cynical: Just recently, there had been some small glimmers that the group was settling in, and she had been discovering some ways to prevent them from exploding whenever she embarked on a lesson. In fact, before this regression, they had appeared to be accomplishing more academic work every day. It still felt to her that for every two steps the group went forward, they took three steps back. But by the first days of November she had actually allowed herself to hope that things might improve by Thanksgiving.

At first, only Jason's and Aaron's behavior began to deteriorate—Jason becoming more unpredictably violent and aggressive, and Aaron becoming more disoriented and bizarre. But true to form, their behavioral problems were contagious, and whenever Jason or Aaron would begin to have trouble, Samuel would become overstimulated and begin shrieking, while Paul would begin mimicking and teasing. Brian needed very little to join in the melee; he had been barely able to function in the past 2 weeks anyway, what with his long-lost mother re-emerging. The result was that the class experienced a "complete regression back to less than zero. . . . And basically . . . no teaching academics at all happened in the classroom. . . . So for almost 2 weeks I did little else than restrain kids all day.[1] And it was really miserable, and really awful." After 2 months of mostly valleys and very few peaks, Anne was at her nadir. She was back to square one. Thanksgiving would come and go, and maybe they could pick up the pieces of this regression. She thought about all the work she'd been putting into building the curriculum, and then she thought about her troubled students and felt "really hopeless and it's really shitty to feel hopeless about 6-year-olds. And it's really hard to maintain the kind of energy that it takes to do this work when you're not feeling hopeful about it."

Then, in one of the great ironies of working with these children, just when her energy seemed to be at its lowest, Jason began to settle back into his routine and to show some of his strengths again. Aaron began to refocus, as well. She had found it often happens that way, but it never stops surprising her. On Thursday afternoon, 2½ weeks after the troubles began, Jason was suddenly involved in a read-aloud story about Pilgrims and Indians, asking question after question about how the Pilgrims kept themselves safe, and Anne found herself smiling at how polite and intelligent he could be. Her energy began to return and, characteristically, she directed it toward figuring out what she could do to improve her teaching.

She had been relieved that the source of the most recent problems was

---

1. Often at Brighton children are out of physical control, threatening to hurt themselves or others. Adults, alone or in groups, will often hold a child in a therapeutic physical restraint until the child regains control. No mechanical restraints are ever used.

outside the classroom. She was usually so critical of her teaching, so willing to take responsibility for what happened in her class, that it was good to feel blameless. Still, over the months since school began, she had come to realize that her overall expectations weren't correctly calibrated for this group. She was definitely part of the problem with getting this group to settle in and learn. She ordinarily set high academic and behavioral standards for her students, believing that it was better to focus on their strengths than on their disabilities; she had been determined that this group would be no exception. However, she hadn't anticipated how much younger and more immature they were than any other group she'd taught. The curriculum and the teaching strategies she had used with past groups just weren't working with this group as she'd intended. She had been acting from wrong assumptions about what the boys could assimilate.

For example, in one particularly frustrating lesson, Anne had attempted to teach about the five senses through an experience with four different kinds of apples. She had done the lesson before with past groups, and she expected the boys to notice that the apples had different colors, shapes, and sizes, distinct smells, tastes, and so on. However, once the first apple was put into their hands, the lesson went awry. Although they had many things to say about the experience, the boys became overwhelmed by Anne's attempt to organize their comments by the categories of sense. For instance, she would ask what the apple looked like, but they were more desirous of reporting what they felt or smelled. Finally, Aaron hit Paul; Paul hit back. Apples were thrown; Samuel began shrieking obscenities at the top of his lungs, and the lesson ended with three children out of physical control and needing to be restrained. She explained what she learned about herself from her mistake.

> [I] didn't really think enough about how different this group is from the group I had last year. . . . These guys couldn't pay attention to four different apples and four different senses and what the difference between seeing and smelling and touching is. What doesn't look like a complicated task at all was much too complicated for this group in a way that it wasn't for the group last year. . . . We needed to cut out like 25 steps. And that's the kind of thing that happens with this group a lot. That I've always taught the youngest kids who were emotionally disturbed and learning disabled and I felt like I had already pared everything down to the barest minimum. And now, with this group I need to go 20 steps below that.

Anne is very self-critical. Others at Brighton were telling her to go easy on herself, reminding her that the group was a really tough one, that she would find the right balance, but she wasn't satisfied. She realized that she should be doing things differently, knew that she had yet to make some sense of this incredibly difficult group. She said:

> In terms of the process of a teacher, this has been a really hard group for me 'cause I've needed to change a lot of things I'm doing . . . I'm constantly critiquing what I'm doing. And the group has been so out of control most of the time! And on one level I know that a lot of other people who have been at Brighton even longer than I have said, "Oh my God! I can't believe that group!" And "I don't know how you deal with them every day." And "This is the most difficult group I've ever had in the art room!" And blah blah blah! So I know it's not me. But at the same time I'm . . . knowing that I *do* need to change what I'm doing and that there *are* things that I can change to make it better. . . . I'm constantly replaying that in my head.

The problems they presented were new variations to her, and she needed new variations on her curriculum and pedagogy to be effective. Part of her work has always pivoted on her ability to comprehend the cause of the boys' difficult behaviors, to see *under* the behaviors, so to speak, and to manage them closer to their roots, closer to their emotional or social underpinnings. Once she understands what is happening with a child, she is confident that she can design learning opportunities that mediate his dysfunctional behaviors; she knows how to make learning fun and interesting for a child by aiming the activities directly at his developmental level, at his strengths not his weaknesses. Unfortunately, these days it was hard to focus on the individual children. She was taxed just trying to keep all the boys safe. It took a tremendous act of will to focus her attention on understanding and addressing each boy separately, while keeping the difficulties of the whole group in mind. Nevertheless, she reviewed each of the boys, listing for herself the quandaries that each presented and those that they presented as a group. She needed to remind herself exactly who these children were, not who she expected them to be, and to "sort out what are reasonable expectations" for them. Only by understanding them could she design a structured curriculum that would get to "the heart of the matter," one that was as close as possible to what made them tick.

THE HEART OF THE MATTER: UNDERSTANDING THE BOYS

Although the boys' behavior was problematic, it was also intriguing to her. In her attempt to answer her question "what are reasonable expectations," she began with Samuel, whose behavior seemed to be the most incomprehensible.

Samuel

At 8 years of age, Samuel is the oldest in the group. Some of the behaviors he presents appear autistic. However, the teachers and administrators in the suburban public school from which he came believed him to be psychotic; he seemed to talk to people who were not present, would scream for no apparent reason, or would climb under tables and refuse to come out. When they could no longer maintain him in school, they recommended he be hospitalized. His parents had Samuel examined on an outpatient basis at a psychiatric hospital. Those professionals explained Samuel's behavior from a different perspective. They claimed he had tremendous cognitive deficits: He was unable to adequately integrate sensory stimuli and organize his thinking. He was neither autistic nor psychotic, but in need of cognitive control therapy. Anne knew that this diagnosis was controversial at the time. It is a relatively recent form of diagnosis and treatment, and still suspect in some circles. It was definitely questionable as far as the public school was concerned.

Because there was little agreement on Samuel's problems or on fitting modes of treatment, Brighton accepted him into the program as a day student with some hesitation. There was a question among the administration and clinical staff whether this was an appropriate placement for him at all. Anne wasn't sure either, given that it was hard to find the patterns underlying his extreme behaviors, and that the behaviors caused tremendous ripples throughout her group. Samuel's specific behavioral difficulties were immediately clear in September. Anne reported then:

> He'll pick a word and perseverate on it, say it over and over or repeat it loudly . . . a word will strike him silly or funny. He'll do hand flapping and rocking and self-stimulating kinds of things [or] he'll impulsively start screaming for seemingly no reason at all. But usually if you look closely there is some small, small sensory stimulation that sets him off. . . . Such as another kid, their hands [moving] or making a noise or something he sees moving across the room. It can be very minute so that sometimes it seems like it's coming right out of the blue. Though my guess is there is something that set it off. But it's something so small that a lot of times you just have no idea. . . . He [also] has very poor fine motor control, he has trouble with visual scanning and organizing his body. He's very clumsy, he is very sort of physically awkward. . . . He's very easily distracted by anything in the environment.

When the boys sit on the L-shaped bench that wraps around the far side of the classroom (the bench constitutes a kind of home base for class activities), Samuel is easy to pick out. Even when he is stationary, he is physically awkward: He moves his head rhythmically, forward and back on his thin neck, making gulping noises; his eyes are sunken into his head and surrounded by dark rings, stark against his grey-white skin. His body is shapeless as if he has no muscles but only a skeleton. His nose runs perpetually as a result of allergies that in the spring turn severe enough to cause dangerous dehydration. When he speaks, his voice is a congested whine; when he yells, it is a sustained shriek. He yells at insects when they fly past him, or he yells into the air when the mood in the room becomes charged; he is like a litmus test of tension: "FUCKER!!" he begins to wail over and over as his classmate Paul is removed to a time-out chair across the room for hitting another boy. That is the word he'll yell out most often and loudest. Paul laughs at Samuel and begins to shout obscenities back at him. This causes Samuel to laugh, too, and to wail even louder. Aaron leaves his seat and begins to wander about the room. Samuel jumps from his seat and tries to run outdoors. The adults are pulled in three directions in an attempt to keep order. For Anne, managing Samuel is a puzzle.

> Maintaining him in a group is [hard]. He's a real puzzle in a lot of ways, diagnostically, to find out what is going on. . . . One of the ways that concerns me is that one of his biggest problems is . . . being over-stimulated and he is in a group of extremely acting out kids. The classroom is very stimulating all the time and the other kids are probably scary to him in a lot of ways. And he's constantly overstimulated and spends large amounts of time out of the classroom. The behaviors that he's doing goes [*sic*] both ways; his behaviors when he gets upset, for whatever reason, are so disruptive to the rest of the group that the only choice in terms of group management is to remove him immediately from the room because otherwise I lose all of them.

Anne's questions about managing this boy piled up quickly: He's 8 years old, but given his disabilities what can I expect from him behaviorally? How can I reduce the stimulation in the class and limit his outbursts? What techniques can I use to de-escalate Samuel's behavior that won't cause him to escalate instead? How can I manage his behavior without losing all of them? How can I get Samuel and Paul to stop setting each other up?

Paul

Paul is somewhat like Samuel, in that he is an overstimulated and overstimulating boy. However, where Samuel's behaviors may be partly attributable to neurological and cognitive dysfunction, Paul's behaviors appear more socially based. Paul is a handsome, round-faced, mahogany-skinned boy who is full of gleeful energy that can quickly turn frightful. He and his family were homeless until just recently; there are ample indications that he was sexually abused in one or more of many shelters where they stayed. He is fascinated by violence, both terrified of it and drawn to it. He is extremely violent himself, quick to lash out physically at others, quick to bring on another's wrath with his sexualized, aggressive provocations. Anne describes him, her voice assuming Paul's machine-gun tempo, as follows:

> He is . . . a combination of a lot of things. He's very, very, very impulsive and very agitated all the time. He can be very disorganized and very confused a lot of the time, [asking questions like] "What day is it? Where am I? What day am I going home? What's going on? I want to be in school, I don't want to be in school, I hate school! I'm a stupid, bad, little, crazy kid and I don't belong in school! I like school." He is very impulsive, he has a very hard time sitting in his seat and is always jumping out of his seat, moving around, moving very fast. And [he] responds very aggressively to any limits. For example, if he jumps out of his seat and I say you need to get back in your seat, he'll say, "Fuck you bitch!" and run out of the classroom. Or he'll jump on a table and start sexually gyrating and scream, "Hump me! Hump me!" and within seconds is in a full face-down restraint because he's become violent and aggressive. Usually toward the adult who is trying to set a limit or trying to contain him. And it happens very quickly and very impulsively and in the middle of something. You know, he looks like he's doing fine and he'll do something wrong and you'll give a calm verbal direction and he'll lose it completely and it will escalate into a major scene!

Throughout September and October, Paul's tantrums and subsequent restraints were frightening to witness. They were "kicking, spitting, drooling, banging his head, wetting his pants, very crazy looking tantrums that takes [sic], you know, two people to restrain him for at times an hour." On many days, Paul had as many as three of these tantrums after he had tried to run from the classroom or had begun kicking or punching adults or children. The resulting chaos in the class was extreme and often frightening to the other boys. Anne tells a story of one day in class when Paul had been doing quite well, but rapidly became violent and uncontrollable. Jason and Brian had had major violent episodes during the morning and were no longer in class, but Paul had been able to avoid any trouble. But when Anne gave him a direction to sit on his bench, he began to scream, run around the room, jump on the bench, and climb on the windowsill. Anne was the only adult with the three remaining boys.

Paul was being very out of control. I stopped him physically and sort of held him on his bench for a while, which, of course, meant that the other two kids basically were on their own. Aaron was in time-out for some other reason [and] was doing relatively okay. And Samuel was shrieking because that's what he does whenever somebody else is having trouble. . . . Paul's behavior continued to escalate, he continued to be assaultive towards me and I went to put him face down on the floor and wasn't very successful. He was squirming and I wasn't strong enough and I couldn't get him into a good restraint position. So we sort of struggled around on the floor for a while with the other two watching until I made the decision that this was bad for everybody involved to have me not being able to safely restrain this kid.

She allowed Paul to run from the room, concerned that not being able to control him physically would terrify the other children. She was left with a number of questions, not the least of which was how she could control violence in the classroom. She asked herself how she could get Paul and the others to accept a simple direction without reacting aggressively. How was she to manage Paul's (and the others') impulsive movements and verbalizations? How could she get them to remain in their seats and raise their hands when they wanted attention? Were there certain behaviors that, although problematic, would be better left unaddressed so that she could zero in on those that were even more problematic? How could she stem the contagious behavior of Paul to other boys?

Brian

Of all the children, Brian is probably the boy most susceptible to Paul's outrageous behaviors and is easily drawn into acting silly or provocatively. Blond, blue-eyed, befreckled, and dressed in overalls, 5-year-old Brian is bright and verbal, cute and appealing. Not particularly aggressive, he is impulsive, unable to sit in one position for more than a few seconds, constantly bumping into another boy, teasing him or taunting him, poking a finger into his side. When he is reprimanded for a small problem, his response is to make it bigger.

A common scenario is he'll be sitting on his bench and he'll stick up his middle finger at somebody or whisper swear words to the boy sitting next to him, or poke the boy sitting next to him. He'll continue to do this despite verbal directions not to, and he'll get time-out and on the way to time-out he'll kick over the tray of magic markers, which will spill all over the floor. . . . And he won't be able to calm himself down in time-out and he'll be removed from the room. He doesn't need to be physically restrained but will need to be physically held in a chair to keep him in one place. And he'll yell and scream and swear for awhile and eventually he'll settle himself back down and get into school. He's usually very motivated to be in school, excited and thrilled about whatever is happening; but has a lot of trouble keeping himself contained.

Thankfully, Brian loves school and is usually motivated to do whatever activity is planned, although he does least well during whole group activities. He is immature and vulnerable, but that is not surprising to Anne. He was abandoned by both his parents 3 years earlier and has been in foster care with his aunt. She was no longer able to manage him, and the public schools in her town could offer very little help in educating him. Like Paul, Brian now lives at Brighton 7 days a week. In September, when he first joined the class, his legal status was pending while his state social worker performed an obligatory search for his mother in preparation for releasing him for adoption. By November, his mother had been found and, outraged that the state would presume to terminate her rights as a parent, began the process of proving her fitness to the presiding judge in Brian's case. These events drew intense feelings and baby-like behaviors from Brian, and lately Anne simply was not sure which of Brian's behaviors could be considered age-expected or age-appropriate. She thinks about what works for him, behaviorally.

If I could put Brian in one of those little things that you carry your baby in and carry him around on my hip all day, he would be great . . . he would be in school all the time. . . . He's been successful when he's on my lap and no other time. So on one hand this is what he needs, and on the other hand I need to say you're a big boy and the way you act in school is you sit on a chair and you keep to yourself. He's going to be six . . . he's not such a big boy.

She smiles warmly and a little sadly when she thinks of her quandary over Brian's behavioral needs. How can she socialize him to school—to following directions, raising his hand, working at a table with another, and staying seated even when he gets excited—when he is so needy? How does she know that her expectations for Brian's school behavior are accurate? He's so young! Moreover, if her behavioral expectations for him are different from those for the other boys, how can she manage those different requirements simultaneously? And finally, how can she even try to help Brian understand, for instance, that he cannot throw the magic markers when he's frustrated, if, in the ongoing chaos, she can't find the time to explain it to him, to talk with him?

Jason

Of the boys in the class, Jason is probably a chief stimulus to chaos. His effect on the group is a lot like Paul's. But he is young, like Brian, and at the age of 6, he is also without parents. Jason was born in prison, has been in nine foster homes, and emotionally is a very damaged child. He has been "deemed unplaceable in a family setting because he was so disruptive and so dangerous. He's extremely impulsive, he's extremely aggressive." Jason displays behavior that points to sexual abuse: When left alone in a room with male adults, he has been known to pull his pants down and offer himself for anal intercourse; when stressed, which is a frequent occurrence, he screams sexually provocative obscenities; he is shockingly seductive with adults. Once, during the aftermath of the sexual activity between him and Aaron in November, he came over to work beside me in the classroom.

"Know what a wiener is?" he purred, glancing out of the corner of his eyes. He turned his olive-colored, slender face toward me and his brown eyes held mine; he arched a brow.

"Yeah, a hot dog," I said, trying to sound as neutral as I could.

"Yeah, well, I've had a lot of *wieners*," he drawled, placing just enough stress on "wieners." He flashed a little smile, glanced away and then back again—a small, 6-year-old coquette with a brushtop haircut.

His precocious sexual activity is combined with wild violence—he doesn't just throw things, he breaks them; he doesn't just lash out at others, he tries to hurt them. During the fall he spent less than 50% of his time in the class. Yet he is smart and verbal, able to argue indefinitely over a consequence he has been given. He loves to listen to books, remembers stories accurately, and retells them frequently. But he has no ability to read and may be a truly dyslexic child. Even at the end of this study, after 2 years of daily one-to-one instruction, he could decode only a handful of words. His attitude toward schoolwork is rarely positive. With Jason in the room, Anne is always fearful for the safety of the others. He is unpredictable: Once, when visitors came to the class as part of an ongoing science curriculum about animals, they brought with them a dog and a mouse. Jason learned that another dog he had been introduced to previously had died. All the boys were sad; but when Brian got to hold the leash of the new dog and Jason was denied the opportunity, he threw a stapler at the dog. The resulting pandemonium frightened everyone and led to a major disruption of the program.

How do I cope with this unpredictability? Anne asked herself. How do I anticipate and manage his sexual aggressiveness? Is there a way to anticipate and avoid his violent episodes? How can I minimize the opportunity for him to engage in legalistic arguments over who should be allowed to sit on the benches, or how many cookies each boy can have, or whether he should sit in time-out for 2 minutes or 5 minutes? How can I manage his panic reactions (like when I said we'll use vegetable oil to make clay dough, and he almost lost control out of an unexplainable fear of oil)? How can I avoid being physically hurt, and avoid having others hurt, when he loses physical control? When I must spend so much time redirecting, and giving consequences for, his negative behavior during lessons, how will I be able to avoid increasing his distaste for schoolwork?

Aaron

Aaron looks "like the highest functioning kid in the classroom. And he probably is the highest functioning kid in a lot of ways." Anne found his academic abilities and achievement to be age-appropriate; when the others would begin to have difficulties, Aaron would be the most likely of all of them to be able to ignore the chaos and keep on task. Slight of build, with round brown eyes staring out from under brown bangs, he is often sitting on his bench with an innocent expression while others are having tantrums. He is eager to please. But in what seems to be a paradox, he is also extremely oppositional, negative and rude, impulsive, occasionally assaultive, and very sneaky.

Adopted by his suburban parents when he was an infant, he is hyperactive and on medication; he is allergic to many foods and must be on a special diet; and, at nearly 7 years old, he is, as one psychologist reported, "in a fragile borderline zone in which very small amounts of stimulation and affect can cause him to look somewhat thought disordered, his thoughts become confused and not well grounded in reality." What Anne could not have anticipated in the fall of 1988 was that his thought disorder would worsen over the next 2 years until he needed to take psychotropic medications to assist in focusing his thoughts. By May 1989 he was on the verge of hospitalization in hopes that it would minimize his chances of self-harm. He is a depressed boy whose major defense is to control adults and peers: Extremely stubborn, his stubbornness often escalates into verbal and sometimes physical abusiveness. Anne reports:

> Aaron is very oppositional. His general response to anything you ask him to do is, "No, I will not!" It can be the most benign thing at all and something that he really doesn't mind doing and he just [has] sort of an automatic response to say "no," sort of like a 2-year-old. . . . Eventually [he] does what you want him to do after a very rude or very negative verbal response. Usually if you give him a 1- or 2-minute time-out for verbal rudeness, he'll do it the right way and he might mutter, you know, a few times, or swear a few times, and then he'll sit down and sit his 2 minutes and then come back and join the group. Occasionally it

escalates into a different problem and occasionally he becomes physically assaultive around those times. It builds up. He becomes more and more verbally abusive and then he becomes physically aggressive.

He is sneaky, as well. When adults turn their backs, Aaron will mutter an obscenity to his neighbors, scribble on their drawings, imitate their movements, and repeat their words in the copycat game that is so maddening to youngsters: Once, Anne turned her back on Paul and Aaron writing stories together at the same table. Aaron made a raspberry sound, and she calmly told him he must go sit on his bench away from the others for 1 minute as a consequence. As he stood to go, he pretended to spit across the table at Paul's work. Paul stood and pretended to spit at Aaron's work. Anne had already begun to return to the table and saw this happening. She touched Paul's shoulder and pointed to his bench. "Now you have 1 minute on your bench, too." He started to yell obscenities about Aaron spitting on his paper, but he stormed toward his bench. The two boys sat on their benches quietly, although Aaron was soon heard to be whispering taunts to Paul under his breath. Then he began to mimic whatever Paul was doing. Paul sat cross-legged, so Aaron did. Paul rubbed the bench; Aaron did. Paul realized what was happening and made a purposeful move; Aaron did the same. Paul complained loudly that Aaron was copying him . . . and on it went.

UNDERSTANDING THE GROUP

Each boy's behavior was difficult to manage taken on its own. But when they were working or playing near one another, the boys interacted explosively. Whenever four or five of them were together in the room, chaos was never far away. Even when there were only two boys, like Paul and Aaron sitting for a few minutes on the bench, the mixture could be volatile. The group behavior was as much a quandary, perhaps more so, to Anne as any individual boy's behaviors. Any social, emotional, or academic learning that was happening in her class was happening in the context of massive group behavioral problems. Anne knew that was the wrong balance. Her goal was the converse, that is, to have social, emotional, and behavioral learning happening in the context of academics.

I think some of the question has to do with this group balancing out each individual kid's academic, cognitive potential versus the behavioral [and] social needs kinds of things. I mean each boy in this group, if I put him in a room with one teacher all day long, could be making more progress academically, probably, in some ways. If they had undi-

vided one-to-one attention to be doing it. But at the same time . . . it's
equally, if not more, important in some ways right now to learn how to
be functioning in a group and to do group lessons and things like that.
So some of it is figuring out how to get them to do what they are capable of doing; at the same time it is keeping in a group and having
reasonable behavioral expectations for the group.

Finding reasonable group behavioral expectations that still foster individual growth is a quandary that every elementary teacher faces. But Anne's
quandary was compounded by the fact that she was juggling too much at
once; the sheer amount of stimulation in even a single instructional period
left her extremely frustrated. Her largest frustration came from not being able
to deal with individual children's needs, behaviorally, socially, or academically,
because of the overriding need to maintain basic safety for the whole group.
The boys turned out to be academically where she'd expected they would be.
Some functioned even higher than she'd expected. She was eager to begin
planning and implementing challenging curricula, characteristically wanting
to push them to do all they were capable of doing. But she admitted they
were the hardest group she'd ever tried to manage, and she was terribly per-
plexed trying to find a way to treat them more therapeutically.

> In terms of behavior and ability to function in a classroom setting at all
> they're a lot more difficult than any other group I've had. And main-
> taining the basic safety and control and keeping the kids in the room
> has become a much more difficult and time-consuming part of the day
> than I expected it to be. . . . That's what I hate most about . . . that's
> the hardest thing about this group. I can't deal with the individual kids'
> behaviors the way I want to because of the group dynamic. So I have
> to do things that I don't think are ideal, therapeutic behavior manage-
> ment. For the sake of maintaining basic control in the group. That for
> me is the most frustrating part of the group. . . . I'm constantly having
> to sacrifice what I think is therapeutic behavior management in order
> to maintain basic safety.

"Therapeutic behavior management" for Anne had required in the past
first that she address each boy directly and individually regarding behaviors
that are impeding his development or success and second that she be able
to address those inappropriate behaviors in situ, when they are most salient.
However, with this group she found that she had to manage two additional
problems. First, the boys had disparate and, at times, opposite behavioral
needs. For instance, Brian needed more leniency in his immature behaviors,
whereas Paul, Samuel, and Aaron needed to have their immature behaviors

strictly marked and modified. But both kinds of needs, disparate as they were, had to be addressed simultaneously in the group context.

The resulting quandary is illustrated by Anne in this example: During a lesson in October, Brian appeared to be playing with his penis through his pants and trying to attract the attention of the other boys. This was a behavior she thought immature, but one that, in other circumstances, would be manageable within the group. However, the current group, especially the older three boys, had a tendency to sexualize gestures or words. If she warned Brian, she would draw the others' attention to him. Knowing that if those boys saw Brian, she could quickly lose the whole group through escalating chaos, she felt she had no choice but to send Brian away from the group as quickly as possible. She was frustrated when she said, "He wasn't doing anything overt. But with the group and with knowing him, that kind of thing will escalate into a much bigger group problem, so he needs to leave." Having him leave fell far short of her goal of teaching Brian something about appropriate behavior in a group. She was able simply to keep the basic safety. Her quandary was clear when she said: "How much [do you] send one kid away from the group for something you think might upset the others in the group?"

Her second problem for managing behaviors therapeutically was related to the first. Each boy had so many behaviors that needed to be addressed that she found she must prioritize the behaviors and stick to the most important ones. She reasoned that if she tried to address every problem as it arose, she'd never have children in class. She knew that with this group of children, to mark any behavior, however small, brought on an escalation of the problem. She wanted to keep activities intact. Her ultimate goal was to manage behavioral learning within the academic context. But at least at the start of the year, the two types of learning appeared mutually exclusive. Thus, if there was any way she could possibly overlook a behavior, balancing out behavioral learning against academic learning, she did so for the sake of keeping the lesson going. However, choosing the behaviors to address was not so easy. For instance, Paul's body was in constant motion, and Anne did not believe it possible or wise to have him limit his activity level entirely. Yet not to limit his impulsive activity almost begged for him to end up in an aggressive situation, and more than his activity level, she was worried about his aggressiveness. At times, she felt she was in a no-win situation as she tried to keep the lesson moving. She explained her quandary:

> You know, if they're involved in the activity and they're interested in what's going on . . . how much to call them on little stuff. Because partly—well, why bother to call them on little stuff if they're involved in the activity? But at the same time if I don't call them on little stuff its

gonna turn into bigger stuff or its gonna spread to other kids. . . . Paul moving his body around a lot is a minor problem compared to Paul being typically aggressive. It's sort of like saving my battles. You know, and if I made a big deal over everything every one of the kids did wrong, they'd never be in class and nothing good would ever happen. So I need to pick which things are important enough to have a struggle over. Because any time a limit is set with this group it is a struggle and it usually means a bigger struggle.

How do I keep this classroom safe? How do I manage the group well enough so I am able to address the individual boys' behavioral problems? How do I manage to keep them in their seats? To not poke each other? Lash out? How do I get them interested in schoolwork when I can't seem to complete a lesson? What kinds of behavior are important enough to have a struggle over, because struggle is inevitable?

Such were some of the overriding quandaries that sprang from the chaos of the first few months of school. When Anne added the quandaries she faced regarding individual boys, the list grew longer: How can I mark Paul's behavior without causing it to escalate further? How can I treat Brian as the little boy he is without giving him the message that he needn't grow up? How do I contain Jason's violence? His sexual acting out? Can Aaron's sneaky behavior be marked without increasing his oppositional behavior? And what about Samuel's shrieking?

Finally, having reviewed the behavioral chaos and quandaries that preoccupied the first 3 months of the school year, Anne returned to the question with which she began her investigation: What are the reasonable expectations I can have for these boys? By Thanksgiving, most years, she could answer that question with relative security. This year, things were different. And Anne realized very early on that she could not rely too heavily on past experiences with other groups. She needed to find new ways of acting and new ways of thinking.

CHAPTER 5

SORTING IT OUT:
SPIRALING INSIGHT AND ACTION

Carter (1990) claims that expert teacher knowledge is "richly elaborated knowledge about classroom patterns, curriculum, and students that enables [teachers] to rapidly apply what they know to specific cases" (p. 299). That knowledge is also highly organized so as to interpret teaching tasks and classroom patterns from a conceptual framework derived in part from experience with past tasks and patterns. Teacher knowledge is also tacit, insofar as it is very hard for an expert teacher to make explicit what he or she does or knows about teaching. Anne is an expert teacher, and her knowledge of teaching is richly elaborate, highly organized, and tacit. However, this particular group of children challenged her specific knowledge and pushed at the edges of it in ways she had not experienced before. In part, the chaos that surrounded the children often made it difficult to focus on the salient details of events and hindered Anne in processing information as she had been able to do previously. But part of the problem was that some of the behavioral, social, and cognitive needs of the children presented altogether new teaching quandaries.

To extend her knowledge and ability to act beyond her current teaching schemata, Anne engaged in an iterative process of observation, reflection, planning, and implementing interventions. This, she says, is her usual way of thinking about her teaching. However, in the fall of 1988, she engaged in this spiral of insight-to-action-to-insight with renewed vigor. By the winter, her thinking had changed and so had her behavioral curriculum and pedagogy, manifested most clearly in three distinct ways: First, she made significant changes in her attitudes and expectations toward herself and toward the boys. Second, she developed more stable goals for teaching the group while simultaneously teaching the individuals. Finally, she restructured the actual school day to de-emphasize what she found to be artificial curricular boundaries that exacerbated the boys' behavioral difficulties.

ALTERED ATTITUDES AND EXPECTATIONS

It was clear to Anne that she had to reanalyze and come to grips with her high expectations for what and how the children would learn, as well as her own desire to be a "perfect teacher." She needed to resign herself to the fact that these children were not at the level at which she liked to teach, or felt particularly prepared to teach. She was disappointed and reluctant to admit that she had to aim at a preschool or kindergarten level when she preferred first and second grade. She eventually came to acknowledge that what she wanted for her class and what the children could do at present were not aligned. Until now, she had been impatient and had been pushing certain activities and certain goals too hard and too soon. It was not that she thought her ultimate goals for individuals or the group were incorrect; rather, she needed to find a different way to reach them.

> I needed to find ways to get all those experiences and all those goals done differently. . . . I think maybe by taking turns a little bit, by not trying to do it all every day, by not trying to accomplish all as quickly as I might have last year. . . . The goals in terms of . . . you know by the end of this year. . . . [They are] the same goal[s]. My feelings about how realistic [they are] go up and down a little bit.

She had to change her expectation that the children would make faster academic gains simply because they were clearly bright and capable. Indeed, she realized that, first and foremost, these boys needed to be learning how to function as a group. It almost didn't matter what they were doing, so long as she could get them to do it together. She said:

> I think in some ways, when I look back on the year as a whole, I will say the first 3 months were spent getting the kids comfortable with the concept of being civilized in a classroom setting. It took that long to have them feel safe in a class and be able to contain themselves well enough to start doing anything else.

She also had to rethink what constituted success for these children and come to believe that success, at least for the present, was having basic safety maintained. She was "hoping that by this point in the year a successful lesson would constitute more than basic safety to make me feel positive." She said, "At this point, if everybody is safe and in school, and doing something, that's really positive."

It was a source of great frustration that Anne could not control the outcomes of her teaching as well with this group as she had with other groups.

She is a woman who has always exercised strong control of her class by structuring the environment in very specific ways. Given the lack of control emotionally disturbed children have over themselves, her assertive, almost stubborn nature is a necessary, perhaps even desirable, behavior in a teacher. However, these particular children were so thoroughly lacking control that Anne's tendency was to over-control them. They challenged not only her control over the safety of the room, but her control over the academic goals, methods, materials, and lessons that she had always used. With this group, what could be considered her strength became a liability at times, especially when her efforts to control them exacerbated an already difficult situation. "Perfect control is unrealistic," she admitted at one point in November, "but perfect control is always what I want to be in." She laughed when she said it, and it seemed like a laugh of self-recognition.

To her credit, she re-evaluated the ways in which she brought her own desires and personality to the work, and examined the things that exacerbated the difficulties of the boys. Doing so opened up avenues for change that she hadn't considered before. This is important to our understanding of her ultimate success with the students: Through self-examination and reflection upon her motives and needs, she was able to put them in appropriate perspective. She was able to reallocate her energy from *determining* the path her students were to take toward her learning goals, to *negotiating* the path with them. In the continuing narrative of her teaching, it becomes clear that this choice resulted in Anne performing complicated and continuous evaluations of the current performance and interests of students, while trying to figure out some way to reach ultimate goals. Negotiating the path of learning with students took the greatest effort of thought for Anne.

STABLE GROUP BEHAVIORAL GOALS AND OBJECTIVES

Quite aside from the insights she gained into her emotions and attitudes toward the work, the spiraling effect of living and learning with the boys made a qualitative difference in how she thought about managing the group's behavior. As the fall progressed, she enhanced old or developed new heuristics for managing the group.

For instance, Anne had a long-standing heuristic about using the *tone* of the class to make decisions about behavioral interventions. In the face of the overwhelming behaviors of this group, this heuristic deepened and changed from what in the past had been a largely undifferentiated "gut reaction," to a more refined understanding of when and how she needed to intervene in the boys' behaviors. As she came to understand each boy more deeply and the effects they had on each other, she found the tone of the class had three general gradations. The tone was chaotic and dangerous when a child was "deliberately trying to annoy somebody else" and that someone else was in a negative mood. In such a situation, Anne had to move toward a swift and sure intervention. The tone was somewhat less dangerous when the child was "not meaning to annoy someone else but doing something that I know will wind up annoying someone else even if that's not what the intention was." In such a situation, her latitude for intervention was wider, although at least initially she could not take that latitude as often she would have liked. Finally, her latitude for intervention was widest when a child's behavior, though inappropriate, was unlikely to upset any other boy or distract the others from their tasks.

These differentiations may seem trivial; however, in the prolonged chaos of the first few months, it was difficult for Anne to find ways in which she could systematically think events through and devise a strategy "on her feet." Using these new criteria as diagnostic tools, Anne was able to structure her responses in a crisis situation or when a crisis was looming. They did not necessarily work all the time, nor did they always assist her in shaping a truly therapeutic response, but they did help manage the chaos.

> Sometimes I have to judge which one of these things [the situation] is and . . . how I should respond to it. Sometimes I don't have the luxury of judging it. I just need to respond . . . if it's in the first or second category, sometimes I can't differentiate . . . sometimes I just have to set the limit and can't even help the kid differentiate "you weren't meaning to annoy him but what you were doing was annoying him so therefore I needed to be really firm and immediately yank you out of the group." Sometimes I'd like to do that but there isn't the chance to do it.

Another heuristic she developed over the fall period was almost paradoxical: As a first step to getting the boys to function as a group, she had to keep them together in the room without major incidents; yet to do so, she had to keep them separated from each other while they were in the room. As she said, "The likelihood of them having a problem when all [five] are together these days has been greater: the physical touching, the amount of them getting each other nervous has been big." With her team members, she refined three general strategies that could reduce the potential for chaos by using methods she said would "divide and conquer" the boys. The first strategy was that a disruptive child would be removed swiftly from the group by the adult who was not teaching at the time and would not be teaching in the next period. The goal was to maintain the integrity of the instructional episode while keeping the class safe. The second basic strategy was limiting how often or how much the boys would physically touch each other (and each other's belongings) during group activities; this was accomplished by placing the adults who were not conducting the lesson between the boys as human buffers. Anne had found that when they touched each other, even in brushing against one another as they sat on their benches during read-aloud time or during transitions, the boys would become nervous and agitated. The goal was to maximize the feeling that adults would keep the children safe. The final strategy was that Anne and Cathy, her teaching assistant, would split the children between them at two tables to conduct the same activities one of them would ordinarily do with four or more children at a single table. The goal was for everyone to do the same activity together, while allowing the adults to give full concentration to fewer children. It also limited the risk of a child stepping into another's intimate space.

These rules of thumb had limited success at first. Problems arose initially because Karen, the classroom childcare worker, and Cathy were new to the team, indeed were novices in the profession. They would hesitate and look to Anne to tell them what to do. They were not as cognizant of the changes in class tone as Anne was and often wanted and needed more of a recipe for action. But looking to her was the antithesis of "divide and conquer," a technique that required every adult to be tuned in to the boys as well as to the signals of the other adults. This frustrated Anne. She said, "Sometimes I do feel like everyone thinks I'm supposed to know everything all the time. Which they probably do think." And then she added, characteristically, "And I probably do something to contribute to that," an admission that her strong control of the class probably affected the other adults as well as the students.

By early winter, Anne's actions in the class regarding the behavior of the group appeared more purposeful, as if she had clearly organized her behavioral teaching goals and devised a stable set of teaching objectives. The overriding goal, she told me, was to have a class of boys that functioned as a group and could do group lessons. She designated three general subgoals:

1. Increase the group's abilities to tolerate close proximity to one another;
2. Teach them to physically move from activity to activity, place to place or adult to adult without becoming agitated and violent;
3. Help them to tolerate a structured group activity where they had to share the adult attention with their peers.

She also had very specific short-term teaching goals, seven in all, that emerged to form the initial content of the daily behavioral curriculum. They were actually what every kindergartner needs to learn to succeed in a traditional school and usually can learn with moderate teacher effort:

1. Raise your hand and stay in your seat;
2. Ask for help then wait your turn;
3. Accept limits without escalating your behavior;
4. Go to time-out without escalating your behavior;
5. When frustrated, don't touch or tease another boy;
6. Perform transition routines without disruption;
7. No violence in the classroom.

As straightforward as these goals and objectives appear on paper, they were difficult to carry out in practice with these boys. This was due to the tension produced by the group needs competing with each individual's needs. Anne's daily dilemma sprung from the fact that not only did all the boys jump from their seats, refuse to raise hands, escalate their behavior, and so on, but each manifested his behavior differently and under different conditions. And if that wasn't enough, each boy had individual troublesome behaviors that were unique to him and needed to be addressed. She handled this dilemma by making the decision, quite simply, to address first things first, by dealing with the disruptive violence that precluded attending to any other goal. She did this by "trying to preserve the classroom space as a safe, calm space. Even if that means that four out of five need to leave it and then gradually come back one at a time. . . . But this . . . space needs to be preserved as a place where learning happens and where crazy behavior can't happen."

She enlisted the help of the principal and the crisis center in demonstrating to the boys the stark differences between being in the class when they were calm and being out when they were violent. Anne knew that separating the boys in this way intervened only in the group-level disruptions themselves, thereby treating the symptom only. It did little to get at the underlying causes of the behaviors—each individual's social and emotional difficulties. But minimizing the symptoms allowed her to get to the therapeutic behavioral management she had been longing to institute, an intervention style aimed at the cause of the behavioral problems in the class.

In the following examples, we can see Anne's therapeutic behavioral management at work with two different children having trouble learning the same group behavior, that is, performing transitions without disruption. Samuel's problems at transition times were often of a different nature and were manifested differently from Aaron's difficulties. Because she had reduced the chaos in the classroom, Anne was able to think about, and to manage, each boy differently, using her knowledge and experience to calibrate her responses as she worked.

Anne thought that Samuel could not perform the regular transition routine without special prompting and practice, mainly for cognitive reasons. That is, he had difficulty separating what was salient in the environment—

the oral directions, the books and papers on his desk, his actual physical desti-
nation—from his inner thoughts, fantasies, and the extraneous stimuli in the
environment. He would manifest his confusion by wandering aimlessly,
chanting the same sound over and over, picking up on a random curse word
he'd just heard and screaming it loudly. I observed Anne's technique for in-
tervening this way: She would first face Samuel, or somehow require him to
look directly at her face. She would then say "Control your mouth right now,
Samuel." (This phrase, "Control your . . ." was a cue that most adults used
with him by agreement. Given the cue, he would usually make efforts to focus
his attention on salient details of whatever action he was to attempt.) Once
he stopped his noise or words, Anne would explain the routine he had to
perform and then ask for him either to repeat it, or later in the year, to acknowledge that he understood. Only if he was unable to gain control over
his utterances or behavior, would she give him an "if . . . then'" ultimatum:
"Samuel, if you cannot control your mouth and stop talking by the count of
three, then you will have to sit in the time-out chair until you can control
your mouth and do the transition." She would then count to three. Careful,
clear, sequential talk, looking into each other's face, maintaining close physical proximity, touching—these were all components of her pedagogy with
Samuel. Knowing that Samuel's difficulties were largely cognitive in nature
invoked very specific behavioral management strategies.

Aaron, on the other hand, often had difficulty at transition times because
he was being asked to stop what he was doing and start something else; Anne
knew that his need to have control over adults was exacerbated at such times.
He could become demanding, "You put the stupid book away!" Or he'd be
abusive, mumbling just loudly enough for Anne to hear, "Pussy!!" Or he
could be defiant, throwing the work he was doing in a heap into his cubby
before crossing back to his seat where he would refuse to sit properly. Anne
interpreted these behaviors as attempts to engage adults in negative interactions with him. I observed Anne using a pedagogical approach for teaching
Aaron new transition behaviors that began by suppressing her impulse to respond first to his negative surface behavior. She knew from experience that if
she chose to deal with his abusiveness, for instance, he might escalate it and
she might never get the transition behaviors taught. She used a combination
of circumvention and ignoring his behavior. She circumvented it by giving
him earlier warning of an impending transition, and more time past the beginning of the actual transition to finish his work and accomplish the tasks of
putting things away and getting to his seat. She ignored as far as feasible his
negative utterances, keeping her discourse with him very spare and focused
on doing the transition. Only if he escalated his angry utterances by turning
them on another boy or actually becoming aggressive did she attend to the
negative behavior. Then she would send him to time-out without any or with

very little explanation. Once his time was finished and he was calm, she would discuss with him what she had expected and why he had been sent to time-out. Giving Aaron extra warning and extra time to comply with requests, minimizing discourse with him around his habitually negative behaviors, maximizing talk about the task at hand, refusing to engage in arguments about consequences, and discussing them only when calm had been regained—these were components of her pedagogy with Aaron. In this case, knowing that Aaron's difficulties were largely emotional in nature invoked behavioral management strategies quite different from those she used with Samuel.

Consistently treating the boys differently—even when they were exhibiting the same type of surface behavior, like not following directions or not performing the transition routine—was one strategy that enabled Anne to manage the individuals and the group simultaneously. But she could not institute this differential treatment fully until she had made the decision to separate those who were most disruptive. It is important to note that Anne considered separation and differential behavioral teaching sufficient only to keep control of the class. As far as she was concerned, the group behavioral difficulties were symptoms of individual social and emotional disturbance. Her goal was to address the causes through curricula and pedagogies aimed directly at the social and emotional causes themselves, not just the surface behavioral symptoms.

A REORDERED CURRICULAR STRUCTURE

By mid-October, Anne had begun to realize that portions of her original schedule for both morning and afternoon activities did not make sense for the children and actually agitated them. In late August when she had originally set the schedule, she was unsure of the boys' academic abilities and she viewed the first month of school as a diagnostic period. Although she had expected she would need to adjust the schoolwork once she was more sure of what they were capable, she had not expected them to have the massive behavioral difficulties that they had. It became increasingly clear that she needed to adjust not only what she was asking them to do in class, but how and when they were asked to do it. Thus, the scope, sequence, and a fair amount of the content of the day were adjusted to meet the boys at their developmental level, behaviorally, and to begin the long trek forward to teach them new group behaviors.

In the original schedule, the children began arriving in class at 8:45 and immediately started a structured, teacher-assigned activity using "the word for the day." After 15 minutes, when all were settled and work was checked, the adults would conduct a formal transition to morning meeting. Boys were asked to sit quietly on their seats and, when they had done so, a period of talk was planned to begin the day. The talk was meant to be about their evenings and what they had done, the date, the weather, any special holidays or announcements; the objective was to teach language skills as well as general information. But word time and morning meeting were very often times of violence and disruption because it was exceedingly difficult to settle these boys. When the boys entered the room and were required to begin a conventional, quiet, organized activity, they were primed for rebellion. Presenting them with what looked like schoolwork brought on the chaos. Anne realized that retaining this organization with the group precluded success.

She changed the organization of the period. Now as soon as they came in, they could choose any quiet activity, the computer if it was their day, games, a book, or their word folder. They could sit or lie anywhere in the room to do their activity, as long as they were cooperative. A formal, announced transition to the next activity, where all the boys moved through the class at once, would not take place. Anne tried to move as seamlessly as possible from activity to activity, keeping as many boys occupied for as long as possible with one activity, then slipping into the next.

The change in the morning meeting period did not affect the curriculum goals for teaching language skills and general information. It did affect the concomitant behavioral curriculum in both content as well as method. Anne had, in effect, stepped back in the sequence of objectives from first-grade objectives to kindergarten and preschool objectives: Originally she had shaped the schedule in this way not only as a means for teaching language; it was also meant to provide practice in first-grade school behaviors, especially group behaviors. The goals were to help the boys settle down and focus on school, and to teach them to begin an individual academic task, finish it as a group, and move to the next, group-oriented task in an organized and orderly fashion. However, the curriculum goal was shifted, and the new schedule for the first half hour of school reflected the needs of a group of preschoolers who would recoil at any change in task, in environment, or in adult caretaker— changes that aroused their behavioral difficulties.

Subsequent morning sessions, where instruction in math and reading were individualized or in groups of two, were less problematic. No organizational changes were made because the group problems were not as prevalent. The next organizational change that affected the whole group involved from lunchtime through the afternoon, when the group was all together for lunch, naptime, writing, social studies, and science. Lunchtime/naptime was chaos. Originally, half the boys remained in class for nap while the other half went to the lunchroom to eat. After half an hour, the groups would switch. The idea had been to minimize the effects on the boys of a busy lunchroom filled with older children. But the boys at nap were hungry and couldn't rest; the boys at lunch had few good eating habits, and adults spent substantial energy teaching the boys what and how to eat, while directing and redirecting their wild behaviors in the midst of a loud lunchroom. The transition back from the lunchroom was often violent, with as many as three boys in serious trouble at one time. The trouble spilled over into the afternoon and it could take as long as an hour "to gradually pull back together." Anne changed the schedule so all the children attended lunch together during the first half hour. She also increased the number of adults eating with the children to help manage their behavior, alternating with Cathy in order to assist Karen in the lunchroom.

After a number of discussions with Alex and her classroom team, she did away with naptime altogether because it did not work as a naptime. With the half hour she added more read-aloud time. Where naptime was never restful, being read to enabled the boys to rest and regroup after lunch. The change in behavior, though not consistent, could be remarkable. The boys were occupied thoroughly by the stories and would cuddle against adults, thumbs in mouths, as the stories were read. For her part, Anne was content to add 30 more minutes of language time to the day and took advantage of this to read a great variety of books.

As well as this period could go, the transition to the second period of the afternoon could erupt badly. It appeared to her that the organization and goals of the period, a half hour schedule for language arts and a half hour of social studies or science, were not appropriate if the whole group was to stay together. This configuration suited the older children she had taught in the past. But for these children the demarcations of time by specific content were artificial. Perhaps they were artificial for Anne as well. When she thought of the afternoon as structured by content instead of by the boys' needs, Anne felt responsible to cover the curriculum. She was not able to address what she came to understand were the real needs of her young students.

> Labels of science, social studies, art, language arts seem very artificial at the level these kids are at. . . . A lot of what they're doing . . . all of it needs to be experiential, hands-on stuff. All of it is increasing their language skills. All of it is increasing their experience of the world. It seems sort of artificial to separate it into distinct blocks of curriculum development at this point. . . . I was feeling like it didn't make sense to have [social studies or science] be a specific thing that happened every day for half an hour . . . it didn't make sense to have a writing period or a language arts period as a regular part of the schedule. But that we would have different kinds of language arts experiences as well as science and social studies experiences within that afternoon block of time.

She elaborated her thoughts from a developmental point of view.

In terms of their attention span and the best way to do curriculum with kids this young, I've been thinking a lot . . . the curriculum that makes more sense for them developmentally, and in terms of their behavior . . . becomes much more of an integration between science and social studies and language arts and art and all of those things. . . . That whole afternoon block has sort of merged together. Rather than [be] two separate activities, it's often actually been sort of one activity that incorporates a lot of those different things. . . . Is it a reasonable expectation to have 8:45 to 2:30 packed with academic activity after academic activity after academic activity? Coming back after lunch and having a 30-minute language arts activity and then a 30-minute science/social studies activity . . . was not a reasonable group expectation.

Slowly, as she saw the children for who they were, not who she expected them to be, she shifted the schedule and the plan of activities to a preschool/ kindergarten style afternoon. The children responded better and felt less pressure to do what they didn't yet understand or feel able to do. At the same time, Anne eliminated the confining feeling she had during half-hour periods devoted to the same thing every day. She felt freed to address the children with what she saw as the sensible approach. The content remained science, social studies, and language—but she taught it more in tandem with their rhythms. She ruminated on the new structure that addressed different behavioral goals.

[I'm not] trying to do it all every day, not trying to accomplish it all as quickly as I might have last year. [I'm] doing sometimes language arts things, sometimes science things, sometimes social studies things. [For language arts and writing] the goals are still there. . . . You know, by the end of this year, the three kids who wouldn't be in kindergarten [the older three children], I want them to be writing. . . . I want them to be writing stories. And the other two kids, I want them at least to be telling stories and maybe doing some writing. . . . But at the same time, it's equally, if not more, important in some ways right now to learn how to be functioning in a group and to do group lessons and things like that.

Part of her decision to make these structural changes was rooted in her desire to minimize the behavioral ramifications of transitions while retaining the transition time itself. It was true that the boys were most likely to fall into negative or dangerous behavior at a transition from activity to activity or place to place. And if a boy fell into difficulties at a transition, he would usually continue to have troubles through the next period. Yet, Anne needed transition times to do direct behavioral teaching. Ordinarily during transition times, Anne lifts the students' behavior from the context of the preceding period to teach the behavioral curriculum in more conventional terms. The transition not only provides a clear ending of one activity and the beginning of another, it also is when boys stop, assemble, hear an adult's estimation of their behavior during the previous period, receive rewards for the behaviors that they are working to change, and hear what will be expected in the next period. It is the time when the behavioral objectives of Anne's plan become the actual content of discussion with the children.

This transition routine is a part of the overall Brighton pedagogy, developed over the years by the school leadership and taught to new teachers through modeling by and supervision with the principal. The routine differs from class to class depending on the age of students and the behavioral management system of rewards and consequences devised by each teaching team for their group. No two classroom behavioral management systems are exactly alike nor are any two transition routines. However, the basic components of stopping, evaluating, rewarding, and setting continuing expectations are present in every transition school-wide. When Anne relieved some of the pressure the boys felt during class periods, she was better able to manage and use the transitions between class periods to teach new behaviors.

HAVING ILLUMINATED Anne's behavioral curriculum, I turn next to her social curriculum and pedagogy, which are its close companions. As I have indicated, whereas the behavioral curriculum is aimed at the symptomatic behaviors of the children's disturbance, her social and emotional curriculum is aimed at the causes. Although Anne had been developing the social curriculum from the first days of school, her thoughts had been preoccupied with the behavioral curriculum. In the first months of 1989, Anne's focus shifted decisively to developing the details of the social curriculum and to braiding its objectives to work concomitantly with the existing behavioral objectives. I use the narrative at the beginning of Chapter 6 to show the observable progression of the boys toward some of Anne's social goals, and then turn to an analysis of the foundation components of the social and emotional curriculum in Anne's class.

CHAPTER 6

GAINING MOMENTUM

It is February 2, 1989. "Ladies and gentlemen! We have *two* authors of the day today! The first book is by Brian." Brian comes eagerly forward from his bench to sit beside Anne and before Samuel, Aaron, and Cathy. Jason and Paul are missing from the class, placed in extended time-out for dangerous behavior. "Do you want me to read it or do you want to read it?" He seems a little shy about reading his story (actually, she knows he has trouble reading independently all the words he has used in his story, but she gives him the option out of respect); he gestures to her to read. "It's called *Dino-Sorcerers.*"

"Read the dedication," Cathy tells Anne.

" 'For Anne,' It's dedicated to me. I'm very honored," she looks to Brian sincerely, as she ceremoniously opens to the first page of the thin booklet. Brian the bold is suddenly Brian the bashful and he casts his eyes toward the floor. Intermittently over the past 2 weeks, he and Cathy have worked to write the story, he dictating and she acting as scribe. He has happily illustrated each neatly printed page of the manuscript with colored markers, and then together they carefully glued it into a cardboard jacket sheathed in shiny golden contact paper. Finally, they affixed the title with stick-on letters. He has been told these materials are all very expensive; he knows the occasion is very special.

" 'These two dinosaurs don't have a family,' " Anne begins to read. " 'This dinosaur is very valuable. He is a baby. He lost his mother.' " She shows the class the picture Brian has drawn in his book, a brontosaurus all alone on the expanse of white. She turns the page and goes on. " 'The valuable dinosaur is friends with the other two. They take care of him. These are two more valuable dinosaurs. They lost their mother too. They visit . . .' "

"STOP!!" Samuel yells out. He has been squirming on his bench. When Cathy touched his leg with her hand to bring his attention back, he disrupted the story—and the mood—by commanding her to leave him alone.

"Part of your point for writing is being a good audience," Anne tells him. While invoking the behavioral management system of the class her voice never changes from the tone she was using reading Brian's book. She reads on.

" 'They visit the other three dinosaurs. The dinosaurs play and read books to each other.'" She looks up to find Aaron perusing his own book instead of listening. "Aaron, your book should be closed right now and you should be listening to Brian's. Closed and behind you." She means he should slide the book behind his back—out of sight and out of hand—which he does without an argument. "That's right. Behind you so you can be a good audience to Brian. Good job."

"'The dinosaurs play and read books to each other. They eat other animals. They run races.'" By now Brian has overcome his bashfulness and is holding the book for Anne, turning the pages as she reads, commenting on how he made the dinosaurs look like they were running. Anne continues, "'Then they get drinks when they are done running races. In the night time the thunder comes. But the dinosaurs don't get scared. The End.'" She ceremoniously closes the book. "Who can raise their hand and tell Brian something they liked about his book?" Aaron's hand goes up. Cathy's hand goes up.

"I liked everything," Aaron says quickly. He is the second author of the day and it looks like he'd rather skip this "what part do you like in Brian's book" activity to get on with reading *his* book.

"Can you think of one best, best part that you liked best?" Anne inquires with enthusiasm, trying to teach what it means to be "a good audience." Aaron gets up and comes to look closely at Brian's book.

"I like that, that, and that," he points to three pictures, "all of them are the best." It's perfunctory praise—but praise nonetheless. Brian is no longer feeling any shyness as he points at Cathy to give him still more praise.

"I like when the dinosaurs all drink together." She is very specific, following Anne's cues, modeling how to be a good audience for the author of the day.

"Samuel?" By now Brian has taken over the proceedings entirely and is polling each person for their praise. Samuel gets up from his seat, comes to Brian, and turns the pages of his book until he finds the page he likes.

"I like this here," he drones. Now Anne raises her hand to be called on.

"Anne?" Brian points to her authoritatively, inadvertently sounding like a teacher, like Anne does herself.

"I like when the two dinosaurs take care of the valuable dinosaur who lost his mommy." Brian quickly flips through his book to find the page where that happens and displays it to Anne for verification. She smiles and gives him a hug as she nods her head in affirmation and approval; he wriggles with satisfaction at so much attention.

The ecstatic Brian, now a bundle of mischievous humor and overflowing energy, jumps up and announces that his next book, already in progress, will "be called *Meanies!!*" He certainly seems motivated to write—but he also is motivated to tease; he has growled the word "meanies" to Aaron, who is waiting anxiously to read his own book. The word (not to mention its delivery) is a provocative one—"meanies" is one of those words that always manages to get the other boys giggling and that changes the tone of the group. The tone turns silly now, extra energy filling the space. But the adults quickly maneuver Aaron to the author of the day chair, Brian to his bench, and everyone's attention to the task at hand.

"Okay, ladies and gentlemen, today is a *very* special day. Because today we have not just one author, but *two* authors!! Introducing Mr. Aaron Blake who is going to read his own book for us." He looks up at her, smiling and squirming with anticipation, his face contorting into a series of strange expressions (contortions that, in retrospect, foreshadowed his progressive inability to manage thoughts and affect). She says playfully, "And don't forget to show them the pictures!!"

"Aaron and the Kitty" commences. Aaron can read his own work, but his reading is somewhat labored, filled with long pauses and sounding-out-the-word hesitations. It's harder for him to keep the other boys' attention—especially Brian's. But he forges on, and the adults keep Brian scarcely in check, alternately squirming and talking out, until Aaron is through and he can ask the others what they liked about his story.

Barely 10 minutes of class time transpired. For Anne, they were 10 minutes spent straining to maintain a basic social activity, that is, to keep just two boys' attention on one boy as he told his story. The list of events and distractions weighing on Anne's consciousness as she worked to keep their focus was varied and formidable: She considered Aaron, who was giving into his anxieties about reading his book to the group; Samuel, who was sporadically giving into, and verbalizing, his fantasies; Brian, who was in the spotlight with his first effort at writing and needed, deserved, very special care—his story was so personal and sad ("It was the saddest story." Anne says later. "It thunders but they're not scared; they feed each other and read each other stories and take care of each other because they have no mommy . . . Brian . . . was telling the saddest story of his life in dinosaur form . . ."); the boys hadn't yet learned the recipe for "being a good audience" and she knew this was an excellent opportunity to model it, except that she worried that one of them might be cruel; she needed to watch Brian carefully because his appropriate excitement and energy could so easily tip over into negativity—he had not yet developed effective emotional boundaries; she could see that Aaron was on the verge of being mean (it was almost inevitable) if he didn't get to read his story in adequate time; and when he finally did get to read, it was of paramount importance that he successfully read aloud with minimal help. Yet, he couldn't keep it flowing, and she saw the attention of the other boys vacillate and then crumble. Brian escalated and could barely be contained; Samuel moaned and rocked. Nevertheless, the little group stayed together; the focus stayed, however marginally, on the accomplishments of each boy. Some of the boys' social and emotional needs got met; some social skills got taught.

A MORE THERAPEUTIC WAY

Later, when Anne commented on the lesson, she mentioned that "things are light years away from where they were in early November in terms of the group." Indeed, this appeared true. As she began to bring the behavior of the group under control, she simultaneously worked to "hook them" on the activities of the class. The boys were by no means behaving and learning as an integrated whole; they were not yet acting like a group (and she was wise enough to know they might never be like a group in any consistent way). But from the chaos of the first months of school, threads of order were emerging, moments of focused learning were happening, and opportunities for therapeutic teaching occasionally presented themselves. They appeared only in snapshots, freeze frames, fragments of stories—but they gave evidence that Anne's attention to the social and emotional needs of the boys might eventually pay off, that she was finding a therapeutic way to teach these boys.

The social gains appeared to be based on the boys' growing trust of Anne and the environment she created. Reviewing some of these isolated events, we can see that she had begun to gain their trust, had created a more predictable and emotionally safe atmosphere. She had been consistently accurate in her interventions and was finding more effective ways all the time, and they were letting her do it, letting her into their worlds.

Building Trust

"I'm odd, don't you think?" asks the consistently rigid and defended Aaron one day as he and Anne are cutting paper and gluing a book together. The rest of the boys and adults are working around them in pairs or alone, talking and laughing, each with their own projects. He sits with her in a pocket of solitude.

"You're what?" she asks calmly, conversationally, showing no sign at how surprised—how *odd*—the question is, coming as it does without warning.

"Odd," he says. There is a long pause. "What does odd mean?"

"Odd means strange," she says as she continues to cut the paper in her hand. At the other table, Brian asks Cathy to write another sentence for him. Samuel is hovering, becoming impatient to receive help from Anne.

"I'm odd," Aaron says with an inflection that sounds like he is rehearsing the new label he has given himself.

"Who told you that?" They never look at each other, only at the paper they're manipulating.

"My mind."

"Your mind?"

"Yeah. My mind told me that I'm odd."

"How come?" she asks. But before he can answer, they are cut off by an impatient Samuel who cannot wait any longer for Anne to help him.

Aaron provided her with the thinnest thread of insight to his sense of self, but it was just such threads that have helped her shape the teaching environment. One can see how, by accruing small insights, she was coming to understand the kinds of challenges that prompted each boy to flounder in an activity or to engage with some degree of success. She continued to build real relationships with them based on respect for them as people, taking into consideration each boy's strengths and vulnerabilities.

In the following snapshot of Anne with Paul, it is clear how her relationship with him and her knowledge of him as a person permitted her to use his blend of little-boy neediness and macho rebelliousness to dare him to read.

"Stop looking silly," Anne says firmly as Paul comes leaping around the room looking loose and a little out of control. That's kind of a code at Brighton. "Silly" is a provocative, hysterical stance that some children often take when they are on the verge of being overwhelmed by their own energy. He pulls himself together immediately and says, "I'm glad I didn't miss my reading because I'd be in *big* trouble!" He had been sent to the school crisis center previously for violent misbehavior, but he had just now worked his way back to class. He is endearing, and it's hard not to smile. Paul looks forward to his one-to-one reading time with Anne very much. Anne enjoys him at times like these, because he can be such a little boy!

Anne whispers to him when he is settled at the table that it is Aaron's birthday tomorrow and that they need to make a card—but they can't let Aaron know. The mock conspiracy of making the card adds to the fun of being social, of thinking about Aaron on his birthday. Paul becomes animated, businesslike, manly, as he demands to write the words "Happy Birthday" himself on the white paper she has given to him. Smiling secretly to herself, Anne follows his orders and says each letter as he demands it. When he is finished, he looks up.

"What's next???" To draw a picture for the card, he is told. His face lights up. "WATCH!" He draws a big orange pumpkin. Lickety-split, he's done and wanting to see what is on his reading "contract" for the day. When he hears that the first thing is to read some short "a" words, he grabs his head, "No, no, I can't do it!" His tough guy attitude dissolves instantly. Anne says, "I know you like doing easy things and you don't like doing hard or new things." Paul looks up, "Yeah!" he says, taking Anne's comment to mean he has been victorious in his manipulation to avoid the work. But very lightly she says, "Don't you want to be a reader?" He retorts, probably thinking about his successfully completed pumpkin birthday card: "I want to be an artist!!"

She puts a word down in front of him and says, "I know you can't do this one!" It is a very easy word for him and she knows it. But with Paul, the name of the game is "I Dare You to Try." He looks up at her with an expression on his face that says he thinks she is nuts. "Yes, I can!" He reads it, and then another. But she keeps teasing and daring, "Get ready 'cause I'm gonna trick ya 'cause I know you can't read *this* one!!"

The review of short "a" is completed quickly, and the two move on to the next item on his contract, and then the next—each slightly more difficult than the previous item. Finally he is given his penmanship page. The letter for today is *K*. He sees it and blurts out, "I HATE K'S!!!" She answers, calmly, "But if you can't write *K*'s, how will you write Karen's name, or Kite, or Kitten?" He tries for a moment but then throws down the pencil, "My brain is broken!!" He's squirming, grabbing the curtains beside his chair, whining; he looks like he is about to explode. Anne is calm, firm; she waits a few seconds and then shows him how. "First you put the pencil here. One, two, three. See?" She makes the three requisite lines that form a *K*. "But it's *very hard* to write good letters." He grabs the pencil from her, determined to show it's not too hard for him to do! He writes the letter and it looks really good. His face cracks into a big smile. He tries again, succeeds, and with each repetition giggles at his success. Finally, he jumps up and shouts, "I'm getting good at this!!" Anne just sits by and laughs with him.

Capitalizing on the Moment

Watching Anne teach, one sees how flexible she can be, how she maneuvers around a child's frustrations until she can find a hook to pull him into the lesson. One can also see how she capitalizes on learning opportunities as they arise.

In the following vignette, she can be seen inserting a quick, precise lesson about rudeness and impatience into a writing lesson because the opportunity presented itself. She could do this because this writing activity was going well, was compelling enough that the boy wanted to get back to the fun activity. He was motivated to pay attention to her brief interlude of social teaching and seemed willing to give up his manipulative behaviors to get what he wanted.

As transition to writing time ends, Anne sends Brian to the round table with Cathy to work on his story-in-progress. Aaron, in a moment of genuine and unfettered excitement, jolting in its intensity because these moments are so rare, claps his hands and jumps up, shouting, "PUBLISHING!!" He knows that today is his chance to begin publishing his newest book, which requires adorning it with illustrations and binding it into a cover. He likes to illustrate, and he is particularly excited about using the black stick-on letters to label his book cover. For some reason stickers, any kind of stickers, have a magic hold on these children. But Anne tells both Aaron and Samuel, who also has a new manuscript ready, that they must first carefully illustrate each page. She tries to impress upon them how careful they must be, overstating how important the illustrations are, dramatically heightening the importance of the task.

"Listen to what I want you to think about. I want you to make the most careful illustrations you have made *in your whole life!* I want . . . no scribbling, no sloppy pictures! But the most careful illustrations . . ." The boys sit at the table together, eager to begin, able to tolerate being near each other and not getting into a fight.

"Can you get my publishing?" Aaron means the shiny cover and the fun stick-on letters. He wants to get to the fun part.

"We're going to illustrate first. What does this page say?"

He ignores her question, will not be redirected to reading his work before making his drawings. He insists that he can quickly draw the pictures and that she must get the materials for publishing so he can start gluing and assembling. He becomes more and more rude with such exchange. Finally, he pushes Anne away; and she tells him he is being too rude, that he must go back to his bench, sit quietly, and then they may be able to start over.

"Okay, okay, I'll stop!" He obviously doesn't want to be sent away and he quickly rallies. But Anne will not be dissuaded and insists that he go. She turns to help Samuel, and so Aaron angrily pushes his crayon box across the table, bumping her hand with it. She ignores him, except to point to his bench as she continues to speak quietly with Samuel. After a few more feeble tries at angering her, Aaron goes to his bench. Some moments later, and after she tells him he is "finally sitting the right way," Anne comes over to sit next to him and to talk.

"Why are you sitting on your bench?"

"Because I was rude," he blurts out, leaps up, and runs back to the table to start his publishing, having given what he knows to be the desired response.

"Uh-uh. Come back!" She has no intention of letting this opportunity slip by. He is extremely motivated to do the activity—a perfect opportunity to make a point with him about his behavior, an excellent time to have him trade in his socially inappropriate behavior for a desired academic activity. When he returns to his bench, she approaches his inappropriate behavior by gently addressing the underlying issue, that is, his impulsiveness: "You're anxious to get to drawing your pictures because you like to draw pictures. But it is important before you draw the pictures to read the words so that you know what the picture is about."

"Why do I have to?!?" He growls it; he has his back to Anne, and has grabbed onto a nearby desk. He is twisting his body against it in frustration at the assignment's constraints and Anne's calm insistence. It is difficult to tell if he is getting her message.

"Because that's the way we're going to do our books." It's really as simple as that, and she doesn't elaborate further.

"And then after that is done I can publish the book?" His body is relaxing a little, less motion, less frustration. It is as if he can see an emerging path toward his goal.

"After all the illustrations are done, then we can publish the book." She reiterates the points, being careful to spell out the whole requirement. This seems to be enough for Aaron, but when he returns to his table he still won't read his page aloud and insists on reading it "in my mind." Anne agrees to this, knowing that Aaron is Aaron: He must retain some semblance of control over the situation if he is to remain in the group. She has made her point and for now must settle for a slight advance in his behavior.

Preserving the Learning Environment

In both the reading lesson with Paul and the writing lesson with Aaron, Anne's individual interventions dug under the surface of their outbursts and aimed at the boys' personality, their immature tolerance for frustration, their impulsiveness. In these interventions, she was taking hold of the situation in an increasingly intimate way with each boy.

She was dealing with the group as a social entity as well. To motivate the boys to stay in the group, the adults had worked hard so that the boys got the idea that the fun in the class would go on without them if they got themselves taken to time-out. The divide and conquer idea was no longer just reactive, meant to separate the boys from each other for safety reasons alone. Now, when the adults separated the boys, they tried to keep them within earshot. The strategy was to let the boy who was in trouble hear just how much he was missing by being away from the group.

At the start of transition after read-aloud period, the energy in the room explodes, as it so often does. Paul throws himself back on his bench, spreads his legs, yells to Samuel to watch, and begins to point at his anus. It is a provocation that never fails, and Samuel starts shrieking and laughing on cue. Jason, not to be outdone, grabs a book off the shelf near his bench and begins mimicking the adults, yelling, "I'm going to read you a book!" Anne takes the book away from Jason, turns to the group, and declares: "I'm going to count to three and I want to see boys doing the right thing," but to no avail. For by now, Aaron is rolling back on his bench and pointing to his anus as well; Jason has grabbed another book off the shelf, this one belonging to Brian. Brian joins the fray to get his book back; Samuel screams more maniacally. Clearly, they are not doing the "right thing."

Without even speaking the three adults move into action: Cathy takes Paul by the arm and moves him to time-out; Karen sits beside Samuel and commands him to look her in the face and to listen to her direction to stop his mouth; Anne tries to hold Jason's hands at his sides, vainly attempting to prevent him from grabbing books from the shelf. His behavior begins to escalate violently and, in an uncharacteristic move, she suddenly lifts him up bodily and removes him to the farthest time-out space, well out of sight. With Samuel finally quiet, Karen moves to the adult transition seat and begins the transition routine with the remaining three boys and forges ahead with the plans. Writing class is about to begin.

Within a matter of seconds, quiet returns to the room. Paul calms himself quickly in time-out; he is clearly motivated to be back in class to do the activity, to see what comes next. He sits in the time-out chair while holding Cathy's wrist, staring at her watch to see his 2 minutes elapse. He soon returns. Jason does not fare so well, and Anne spends a few minutes settling him into time-out. By the time she returns to the group, they are all in control of themselves; Karen has finished the transition routine completely; Cathy is sitting on the bench beside the reinstated Paul. He is sucking his thumb with one hand and holding her arm with the other, leaning against her so tightly that if she moved he would surely topple over without her support. And so the next fun lesson begins, with four boys in attendance and one within earshot.

In these few scenes from Anne's class, we see and hear the children give evidence of their social and emotional disabilities—disabilities that have been summed up elsewhere as the "pervasive inability to trust, depression, impaired tolerance for frustration, and failure to interpose thought between impulse and action" that ultimately result in these children having "severe difficulty making and maintaining basic human connections" (Small, Kennedy, & Bender, 1991, p. 331). These are the disabilities Anne sets out to address, and in the vignettes above we can see a small sample of her interventions. Almost in direct response to Small, Kennedy, and Bender's conceptualization, we can see her making efforts to build *trust,* we see her attempting to foster *relationships,* we observe her attempts to *capitalize on moments* to socialize the boys, we watch her efforts to *preserve the primacy of the group,* and we hear her use, again and again, very specific *language*—all in an effort, I maintain, to "interpose thought between impulse and action."

MEETING THE SOCIAL LEARNING CHALLENGE

What emerges from these stories, as well as from the evidence to come, is a social curriculum and pedagogy that are meant to teach something about both *doing* what is social as well as *being* what is social in order to maintain "basic human connections." Within this curriculum effort, Anne explicitly teaches what is social and she implicitly models what is social; it is the implicit qualities that are hardest to capture. The social curriculum resides largely in the ways Anne insists that life gets lived in the classroom. The curriculum is imparted through the values she places on certain social activities and attitudes, on valuing not only what gets done, but how it gets done. Establishing such an environment with these children is difficult at best.

In quite ordinary circumstances, it takes time to build a classroom environment where youngsters learn to be social and to do what is social. In developmentally oriented elementary classrooms, teachers work hard to foster a spirit of cooperation, collaborative and individual effort, and respect for the differences of others. While building momentum toward those goals, teachers make use of the different threads of social ability and understanding with which children present themselves, such as the emerging sense of self and autonomy in most children; their ability to tolerate a modicum of frustration; their ability to control their most primitive impulses; their ability to engage in parallel activity; their basic trust that the world will not do them harm.

Unfortunately, Anne's students presented themselves as having few such threads of socialized behavior with which to work, and it was she who was being asked to help weave them from meager resources. This was no small challenge, for while the social understandings and competencies of Anne's students remained largely undeveloped, the children themselves were growing older. The inevitable social requirements placed on them by peers, families, schools, and their neighborhoods were advancing quite independently of their ability to meet those requirements. Each child's inner conflict between social ability and social expectation could be seen in some aspect of his difficult, sometimes wild, behavior.

In Anne's mind, the behavioral and social aspects of the children's personalities overlap and interact with each other, and as she works out her social curriculum and pedagogy with any class, she perforce addresses behavioral issues. Moving deeper into Anne's thinking and action in this case, we can see a complex shifting back and forth between behavioral and social domains, and a fair amount of lingering in the common area between them as well. As Anne gained momentum in dealing with the behavioral issues of the class, she also gained momentum in addressing the social underpinnings of that behavior. But the reverse was also true, and as Anne worked with the threads of a social curriculum in her class, she was at the same time weaving them with the behavioral curriculum she had begun to establish.

CHAPTER 7

SHAPING A SOCIAL CURRICULUM
AND PEDAGOGY

Anne's social curriculum and pedagogy revolve around three key premises that, for her, constitute a therapeutic means for increasing pro-social behaviors. She insists that in order for children to learn to be and to do what is social, they must live and work in groups. Only in a group context will their social strengths and weaknesses be revealed, thus giving her the material for teaching and learning. She also believes strongly that children's work must be meaningful. Only if they involve themselves in meaningful work can she hope to teach them anything at all—be it social or academic. Perhaps the most subtle aspect of the social curriculum resides in Anne's ability to use specific language as the most potent means not only to communicate her thoughts to the children, but also, eventually, to "interpose thought" between the unchained impulses of the children and their subsequent actions.

LANGUAGE AND THERAPEUTIC LEARNING

Early in the life of this project, as I videotaped the children during a writing activity, I observed a curious verbal interchange between Cathy and Brian that left me wondering about language and how Anne used it in her teaching. Brian had been directed to settle down to work on illustrating his book. While crossing in front of me on his way to retrieve some supplies, he became momentarily distracted by the video camera. He made a smile for the camera and struck a pose, the kind of thing that the boys would do for the camera from time to time. Cathy gently said to him, "Come on, Brian. Remember how Anne told us we have to do good ignoring of Joe when he is here? I want you to ignore Joe." Brian cocked his head and with a confused-sounding voice said, "Why do we have to ignore him? Did he do something wrong?" Cathy seemed nonplussed; Brian's question had left her exposed. Until now, "ignoring" was something that Anne told the boys to do (and therefore novice teacher Cathy told the boys to do) when others were not

81

doing "the right thing"—like when Paul was rolling around the bench and pointing to his anus, or Samuel was shrieking. Joe was clearly doing neither.

Brian's question was apt because Cathy had inadvertently introduced a whole new meaning for the word, and thus a whole new social expectation. When she finally found her words, Cathy explained that Joe hadn't done anything wrong, but (and at this she hesitated and visibly grappled with her explanation), "we don't ignore others only when they're doing something wrong. Sometimes we ignore people when we should be paying attention to something else." Brian thought about that for a moment, then shrugged and went to work on his drawing.

I though about Cathy's explanation as well. From an adult's perspective, her explanation clearly was incomplete and simplistic. We ignore people for many different reasons, some of which are contradictory: We don't always ignore those who are doing something wrong, because the results would be tragic. Sometimes we ignore others when they are doing something wrong to get our attention, as in the case of a child who is acting naughty. And we have learned to ignore others who are doing nothing wrong but who might make us uncomfortable or put us into danger. Yet, we have also learned that to ignore another person is rude. The word remains the same; its social uses and meanings change with the context.

Anne's language is peppered with such vocabulary and expressions as "that's good ignoring," "you're doing good listening," or "you're doing the right thing." Each of these expressions, when used in her class, appears simplistic at first. Anne herself says they sound funny to her ears, "a little ridiculous" sometimes. That is because they are used narrowly and function as encapsulations of very complicated social concepts; they are reductions of behaviors and attitudes that constitute aspects of socialized behavior. But in the context of the classroom over time, the children confront the words in new and increasingly complex circumstances, and consequently they confront deeper social meanings. For instance, Brian's puzzled question and expression when he was told to "do good ignoring" revealed a bit of the complexity of what it means "to ignore." He confronted what adults have already learned, that no matter which way one slices it, the whole idea of ignoring another person is socially complex: Why do we ignore others? Whom do we ignore and under what conditions do we ignore them? When is ignoring another person socially appropriate? Socially necessary? Socially desirable?

It is difficult to teach social behavior, particularly to these boys and children like them. They have little, if any, positive experience and clear understanding, or, as in the case of Samuel, the cognitive maturity on which to build socially appropriate behavior. Anne, and teachers like her, are given the task of socializing children who have been minimally socialized to date, or whose socialization has been skewed by their early environments.

Anne's repeated interjection of certain words and phrases into the social milieu of the class was, at least at first, an interposition of *her* thoughts between the boy's impulses and actions (to borrow again from Small, Kennedy, & Bender, 1991), eventually leading to the boys socially thinking for themselves. For instance, Brian at first had no cognitive or affective tools at his disposal with which he could resist Paul's wild, sexual gyrations. Anne inserted "ignoring" as a tool he could use to stay out of trouble. But only over time and with practice did Brian actually learn what she meant: The social goal was not to ignore Paul per se, but to choose to avoid the trouble through the act of ignoring Paul's behavior. Only over time did the word "ignore" become thought for Brian—thought that mediated his impulse to involve himself in others' difficulties and caused him to choose alternative actions. Nevertheless, having learned what ignoring meant in regard to Paul's behavior, he was suddenly confronted with ignoring in a new context, that is, ignoring Joe as he videotaped. And so began the process of learning the new social meaning, and eventually the new social behavior, encapsulated in "ignoring."

There were two interrelated ways in which this kind of language helped form the social curriculum and pedagogy of Anne's class. First, we can characterize some of the vocabulary and expressions that Anne used as content in the social curriculum. This language is used to encapsulate, and then teach, what it means *to be* social as well as what it means *to do* that which is social for a 6- or 7-year-old boy. Second, Anne's use of this limited lexicon amounted to a type of social drill and practice. Drill and practice in this context were evident in such instances as her labeling "good listening" when it occurred in order that the boys might have tangible evidence of what "good listening" actually was; and in eventually giving them practice in making age-appropriate social choices in ways she had modeled for them.

This two-stage process, I think, is not unlike what Vygotsky (1978) called internalization or "the internal reconstruction of an external operation" (p. 56). Internalization, he maintains, proceeds through three "transformations": The first is that "an operation that initially represents an external activity is reconstructed and begins to occur internally," resulting in "development of practical intelligence, voluntary attention, and memory" (p. 57). The lack of this operation in Anne's students is, I believe, roughly equivalent to the "failure to interpose thought between impulse and action" (Small, Kennedy, & Bender, 1991, p. 331). Anne's effort is to provide enough socially appropriate external activity so that it is possible for the boys to build internal recognition of those activities.

At the second level of transformation, Vygotsky states, "an interpersonal process is transformed into an intrapersonal one" (p. 57). Thus, he says, a child's cultural development first happens between people, and only later within the child. Anne's repeated use of certain language, as well as her efforts at arranging suitable practice in socialization, carries with it the hope that eventually the boys will be able to be social without all of the scaffolds she provides. As she says, she hopes that "all the time and effort and energy . . . is going to mean that 10 years from now [they] can lead some sort of productive, more normal lives where [they are] not overrun by sexual and aggressive impulses 80% of the time."

Finally, her notion that the socialization process will take a long time links directly with Vygotsky's third idea about cultural transformation in the child, that it is the "result of a long series of developmental events" (p. 57). As we can see from Anne's comments above, she is aware that she is in this for the long haul—that it will be years before these thoughts and behaviors become automatic (and perhaps they never will).

Vygotsky's (1978) concept of the *zone of proximal development* is helpful in understanding both the time it will take for Anne's students to become social, as well as the method she uses to teach them. The zone of proximal development is the area of potential growth an individual possesses for a given behavior. Although a person who is in the lower region of such a zone of development cannot be expected to understand or perform independently in highly differentiated ways, he or she can be expected to do so given external structure or *scaffolding*. Anne provides her students with the scaffolds for social behavior through her habitual use and explanation of such things as "doing good listening" or "doing good ignoring." Over time, and through a vast variety of social experiences, the students begin to work up through their zone of proximal development and internalize what was once external, thereby transforming learning into practical intelligence.

More time for learning such social content is needed for these students than for more typically developing youngsters. The reasons for differences in rate of development vary in type and complexity. For Samuel, for instance, Anne knows that his cognitive integrative difficulties confound his practice at socialization. For Paul or Jason, whose early lives were spent in violent or highly disorganized social environments, many new social experiences must be presented that will be contradictory to those they have already come to understand. Thus, Anne is aware that her students' organically based or socially constructed difficulties have, in a sense, constricted their zones of proximal development. Nevertheless, by providing the content of social learning as she does, and adequate practice using that content, Anne is confident that, over time, her students will make the necessary steps in their social development.

Language as Content in Social Learning

Much of the language Anne uses to scaffold students' social learning is the language of "groupishness." Groupishness is that quality of classroom life

that Anne says she aims to achieve where everyone is "on the same agenda
. . . everyone is focused on the same thing . . . [where] we're interacting with
each other." Her language use clusters roughly into three groups. The first
group are words or phrases that are intended to teach pro-social behavior; the
second group consists of phrases used to teach the boys what not to do, or
how to avoid socially troubling behavior; the third group of phrases provides
information on what adults expect from the boys socially.

In Anne's phrase *be a good audience* we hear a good example of language
to teach pro-social behavior. When author-of-the-day Brian reads his sad
dinosaur story, we hear Anne admonish Aaron to be a good audience. It is a
recurrent expression in writing class. As Anne structures it, writing is a class
that lends itself to teaching a number of social lessons in addition to writing
itself. For instance, in writing class, being a good audience requires the boys
to put away what is personally important, in this case Aaron's own story, and
fully attend to another person's story. Brian's story, she told me, was "the saddest story of his life" and it was important to her that Aaron leave his own
concerns behind, at least temporarily, and be attentive to his classmate. Being
a good audience is also the act of being trustworthy, something especially
important to the process writing approach that Anne employs: The writer-
storyteller must trust his audience to be benevolent, and the listeners must
be trustworthy. A rule of writing is that students "say something you liked
about the story; something that's good." Anne says one of the primary goals
of writing class is for the children to begin "valuing their own creative expression." From Anne's perspective, to be a good audience is clearly to value another's expression. Through reciprocating, they will also value yours.

Being a good friend is another goal of "groupishness," used most often to
label pro-social behaviors that show sportsmanship, social perspective taking,
sympathy, and so forth. For instance, Paul and Aaron plopped in the middle
of the floor and played *Candyland* together one December morning. Anne
played but she didn't need to direct the game. However, when Aaron began
to win, Paul erupted. Anne put her hand out, touched him, and said, "Slow
your body down, Paul." He settled down immediately and the game got back
on track. Anne told them, "You're both playing really fair. You're *being good
friends*!" Aaron then tried to show what a good friend he was when he looked
at Paul and told him, "You know, first is best and second is best, too!" At
transition time, Aaron received an extra sticker as a reward for being a good
friend. "Anything pro-social," she tells me, "in some ways is more [important]
than anything academic that can happen with . . . these kids." On another
occasion, Aaron helped Samuel use rubber cement to paste a book together
instead of doing his own work as he had been told to do (Samuel hated the
smell of rubber cement; "It smells like the hospital," he said). Anne commented on why she didn't redirect Aaron to his assigned work: "Anything
socializing, anything that is treating other people nicely and functioning like

human beings is . . . important. . . . How can I tell them to stop the primitive attempts that are appropriate social behavior?" She rewarded Aaron by praising him for "being a good friend," and tousled his hair.

Doing good waiting is a phrase used like a mantra, to label for the boys a behavioral manifestation of tolerance for frustration. At a transition after a January writing class when all the boys had been involved and active, Anne tried to teach about waiting. They had pulled her in many directions during the period. Anne called it "the classic writing period" where boys were in such need of attention that she had to "pretend to listen" to one so she would not frustrate him, while really attending to another. When she brought the children together at the end of class, she finally got their full and simultaneous attention. She said, "During writing time there are a lot of different things going on. And sometimes kids need to wait. Everyone is excited about what they are doing. But sometimes you just need to wait for an adult to help you." With this announcement, she had introduced a new social behavior, and in the future she began rewarding good waiting and was often heard to ask, "Is that *good waiting?*"

In the second category of language, the phrase most frequently used to teach ways of avoiding social difficulties was a variation on the phrase *set up.* "Don't let him set you up," Anne told Paul while Aaron was mimicking him. In this situation, the important social lesson is to learn how not to allow yourself to be set up by another. But Anne uses the phrase in other situations as well, when she wants to teach the importance of not setting anyone else up. And for some of the boys, the toughest thing to teach is not to set yourself up by acting like a baby or being an easy mark for teasing. All three kinds of setups are prevalent in this class because the boys get each other nervous, she says. Their physical proximity to one another appears to erode their meager emotional or psychological boundaries with each other; it washes away their ability to resist or manage their affect when energy rises around them. As a result, Anne says, "the likelihood of them [the boys] having a problem when all [five] are together . . . [is] greater." When they are most nervous, they are most likely to go on the offensive, to call out the worst in each other through displacement, to prey easily on each other's weaknesses.

Yet, regardless of who is setting up whom, what is interesting and revealing is the way adults speak the phrase, the tone of voice they use in each circumstance. When they speak to a boy who has been set up, there is often an incredulous quality in their voices, almost shock that the boy would allow himself to be drawn into another's foolishness. When adults use the phrase to label the behavior of one who is setting the other up, the tone is critical, impatient, final. Setting up another is wrong, they seem to say, it is unacceptable, it is selfish. And when it is used with the boy who sets himself up, it is often instructive, as if to say, "This is what it is that you do to bring pain on yourself." At other times it is admonishing, as if to say, "You really should be more aware of this by now."

Two phrases often accompany setting up: You should do *good ignoring* and you should *take care of yourself.* I discussed good ignoring above. Taking care of yourself is a phrase Anne uses that often transmits a sense of her confidence in the boy to know what to do. When they sat on their benches and Aaron mimicked Paul's every gesture and move, Paul yelled to Anne, "Anne, Aaron is setting me up!!" "Well, then take care of yourself," she said. "You don't have to pay attention to him." She seemed to be saying that Paul was halfway to managing the social situation on his own simply by knowing that he was being set up. He needed to focus on anything other than Aaron.

Another way to avoid social difficulties is by not *being silly*. Being silly is the hysterical stance boys take in charged situations or when feeling overwhelmed by their emotions. At those times, Anne might tell them that they are *looking a little loose*. It's an accurate behavioral description: Samuel, when illustrating his story, draws his dog with no legs and a body floating in the air. Anne gently admonishes him, telling him that if he wants others to understand his pictures, he has to be more accurate. He doesn't like being told his picture is inadequate and that he has to try harder. He flops down like a rag doll might and begins making a series of meaningless, shapeless noises. For a few moments he appears to have melted into a heap. Anne says he is being silly, and later she describes him as looking loose. Such behavior usually sets him up with the other boys, and they tease him or incite him to engage in even more bizarre behavior. It also sets him up with adults. Indeed, his public school teachers thought he was psychotic; Anne has learned he is quite capable of gaining considerable control over looking loose and being silly.

"I see boys doing the right thing." More than any other expression, *do the right thing* (and its converse, *do the wrong thing*) is the expression Anne uses to label the desired social behaviors of the boys. It falls into the third type of phrase that adults use; it is used to tell the boys what is expected and where they stand. Simplistic to an adult's ear, "doing the right thing" is a phrase scattered across the day, useful in teaching behaviors to the whole group as well as to individuals.

After an early and mostly successful writing period, the boys became rambunctious while Anne scooted them to their benches for a transition. They were not settling down quickly, and so she began her usual strategy for bringing calm: "I'm going to count down from five to zero, and I want to see boys who look ready for transition." She put her finger to her lips in a gesture of quiet, and as she counted down, the boys rushed to sit upright on their benches. "Brian is doing exactly the right thing. Samuel is doing exactly the right thing. Paul is doing the right thing." With each comment, the boy gets his transition sticker as a reward. To Anne, the right thing happens when a boy focuses on, and then chooses to do, the appropriate social activity or response within the chaos of the rapidly moving transitions. These boys have limited attentional abilities and equally limited motivation to be pro-social.

Finding the right thing, and then choosing it as a course of action, is no small feat—even for adults. Aaron, Anne says during the first stages of the study, is the most likely to "stay focused on the right thing and doesn't fall apart completely like the other kids." Brian is less likely to focus on and do the right thing, especially when he is emotionally upset. And Samuel simply can't locate the right thing at all in the constant rush of stimuli. Thus, in the day-to-day activity of the class, the right thing is Anne's way of labeling for the boys what has probably never been pointed out to them before: Saying good morning is the right thing. Walking away from an argument is the right thing. Listening to, and then following, a teacher's direction is the right thing.

Being perfect is hard to do. But when a child did *exactly* the right thing and needed to know it, or when it was time to test a particular social behavior and expectations for performance needed to be set, Anne often would use the word. Perfect was a changeable thing as the year went on. "What I'll accept as perfect right now is quite far from what perfect hopefully will be at some point later on," she says. She points to an incident where she told Brian she wanted to see him have a perfect transition.

> I give him a direction to go to his bench and he first knocks the garbage pail around like four times and then we stand there and discuss it for a while. Then he ultimately winds up on his bench—so that's perfect enough!! Whereas with an older kid or later in the year that would not have been perfect because too much other stuff went on between the direction being given and the direction being followed.

This quote provides a good example of the differing contexts and conditions under which certain social behaviors may or may not be acceptable. Words like perfect, as well as the others in the representative list discussed above, maintain the same form throughout the year, but their function changes as the seeds of social understanding grow in the children and new social connotations emerge.

Language and Socialization Practice

Anne employs certain vocabulary in teaching certain social concepts, and I characterized those concepts as part of the content of her social curriculum. She also employs a particular pedagogy to help the boys understand and use those concepts in actual classroom situations. Four strategies for socialization

using language are most often used: First, she continually *labels* both appropriate and inappropriate instances of social behavior as they occur; second,
she frequently uses statements and questions that provide *limited social alternatives* for the boys between which they must choose; third, she uses statements that *explicate the means that must be taken to reach desired ends;* finally,
she uses questions that are intended to *prompt reflection* in the boys, questions
that make the boys stop and think.

Labeling. Labeling, of all the techniques in Anne's class, is the one used most
frequently and functions in a number of ways in the social curriculum. In the
initial stages of teaching a new social concept, labeling is a way to connect a
word with a behavior. For instance, "You're setting up Samuel," she says to
Paul when he is doing his wild sexual gyrations. But it is also a way to give
children language for what they feel. "You're frustrated right now," Anne says
to Samuel when he becomes explosive over being told his drawings are not
complete. "You're angry because you had to stay in for recess," she says to
Jason who has called Cathy a name one too many times. "You're feeling nervous because your mother is coming today," she says to Brian who is laying
across her lap, chanting nonsense syllables and rolling his head round and
round. With these kinds of labels repeated innumerable times throughout the
day, a vocabulary of feelings and behaviors begins to coalesce in the class,
eventually leading to the children attempting to label their own feelings and
behavior.

Limiting social alternatives. "You can be a good friend to Brian, or you can
sit and work at your bench alone," she says to Jason who is being disruptive
at the table with his peer. Angry at the limits, he ups the ante by replying that
he wants to go to the crisis center instead. "That's not a choice. You can either
be a good friend or go to your bench to work." By giving alternatives such as
these, Anne tries to teach the boys that there are alternatives to creating disruptive social situations and that certain decisions are for adults to make, not
boys. The former lesson is an important one for boys who can usually see only
one path toward a goal, if they even see a path at all. Boys such as Jason
usually act on impulse and without any thought. By laying out two worthwhile alternatives using language from the class lexicon, Anne attempts to
organize Jason's impulsive behavior into discernible alternatives from which
he can reasonably choose. Of course, the ultimate goal of limiting alternatives
is that the boys might be able to generate them without her assistance.

Means to an end. In the short vignette at the beginning of Chapter 6, where
Aaron wanted to begin publishing his book before completing his illustrations, Anne was explicit about the exact behaviors he was to perform to get

what he wanted: He had to work carefully and completely, illustrating each page. Thus, she attempted to teach him that if he could tolerate the frustration of working carefully, he would be rewarded by getting to the fun part. In another example, Paul escalated rapidly from whining, to stamping his feet, to feigning that he would run from the room, all because Anne was helping Aaron for a moment and had asked Paul to "do good waiting." "If you want me to help you, you must talk to me politely," she explained firmly and continued to work with Aaron. After sputtering and fuming for a minute longer, he said (still with a pathetic whine in his voice), "Anne, I'm getting frustrated! Help me!" As if to prove that his polite request was nothing less than magic, Anne immediately turned to him and began to help, no questions asked. Doing this, Anne reinforced the fact that there are certain ways of asking for help that will almost always get the desired response.

Prompting reflection. After an initial period of labeling behaviors in situ, Anne begins to prompt the boys to reflect on their actions. She uses such phrases as, "Are you going to imitate someone doing the wrong thing?" when Brian has begun to make obscene gestures back at Jason who is already in time-out for being disruptive. She asked Aaron, "How does a good audience act?" when he began to make fun of Samuel's illustrations when Samuel was author of the day. She said, "What should you being doing now instead of crying?" when Samuel clearly needed help with his work, but had failed to ask for it and had resorted to an old inappropriate behavior. All of these questions serve as reminders to the boys to call up learned behaviors from their memories.

I observe three important principles being taught with these four strategies. First, by giving labels to the boys' acceptable and unacceptable behaviors, Anne is teaching them to define and differentiate cognitive categories for single social behaviors. Within each boy, singular cultural definitions are slowly being constructed. Second, Anne increases the amounts of social experience and thereby increases opportunities to label the various connotations of a particular word in different contexts. She also begins to show the interrelatedness of words and concepts, to braid a number of constituent definitions together into a whole social expectation. We hear this most clearly with Samuel, for instance, when Anne says to him, "A big boy can pay attention to his own work and ignore other boys who are having difficulties." She braids the previously learned phrases of *big boy, paying attention to self,* and *ignoring* into one social expectation. Eventually, she begins to prompt his reflection by asking him, "Is that something a big boy would do?"

The third social lesson being taught is what constitutes social consequences—positive, negative, and neutral. There is a social consequence, for instance, if you do as Paul did one day when he heard a dog bark outside the class window. He jumped from his seat, yelped himself, and began to rush toward the window, upsetting his quietly working classmates. Anne took him aside, calmed him, and carefully explained that "it is not okay, it is not the right thing, to upset the whole class because *you* are very excited about something." The consequence of doing what he did is not just that he got himself into trouble; more important is the fact that he disrupted others who were hard at work. Socially, that "is not okay."

Anne's uses of such metacognitive strategies as labeling, limiting social alternatives, means to an end, and prompting reflection are consistent with her constructivist notions and are closely related to Vygotsky's (1978) theory of socially mediated learning, described previously. Paris and Winograd (1990) have described several properties of metacognitive strategies.

> Megacognition focuses our attention on . . . awareness . . . and management of our own thinking . . . helps learners become active participants in their own performance, rather than passive recipients of instruction and imposed experiences . . . it is oriented toward individual differences in cognitive development and learning . . . the constructive, personal, strategic thinking involved in metacognition is amenable to classroom instruction. (p. 8)

Thus, through the use of what amounts to a core vocabulary, Anne teaches about human behaviors in context. She exhibits a disciplined use of language, a specific and structured way of lifting from the happenings of the classroom the most important social material when it is most salient. Anne's pedagogy labels and explicates both intrapersonal and interpersonal processes as they occur, and then structures those processes more effectively. This is a difficult and subtle pedagogy, and markedly different from pedagogies that abstract social principles and then attempt to teach them in structured lessons on listening, for instance, or turn-taking, or conversation skills. Anne chooses instead to address social skills in the context of social activity, using language as a fundamental element for shaping the social thinking of children.

THE PRIMACY OF THE GROUP

Throughout this study, I found Anne to be consistently preoccupied with finding ways to meet the needs of individual boys and still have a group learning environment. There is ample evidence that learning in groups is a primary goal of her teaching; her language is filled with pro-social and pro-group concerns, and her actions in the class corroborate that she did considerable thinking on the subject. From our first interview in October 1988 through our last in June 1990, she spoke repeatedly on the subject. She began our first conversation by ruminating at length over the quandary she had in keeping all the boys safe yet in a group; she rejoiced, later that fall, over the tiny conversations the whole group had regarding an interesting book or film; she grieved when the group fell apart in November as a result of the sexual acting out of Aaron and Jason; during that winter she spoke at length about getting boys to sit at a table together without incident, of them finally "being civilized in a classroom setting"; later still, she related how she had decided that "anything socializing, anything that is treating other people nicely and functioning like human beings is . . . important"—even more important than academics.

But it was not until the late fall of 1989 that Anne spoke in any depth about why learning in a group was so important to her teaching. Until then, when she had spoken on the topic, it had been anecdotally, in the context of sharing her quandaries around teaching and their resolutions. By the beginning of the second academic year, the group was performing better, and her thoughts turned to explaining why her emphasis on learning in a group was so strong; she began to reflect on why she emphasized the primacy of the group. The reason this conversation hadn't begun sooner can be partially explained by my research methodology. Because our conversations were elicited from the videotape, Anne determined the course of conversation; my function was to probe her thinking, not redirect it. When, during the beginning months of the work I would ask her why her emphasis on group learning was so strong, my questions would go unanswered; Anne was considerably preoccupied with explaining how she taught and was less apt to reflect upon why she taught as she did. And although it was quite apparent that she placed unusually high importance on group learning, it was not until the October 1989 conversation that the opportunity arose to define what it was she had been trying to accomplish with the group. At that time, she lamented that the boys had been less "groupish" of late. Yet even then, when I asked Anne to define "groupish" she said, "I don't know if I can . . . define it. I might be able to give you examples!"

As difficult as it is for Anne to verbally define "groupishness," it is a palpable goal in her work, embedded in her discourse and action. What follows is the section of the conversation where we pursued her reasons for maintaining the emphasis on group learning. I include the conversation transcription for two reasons. The first is that, although she begins by saying she can only explain the meaning of "groupishness" anecdotally, she ends by being quite specific about its meaning and its value to her as a teacher. When she shifts from anecdote to self-analysis, we hear a trademark of her thinking style. That is, Anne may not have articulated her social goals and objectives verbally until this time, but they resided quite near the surface of her consciousness. Talk brought her thoughts quickly into consciousness, and when they emerged, they were clearly ordered and cogent. This clarity and cogency supports my contention that the group learning goals were indeed hard to verbalize, but were explicit thoughts nonetheless, and essential to her method of teaching. A second reason I include these passages is because Anne's voice as a thinker is very strong and they afford the reader an opportunity to hear that voice clearly.

Interviewer: [Let me] ask you a question about "groupish." Can you define "groupish"?

Anne: Groupish is when five boys are clustered around me holding a jar with a butterfly, and they're all completely intent on talking about the butterfly. And it's not mattering that their bodies are touching each other. And it's not even occurring to anyone to set each other up or to have a problem. Because they're all so focused on what the group is talking about, and they're listening to each other and talking to each other and being normal.

Interviewer: Do you value that?

Anne: Yes.

Interviewer: Why?

Anne: Because it's normal, because that's what little kids . . . I don't know . . . because it means that they're focused on something positive and developmentally appropriate and normal. And they're not . . . I mean I think I would value it for any kids, but I think I value it especially for these kids for that reason. I mean that social interaction, being able to work as part of a group, are important goals for any elementary school kids. And it's so rare for these kids.

Interviewer: Do you think that being able to work as a group . . . means that the focus is on an object?

Anne: No, that was the first example that sprung to mind. There have been other times when we've [the class] had discussions, which is something that [we] would never have had last year, where we've read an article . . . about not taking candy from a stranger kind of thing. And then five boys raised their hand and took turns sharing experiences, and listening to each other and asking each other questions about their experiences. And having group discussion.

Interviewer: What is the focus in that, is it different than the jar of butterflies?

Anne: . . . It's not as concrete a focus. There was a focused topic of discussion, but I guess the focus is the other people in the group. They were listening to each other and hearing what each other said. About a topic. But that is something that is very exciting for me when that kind of thing has been able to happen.

Interviewer: Why?

Anne: Because it's a higher developmental level to be able to . . . because they're not just so focused on their own needs and their own issues. And they're able to sometimes share the focus with other things.

Interviewer: Why is that important in the work you do?

Anne: 'Cause it's part of normal development. It's part of the normal tasks of childhood. It's something that most kids have accomplished by the age of 4. And you know last year there was [only a] little glimpse that [they] would even get kinda close to the level that they could do that.

Interviewer: Do you think this is a very high goal for you? Or is it a medium high goal for you . . . ?

Anne: Groupishness! [she laughs] Group cohesiveness!! . . . Yes, I think so, because I think a lot of learning happens with kids . . . I think in good elementary school classrooms, kids learn a lot from other kids. Kids learn a lot from listening to other kids. And I value cooperative kinds of learning, anyway. And I think I would value that with any group of kids I was working with. But for these kids, it's even more important, or even more difficult, or even more something. So I value it even more. So, yeah, I think a lot more learning can happen when kids are able to share it together. [That] is the highest reason why I probably value it. I think also it is a necessary prerequisite for movement to a less restrictive placement. That kids be able to function as part of a group. Whether that less restrictive placement is classroom two [at Brighton] where there are more kids [or in a public school].

Interviewer: How large does that reason play with you? That sounds political.

Anne: Right. But I think both are real. I think there are sort of the idealistic goals and there are the more practical goals. And they both fit together, I think that both are true. I want them to be able to go on in a classroom that is not entirely one-to-one based. So I want them to be able to function in a group. And I want that both because that's the reality of the way the world is, but even more because I think it's a good [laugh] way to be.

Interviewer: Is groupishness a goal that's conscious in the same way that you have a plan for, say, Brian?

Anne: I think so.

Anne emphasizes moving the children from the behavioral fringes to the behavioral norm. Crucial to that movement is the ability to work successfully in groups, to have the requisite skills for eventually being in a regular classroom or at least in less one-to-one situations. The ability to work in groups with some success is a developmental task that any well-adjusted human being must master, she says. She values and will teach the boys to value being co-operative, listening to others, giving attention to another, sharing with another, and helping another. These she considers to be "normal" goals for these or any children, and she is stubborn in her insistence that they be part of her curriculum.

Teaching boys in groups was always a primary goal for her class, and she was not willing to create an entire day of individualized learning. Her notions about what is pedagogically necessary to teach socialization skills to these children run counter to conventional wisdom in special education. That wisdom suggests pedagogies that circumvent the social problems troubled or learning disabled children have by exhorting teachers to separate the children from each other for their academic work. Thus, in many special education classes, it is quite common to have the children each working through a packet of academic material at separate tables or in carrels in order to avoid bringing the students together for group-style lessons (see D'Alonzo, 1983; Hewett & Taylor, 1980; Mastropieri & Scruggs, 1987; Stephens, 1977). Often, socialization skills are taught in a class period by themselves and in a presentational format.

Anne groups her students in two-to-one, and sometimes one-to-one, tutorials for work in reading and mathematics. But she keeps the group together for all other classes, mostly to address the goals of her social curriculum in the context of normalized classroom learning. These differences are consequential; they reflect important paradigmatic differences between Anne and many authorities in teaching troubled children. Those differences can be located in the way Anne conceptualizes the abilities and needs of her students, the types of environments from which they can benefit, and the relationship a teacher ought to develop with troubled students.

Not only are these differences apparent in Anne's emphasis on the primacy of the group, but, as we've seen, they are clear in her use of language as a tool of socialization as well. They are also evident in the weight she places on children working together at meaningful tasks. If these three aspects of her social curriculum had not functioned simultaneously, then working as a group probably would not have been successful.

SALIENCE AND FUN

With all the difficulties the boys had from the first day of school, the one thing they were good at, the one thing that they loved to do, was listen to books. Anne had not anticipated that they would become enrapt with books in particular, but she quickly realized that their love of reading and writing books could be her pathway toward learning with this group. The first thing she did was change the classroom schedule to accommodate more time for reading. Originally half the boys alternated going to a 30-minute lunch while the others napped. This alteration had proved disastrous because sometimes as many as three or four of the boys ended up in trouble during the transition times. But when Anne started sending all the boys to lunch together and made naptime into a time for read-aloud, she created the most successful whole group activity of the day. All the boys attended to the story and actually did use the time for rest. Not every day was calm, and all boys were not always present (usually those who were not had gotten into trouble in the transition after lunch), but the calming influence the reading had on the boys, thumbs in mouths, leaning forward to see every picture and to hear every word, was quite remarkable. Teaching boys to be literate had always been one of Anne's first goals as a teacher. So by taking advantage of the opportunity presented by these boys' love of books, she not only quelled a storm in the middle of the day and gave the boys more of what they liked, but she also added substantially to the time spent on language and reading. In fact, rearranging the schedule increased the total time spent listening to or doing group activities with books, from the half hour spent with Big Books to a full hour every day. Together with the one-to-one or two-to-one formal reading instruction each boy received for half an hour every day, the addition of read-aloud meant Anne spent 35% of the day on literacy activities.

In general, the boys retained the information from the books, and, with more information, they began to talk more about the content of the books. Even around Thanksgiving time when the class was in an uproar, books provided a center of gravity. On one occasion, Anne was reading about Pilgrims and the book mentioned that the first Thanksgiving feast lasted for 3 days. The next day, Anne was reading a new and different Thanksgiving book. When it came to the part where a feast was happening, Jason, sounding like any first grader, yelled out, "And it happened for three days!!" Anne, surprised and pleased, said, "Yes, Jason! That is good remembering!!" Emboldened by his first attempt, he later talked about the dangerous mushrooms that were pictured in the book, and how he hoped the Pilgrims did not eat the mushrooms. Anne responded to his worries, and a short conversation ensued.

Later, Anne pointed out that his comments were important: They were his attempts to talk about something other than himself or some inappropriate activity. It was a small discussion, she admitted, but the beginning of a trend, she hoped. She saw this small interchange as something new on which to build, a new way to increase the connection of the boys with her, with the classroom, with learning, and with each other. It was a type of groupishness.

Reading was enjoyable, but certain subjects truly captured the boys' imaginations. When she realized this, Anne placed more of that kind of thing in their path. She told me that there were "these really salient things . . . they had been powerful or exciting or different experiences" that the children responded to. For instance, a group of naturalists came to her class periodically with wild, but injured, animals that the children could interact with. The class took a field trip to a hands-on science museum where the exhibits got the boys thoroughly engaged. They watched many filmstrips in class about nature, and eventually they became very excited about dinosaurs (especially Brian, whose inner world was opened by his identification with these primitive beasts). Anne would couple these exciting experiences with some writing and language activity. The more writing they did, the more they wanted to do. When a filmstrip was very interesting and successful, she would ask the boys to draw a picture of their favorite part. They would then dictate a sentence to her or to another adult, who would write it underneath the picture and give the filmstrip a new title. In the first week of January, on one wall of the room were 10 or 20 primitive drawings, results of the activity, each with a label and a sentence beneath. These were fun, meaningful activities to the boys.

> We had done it once or twice. It was actually a sign that they were
> ready for a more formal writing program. They were loving this activity
> and doing well at it. . . . They wanted to write their own sentences;
> they didn't want me to write them.

By mid-January, there were signs that they were ready for a formal writing program, ready to abandon the free-flow, preschool schedule of the afternoon and participate in an organized activity. Probably the most interesting indication was their request to write and make books of their own.

> They wanted to make books. They were very interested in words and
> writing and wanted to do it themselves. "I can write that word! I want
> to write that word!" [They made] more careful drawings and pictures
> and [were] more able to sit still and work on a product like this, a more
> representative picture . . . [they were] able to not sit down and scribble
> for a few minutes, but to draw a picture that tells a story and then have
> a story to tell about it.

The process had begun back in November, when the classroom was still in an uproar. Anne had noticed that, on occasion, a boy would ask to make a book during his free choice time. She hesitated then to push the idea of setting up a formal time to write books. She decided instead to let the excitement of making books brew and build. Whenever an opportunity came up informally, though, she jumped on it. If the boys showed particular interest in the animals, or a book they had read, or dinosaurs, Anne would stage an impromptu writing lesson during the afternoon period. After visiting the museum, for instance, Anne made a picture book out of the drawings the boys had made about the museum trip. Before assembling the pages and binding them, she conducted a successful group lesson wherein the boys told what they were doing in each drawing, and what they liked best about the experience. The book was bound and read to the whole class the next day and ceremonially put on the class bookshelf. The boys were very excited. Then she helped them to write a group thank-you letter to the museum.

> It seemed like too good an opportunity to pass up! That they had been really excited . . . so I wanted to be able to capitalize on these things happening and to get them to do this [writing] . . . as an initial step. . . . If they're gonna be able to do it [writing] at all, they'll be able to do it best when there's something they're really excited about.

With opportunity after opportunity, Anne planned ways to match the children's interest with salient activities from her already existing cache of ideas. These lessons worked somewhat better; they were unlike the unfortunate presentational lessons of the first weeks of school. She listened and watched more carefully before she instituted many of her lessons. She waited, "looking for the clue from them that they were ready to do it." She didn't know when the clues would come. When it came to writing, she knew she wanted the older three boys to be writing their own stories by June, and the younger two boys to be dictating whole stories, at least. She also knew that she wanted their first writing experiences to be fun ones; she did not want to be responsible for turning out students who did not "value their own creative expression." So she continually looked for opportunities.

Fun played a big role in activities other than writing and reading, and was especially important in tutorials and two-to-one math and reading groups. Games were fun to use with the boys—even when they didn't go completely according to plan. *Sea Monster,* for instance, is a game for learning about adding and subtracting numbers up to 10, which Brian and Aaron played one day in math class. Anne put 10 goldfish snacks in cups for each of the boys. She then gave them blue, laminated playing boards with waves drawn on. "There are four fishes in the sea," she said. They both quickly counted out four fishes from their cups and put them on their cards. "But two got scared and went home!" The boys scooped up two and put them back in the cup. "How many are left?" Aaron: "Two!" Brian: "LET ME EAT THEM!!!" He was so excited and tantalized by the edible fish, he was dying to eat them; but Anne pushed forward with the game, with a lot of laughter and teasing. Finally, Anne said the Sea Monster was coming! "There were 10 fishes swimming together. But the Sea Monster came and gobbled up four!"

The idea was that they would scoop up four goldfish and pop them in their mouths.

But the waiting had been too much for Brian. He grabbed the whole bag and ran, stuffing a handful in his mouth as he went. He had so many in his mouth, he blew the dry crumbs out into the air as he breathed. Some even hit Anne in the face. The game and the period came to a close with Brian in time-out. He went without argument; he knew he had exceeded the limits. He also knew that his recess was next and his motivation was high to do well in time-out. He had lasted through the entire period and showed a good understanding of the meaning of "ten." So Anne didn't make too big a deal about his ending. After all, she figured, there is only so much a little kid can take of all this excitement!

Work is a fundamental social activity and it can be meaningful and fun— this is clearly a value of Anne's and a foundation for her social curriculum. She intends for the boys to learn that working in a group is desirable as well and that doing so need not cause them anxiety or reinforce behavioral prob- lems. Even while working in a group, boys can get their needs met; it can be just as stimulating to be *out* of trouble as it is to be in it. Conveying this was no small feat with boys who found negative attention from others to be more powerful and rewarding than positive attention. But with fun and salient ac- tivities going on in class, Anne hoped to make work compelling enough to lure the boys away from their negative acting out. As she said, "If they're gonna be able to do it at all, they'll be able to do it best when there's some- thing they're really excited about."

Once again, Anne scaffolded (Vygotsky, 1978) student development by providing meaningful and enjoyable work. This enabled students to work within their appropriate developmental range and to limit interference in the learning process from boredom and distraction. Of course, being excited about their work did not suddenly and singularly cause their social difficulties to abate. Indeed, in some respects, by choosing this path for teaching social- ization skills, Anne drew into sharper relief the boys' inabilities to delay grati- fication, to trust in adults, to maintain intellectual focus, and to resist displac- ing their frustrations onto each other. Yet, when she caused those social difficulties to manifest more clearly, Anne was able to address them more pre- cisely. Anne needed to use her behavior management skills therapeutically, as in the case of Brian and the goldfish. She had to be wise about her choice of interventions and judicious in how she carried them out. Above all, she had to be patient and take the time necessary to build a solid social foundation in the classroom.

As Anne began moving beyond the struggle and chaos of the first months of school, she slowly organized the class into more of a teaching and learning environment. Her thinking about the behavioral curriculum goals

became more organized, and she became increasingly preoccupied with finding a more therapeutic way to address the needs of the boys, that is, she began
to mentally process her social curricular approach. When we arrange the social
curriculum and pedagogy discussed in this chapter side by side with the behavioral curriculum and pedagogy discussed previously, we can begin to see
the important connections between the two. Managing the boys' surface behaviors and training them to conform to the structure of her classroom was a
necessary but insufficient teaching strategy for Anne. She wanted not just to
control their behavior, but to help them grow in their own self-control and
self-initiative. To do so, she reached under the dangerous and maladaptive
surface behaviors of the boys and tried to work at what she considered the
root cause of many of their difficulties—an immature social understanding
of the world. Thus, the social curriculum and pedagogy initiated the boys'
movement from egocentric ways of thinking to emergent sociocentric ways
of thinking. Yet, her socializing efforts are braided closely with her efforts to
reshape surface behaviors in the boys, and together they undergird her teaching efforts and assist her in what she calls "pushing to the next level"—the
academic curriculum and pedagogy. This ability to braid the three curriculum
areas is the crux of her teaching effectiveness, and clearly where she exercises
her greatest effort of thought.

CHAPTER 8

LITERACY AND NUMERACY . . . AND PLENTY OF TALK

Slowly, things came together. After all the months spent struggling with Paul's tantrums, Samuel's shrieking, and Jason's assaultiveness; after the weeks spent frustrated because a "surefire" plan for intervention failed; after the days of having 20 minutes out of each 30-minute period spent managing behavior; after not getting to the neat curriculum she'd planned, things came together. By March 1989 the predominant activities in Anne's classroom were becoming academic. Reading, writing, mathematics, science, social studies, language arts—activities that Anne had been striving to make the substance of the school day since September—gradually moved into the foreground. The behavioral, social, and emotional needs of the children became increasingly manageable in the context of those academic activities and became less likely to bring the activities to a complete halt. The boys remained in class for full instructional periods; activities had beginnings, middles, and ends; and there was a gradual shift in the discourse of the class, from one that regularly was dominated by behavioral teaching and intervention, to one that more often was dominated by academic instruction and dialogue.

A TRADITION OF "NEAT CURRICULUM"

The day was running as it had been planned, full of language-based academic activities divided into half-hour segments: Word time led to morning meeting, which led to math groups. After math, some boys would go to recess while the remaining boys were divided between Anne and Cathy for reading; at the end of half an hour, those at recess received reading instruction and those who had had reading went out to play. When everyone reassembled, it was time to read Big Books and then go to lunch. Back from lunch, it was another read-aloud time, then writing, social studies, and science. Finally, at 2:00 the boys had "free choice" for half an hour—unless work was left unfinished or they needed to "sit minutes" for earlier misbehavior.

Anne inherited this half-hour format as well as the shape of the curriculum from the four teachers who had gone before her. She knows that the language-intensive, hands-on approach to learning began a decade before with Barbara, who had established the youngest classroom as a language-based program for first and second graders with learning disabilities; when Amy followed Barbara, she introduced the process writing approach, along with whole language activities; next, Joan established the hands-on, experiential math program; Sally taught the class only one difficult year, but during that time still was able to write much of the math curriculum into activity guides. Anne's contributions to this class history are several. During her tenure, the emotional and behavioral difficulties of the boys entering the program have worsened dramatically, yet she has been able to maintain the academic focus of the class. Without altering the core purpose of the program, she has been able to refine both the curriculum and the pedagogy in response to the students' changing cognitive, social, and behavioral needs. She has altered the schedule where necessary, and because the children in the class have been progressively younger she has extended the scope and sequence of the academic curriculum downward to include the preschool and kindergarten goals and objectives heretofore unnecessary.

Like all the teachers at Brighton, Anne knows the history of the academic program in her class, how and why it evolved as it did. She did not invent this curriculum; she has adopted its purpose, shape, and scope from her predecessors. Anne and her colleagues have been trained in this academic tradition, with the strong guidance of the principal. Over her years at the school, she has refined the curriculum and pedagogy and made them her own, but only within the school's stated purpose. The institutional foundations of the academic curriculum and pedagogy are very strong. Without them, it is doubtful that Anne, or any teacher, could have been effective with her troubled children.

Word Time

It's June 8, 1989, 8:45 a.m., and it's word time, a period that has been "consistently one of the worst parts of the day all year." Even on a good day, it's a hard period to manage, not because the curriculum is particularly complex, but "[be]cause it was the first time they all were made to sit down, and listen, and to all be together." Today is not so different from other days of late—the boys don't arrive ready to work as a group, and each is moving fast and in his own direction. This is the time to pull them together for schoolwork.

"Take a picture of our tadpoles!!" It's Aaron and Paul—and me with my video recorder—huddled at the aquarium tank. The boys dashed into the room and almost immediately went to peer in at the tiny frogs-to-be darting about in the water. Aaron enthuses, "Take tons of pictures!!" I zoom in for a close-up as Paul dashes off toward some other activity. Aaron remains. "Did you get the picture?" he asks. But before I can answer, he is asking Cathy about the jelly-like substance he sees in the tank and whether it contains snails eggs; he seems to have forgotten that he asked me a question at all.

In the meantime, Samuel has come into the room and is agitated because he can't find his yellow raincoat. He is whining loudly and throws first his coat and then his book bag across the room—away from everyone else and really not very far. He is clearly in control of himself and looking out of the corner of his eye to see what effect he's had; it appears that he just needs some attention. Anne tells him she can't help him when he is throwing things. He immediately picks up his belongings and comes over to her for a hug, which she gives him with real affection.

"Now, can we start all over again? Can you walk in and act like a big boy instead of acting like a baby?" With a very kind tone of voice, she not only tells him how she expects him to behave, but is quite explicit about what she doesn't like about his behavior. They walk toward the classroom door together, and Samuel goes out while Anne waits for his return. The door swings back open and he comes in crying and wailing louder than before! But he can't keep the folderol going and starts laughing at his own joke. Anne laughs, too, and then goes out and in the door, good-natured as she models for Samuel how it is done. "Good morning, Anne! How are you?" He dissolves further into laughter at her charade—but finally lets her direct him to the computer. It is his morning to use the software. By now he has forgotten about his worries over the yellow raincoat altogether—if he ever was really worried.

Just outside on the porch steps, Jason is sitting with Sandy, the adult with whom he had some trouble at breakfast. They seem to be finishing their conversation about the incident (what Brighton staff call "processing"), but suddenly Jason erupts in anger and storms off to the crisis center after all; Sandy follows. The school year is almost over, and Jason has been able to make it to school 50% of the time, usually getting into trouble before finishing breakfast. That statistic is hard for Anne to face, and she has made a pact with herself to find some way to increase his time in school next year. By now she knows that she will have all the same boys in her classroom next year, with the exception of Paul.

Brian has not arrived yet, and a phone call confirms that he is starting his day in the crisis center as a result of trouble at breakfast. These days have been a little harder for him, what with his mother becoming progressively more active—and troublesome—in his life. But overall he has done well and usually makes it to class, so Anne is not particularly concerned about him.

And so the daily routine begins with three boys in the class—and their energy is high. After a short period of unstructured play, the adults push forward into the academic day, asking the boys the same question they've asked for 9 months of mornings: "What is your word going to be this morning?" "Armor" is the word Paul wants. Aaron chooses "half-dollar" as his word. Samuel is at the computer so he'll skip word time today. From a nearby shelf, Anne takes each boy's plastic file container full of materials for word time, and distributes them. In the containers are long paper strips on which Anne has written the words the boys have chosen throughout the year and a three-ring binder that has become a dictionary of all those words. The activity itself is based on the work of Katie Johnson (1987) and works this way: A boy chooses a word that interests him, such as "armor." Anne copies the word for him in large letters onto a strip of paper approximately 3 by 12 inches. The boy traces the word on the strip with a colored pen, then copies the word onto paper specially prepared for this purpose. On the top of the paper is an open, white space; the bottom is ruled for a primary student. Once the word is successfully copied, the boy draws and colors an illustration on the page that matches the word. He then places the page in its correct alphabetical place in the three-ring binder. The binder serves as the boy's personal diction-ary, which he can use during writing class or at any other time.

Beginning the day in a freer format, then carefully easing into an individ-ualized activity like word time, suits the boys' needs in the morning: It pro-vides them with an activity where they have a lot of choice—over the words they choose, the drawings they make, the colors they use. But it is also an activity that is carefully structured to help focus their attention. It requires them to follow a simple procedure from beginning to end; it results in a tan-gible product. Most important, it is language-based and instructive. The chil-dren are able to build their vocabulary from words that they've heard before and now seek to make their own; they learn something about the spelling of those words; they get practice in near-point copying; they get practice in alphabetizing their pages. Quite aside from its intrinsic teaching power, the activity in this short period is intended to help funnel the boys' undirected energy into schoolwork, to provide a transitional activity from 18 hours in the lifespace to 6 hours in a structured classroom; therefore, it has enough choice to assuage their need for control, yet enough academic learning to ease them into the structured day.

Of course, its effectiveness in funneling the boys' energy is variable by day and by boy—and the social, emotional, and behavioral circumstances. For instance, this morning, Paul seems like he is in good shape when he asks Anne is she has a picture of armor that he can use to copy. But when she doesn't find one that satisfies him, he loudly and suddenly accuses her of not listening to him or to what he wants. When she tries to respond, he breaks into an impromptu rap song: "You talk too much/You better shut up/You talk too much." She brings his song and dance to a halt when she looks him in the eye and firmly tells him he is "doing the wrong thing." He accepts her intervention readily, and he immediately returns to his task, a sign that he might still have a good morning.

Aaron meanwhile has looked in his dictionary under "H" and discovered he has already used "half-dollar" at some other time. He hears Paul talk about armor and decides that he will take "knights in armor" as his word. But Anne is concerned that he is not thinking for himself, and is just mimicking Paul. Moreover, he is being demanding and whiney. She asks him to sit down and to "think for 30 seconds" if there is any other word he would like to choose. He comes up with "knights on horseback." These words seem more his own, so she agrees. Always looking for opportunities to teach something new, she writes the words on his strip but reminds him that "knight is one of those funny words that begins with silent *k*." He remains edgy and sullen over his new words and clearly may need more help later in remaining focused on the schoolwork.

A tenuous moment of academic work has actually begun when Brian shows up, escorted by Karen, and is led to the time-out chair (which is the usual routine the adults follows when a boy makes a transition from the crisis center to the classroom). He is still agitated, and he yells a few times, something about how he will not make up "his fucking homework." Apparently he has lost his homework from the night before. Anne goes to him and speaks with him for a moment, leaving Paul and Aaron alone. Predictably, Aaron begins to call Paul names beneath his breath; Paul, agitated, starts rapping his pen against the tabletop. Anne returns quickly and tries to redirect them to work. But Aaron escalates and calls more names and, when Anne sends him to his bench to sit quietly, he uses his felt pen to draw on her buttocks as he passes her.

"I wrote on her bum!!!" he blurts out and then begins flicking his tongue in and out of his mouth.

"Now you will have to sit for 5 minutes instead," she tells him.

"He's talking sexual," Paul says breathlessly.

"You take care of yourself," she says firmly to Paul, using the language that addresses her social goals for Paul. She quickly turns her attention back to his drawing. "Good, there is your knight on horseback. What color is his armor?" Paul begins to work, conscientiously drawing the armor. Anne has successfully navigated him away from Aaron's attempt to set him up. Aaron, for his part, is not yet finished and is sitting on his bench making his felt marker protrude from his fist as if he were sticking up his middle finger.

"Look, Paul! Fuck you!" But Paul only glances at him and continues to work on his drawing.

"I'm glad you're ignoring him," Anne praises his self-control, "Ignore him completely."

"Ignore him completely/Ignore him completely . . ." Paul begins to chant a new rap, sotto voce, almost like a mantra that keeps him focused and in control, as he continues to work on his word and picture. A 5-minute period of calm ensues. Eventually, Paul's song makes a segue into a conversation with Anne about the armor that he had seen and tried on when he recently went to the museum with his residence group; Aaron sits without disruption; Samuel plays his computer game; Brian sits in time-out without saying a word until finally both Aaron and Brian, quiet and apparently in control of themselves, join the group at the table and begin to trace and draw their words. For a few moments, it appears that the period is "working" and that all the boys present might finish their words by period's end. They do—but not without Aaron escalating once again, first in a frustrated outburst about not wanting to trace his words, and second when he is told to put his work container away and instead lets it slip off the table, spilling its contents all over the floor. Samuel, too, has some moments of trouble when he passes Brian on his way toward his bench and inexplicably hits him. Karen intervenes in this altercation, while Anne continues to monitor Aaron picking up his materials from the floor. Paul's voice gets progressively louder, and his body moves faster with all the negative energy in the room.

Anne moves back and forth between boys, setting a behavioral limit on one, reinforcing a social goal in another, teaching about "silent K" with another, only to set another behavioral limit—all in an effort to begin a day of academic work. And at 9:15, after half an hour of effort, the tone in the room isn't yet conducive to productive schoolwork in a group. Paul can't stay in control with so much activity around him and escalates his noise and movement so that he is removed from class for a brief period. Anne, seeing that the group is still shaky, makes a small change in plan by quickly taking out a picture book the boys like and begins to read to them. It is a 2-minute detour into a favorite story about a crocodile. Within seconds, three boys are leaning forward to see the pictures, and they're talking about how the crocodile was born and what he'll do with the monkeys in the jungle. Her intervention has worked; with a book being read to them, the boys are being more groupish, and she takes advantage of the moment, quickly turning to the next academic activity, morning meeting.

These quick shifts in plan are a mainstay of her pedagogy, a chief means for keeping the boys on the academic track. Anne intends for the day to stay on schedule and for all the planned activities to get done. Thus, the detour into a book about a friendly crocodile is an intervention, and not a lesson per se; she doesn't stay with the book for long. Without being tied to the schedule, she will nevertheless keep to it closely, knowing that it provides both a predictable structure of time for the boys (a valuable lesson in itself) as well as a strong expectation for doing all of the schoolwork planned. Anne always works on the overarching goal of doing what is normalizing in hopes of bringing the boys one step closer to succeeding in a public school.

Morning Meeting

Morning meeting is one such normalizing activity. It is a group activity one can expect to see as a first activity is many primary classrooms. But with special consideration for the special needs of her boys, Anne begins her day with the parallel play of word time and only gradually moves the boys toward a group activity. "I'm going to look for guys that seem ready to help me with the calendar. Brian, what month is it?" Brian is a little silly in his response when he yells out "January," and so she calls on another boy without missing a beat or changing her expression; it is a technique that invariably works with Brian. Just going to another boy for the response causes Brian to rally and he yells out the correct answer.

"JUNE!!" But, ever impulsive, he can't stop himself. "And then comes July, August, September . . ."

Every day, morning meeting is an activity used to help orient the boys in time and place. During this period, the goal is for them to learn not only to tell time, but about time; it's used to teach what month they are in and what day of the week it is, to help them notice the weather, to anticipate events and holidays. Most of the activities are structured using a series of charts and graphs on which the boys plot information, and therefore they have a real-life mathematics and science component. By the end of every month, for instance, a complete log of sunny, rainy, cloudy, and partly cloudy days has been made using cutout weather symbols. With it, the boys can do counting activities, or they can predict how many sunny days will happen during the following month. The temperature graph helps Anne structure the same kinds of predicting activities or gives her an opportunity to teach about more and less, or new vocabulary, such as Fahrenheit. The oversized calendar has important days written in, like birthdays, planned trips, and school holidays. Anne leads boys to count how many days until an event and to translate that into weeks. The content is what primary teachers call "general information," foundation knowledge providing orientation in time and space, and knowledge of physical science and mathematics. The pedagogy is straightforward conversation and simple data collection, and is an attempt to emulate morning meeting in regular primary classrooms. But, as with every effort in Anne's class, the academic pedagogy cannot be separated from the behavioral and social pedagogies.

"Aaron, what day of the week is today?"

"I'm not saying it!!" he whines pathetically. He seems unsure of an answer and mumbles "Tuesday." It is not Tuesday, and so he guesses Wednesday, then Thursday. Finally right, he can come up and put the "Thursday" card on the chart.

"Thursday the what?" He checks the chart and sees the seven on the day before and seems sure about today being the eighth. Brian yells out the entire date, and Anne offers a rejoinder.

"Seven days to our Walden Pond trip," she says. "And 16 more days until graduation." On the last day of school there will be a ceremony and party for the boys who are leaving Brighton.

"Can my mother come to graduation?" Brian asks anxiously. His mother is never far from his thoughts, and Anne pauses in the lesson to answer his questions and console him about missing her. Then it is on to the weather, with Samuel charting that it is cloudy, even though he wishes there was a category for "muggy" because that's what it really is like outside; Brian adds that it is breezy.

In the middle of it all, Samuel starts doing a bizarre dance, flapping his arms and yelling loudly. Anne intervenes brusquely, mock shock in her voice, telling him he will have to sit another minute at recess as a consequence for disrupting the group. He starts whining, goes to the window, and sits with the curtains pulled over his head, mumbling and yelping. But Anne just goes on to the next activity, which is swiftly giving out points for the first part of the day, explaining to each boy the reasons for the reward or the withholding of points, teaching behavior explicitly.

She addresses Samuel first, telling him he gets both points for computer time (one for his behavior and one for doing his work), but that she is holding her judgment on morning meeting to see if he is able to take his head out from under the curtains and sit correctly.

Aaron gets only one point for word time because of his rudeness and disruptive behavior, but both for morning meeting because he bounced back so well.

Paul gets both points for word time, but none for morning meeting because he was unable to manage transition time and stay with the group.

Brian gets one point for word time because he didn't start with the whole group, but both for morning meeting because he started to have a problem, yet turned it around into doing the right thing.

In the first 45 minutes of the day, Anne has accomplished a number of academic goals, as well as social and behavioral goals. The day is constructed such that these initial activities can help lead the boys from the relatively un-structured time in the lifespace into the structured time of school. Word time allows the boys to work alone while remaining in a group. By morning meet-ing time, Anne is working to bring each boy's focus away from his individual task and onto a common task. Funneling their attention this way is difficult, requiring that Anne give attention to myriad individual behavioral and emotional difficulties, and that she use a variety of behavioral, social, and academic pedagogies. Although she must continually shift among these three goal structures, she keeps her equilibrium by maintaining her focus on the academic activity. This fact is crucial. Given any one of the serious social, emotional, or behavioral issues that emerge on any given morning, Anne could easily be sidetracked from teaching about knights in armor or the days of the week. But instead she balances those issues and pushes on to the next level—math class.

Math Class

9:30 a.m. "Who remembers that fancy word for math that's [all] about shapes?" There is mumbling and a fidgety rustle among the boys for a few moments until Brian ventures a guess. I recall how back in September a question like this from Anne, directed to the whole group, would invariably cause the boys anxiety that was too great to contain.

"Psychiatrist??" he bursts forth off his seat for a foot or two, and recedes to his place.

"No," Anne has that tone of voice that teachers get when they must say "no" to a student's earnest but incorrect answer. His choice of word is funny and ironic, but there is no recognition of either in Anne's response. Brian gets his thinking look on his face and pauses for a moment or two.

"Ghee-ometry," he tries again, slowly pulling the word out of his mind, saying the initial *G* as a hard sound. He has encountered this word both in writing and in Anne's talks about it. Given his pronunciation now, it is probably his visual memory of the word that helps him answer Anne's question.

Anne has recently introduced geometry as the math subject for the month of June, telling them that it is learning all about shapes. This morning, she tells them that everyone will be playing a game, called shape dominoes, one that some of them learned yesterday for the first time in a small group. She sits on the floor and invites the boys to sit in a circle, telling each where she wants him to be, trying to form the least volatile configuration. She deals out the game tiles to the four boys, Karen, and herself. Each tile is about 3 inches by 5 inches and has two shapes on it, for instance, a red circle and a yellow parallelogram. The object is for the boys to match either the shapes, the colors, or both on their own tile to one on the game table, just like in dominoes.

"How many tiles do you think each boy will get?" Anne asks for estimates as she deals the tiles. Aaron, who played this game yesterday for the first time with only three players, begins guessing numbers that are very high. The expression on his face says that he is up to something as he glances at the other boys to see what effect he is having by mentioning big numbers. He has a propensity for turning fun situations into unpleasant competitions. Anne tries to redirect him when she asks him to think if he will have more or less than he had yesterday. But her question doesn't distract him from trying to set the group up.

"I don't want Karen to play," he spits out in a hurtful tone just as the game gets under way. Karen tells him it is not a choice he can make. Thwarted again, he reverts to competing about how many tiles each boy has and announces that he has five tiles when actually he has four like everyone else. This creates a small ripple among the boys, and Anne intervenes quickly again, determined that this will be a successful group activity.

"We're going to ignore you because we know you're not telling the truth." Moments later when it is his turn, he tells everyone that he is not going to put his tile where it belongs, but he is going to do what he wants to do. Each of Aaron's comments gets the attention of the whole group; there is a discernible pause in the action, with boys looking to the adults to see what they are going to do. For their part, the adults consistently downplay his comments by saying, "That's not true," by redirecting his attention, or by pushing the game forward and ignoring him outright. This morning, the others are enjoying the game enough that she can quickly get them re-involved with it and away from Aaron's negativity.

The object of the game, at least at the level Anne played it that day, was for the boys to match one of their tiles with one on the board by shape but not color. That was the easy part. The great initial challenge of the game was to place the tile where only one of its sides would match one side of another domino. Often, a boy would place a tile so that both of its sides touched another domino, with only one side creating an exact match. Anne tried valiantly to get all the boys to follow this rule; Paul and Brian understood the rule quickly, but Samuel and Aaron did not. Eventually, Anne, Paul, and Brian agreed to "bend the rules" for the game and allowed some tiles to touch. Otherwise, they would have bogged down and never finished.

Besides teaching about games having rules and that boys must take turns, Anne uses this game to introduce a number of geometry skills and facts: It introduces the variety of plane geometric shapes, helps the boys develop vocabulary, gives practice in pattern matching, and gives opportunity for rudimentary geometric proofs. In the case of pattern matching, for instance, the boys must look carefully before trying a match, because the tiles have a variety of geometric shapes. Paul, a very attentive student during this activity, is the first to attempt a polygon match. He begins by placing his tile in one spot and then another, counting the corners of the figures to see if there is a match, a strategy for which he receives ample praise from his teacher. On the third try, he finds a correct match. When the others hear and watch him find a match this way, some of them try to emulate his strategy, with good success. To substantiate their choices, they begin to "prove" their matches by counting corners.

As the game nears completion, the excitement among the boys mounts. No one can predict whether the last person to play will be able to make a satisfactory match. But the last tile is played with ease, and everyone jumps up and begins to move fast throughout the room. Anne quickly calls for the boys to sit on their benches.

"I want everybody on their bench by the count of five." They do it— with a fair amount of whooping and yelling. She asks for 1 minute of silence to show that they are ready for the next activity. One by one as they settle down and are quiet, she mentions which of them now "looks ready for the next activity."

She divides them into two smaller groups. Samuel and Paul go with Cathy; Aaron and Brian stay with Anne. Moving from the whole group to smaller ones is typical of math time. With two and sometimes three adults in the room, Anne says that "we can do things in a whole group for like 3 minutes and then once I set the base, the groundwork for the activity, we can split out into . . . groups and do it." Today she gives each group a big bucket of pattern blocks. Pattern blocks are varied geometric shapes, about 2 inches in size, cut from wood and painted bright colors. The boys pour these out onto the tables, and Anne tells Aaron and Brian that they can make their own design for 5 minutes. She has learned that they must have this opportunity to play before she can hope to involve them in her planned activity. Aaron, after a brief burst of obscenity, sits down to his work and makes a graceful and balanced mandala; Brian makes a fat, tall man, names him Ralph, and begins to compare him with one of his residence child-care workers whom he dislikes. This sets up Aaron who renews his obscenities, only now about Ralph. Anne stops this behavior by swiftly giving them a firm ultimatum: Either stop talking about Ralph and anybody else at Brighton, or sit out the remainder of the period doing nothing. They choose to stop. I recall how, earlier in the year, if she had given such a strong ultimatum, she would have caused the boys to escalate their behaviors even further. Now, such strong and direct interventions work, at least some of the time.

Even on the best of days, Anne must constantly shift her teaching focus between the boys' social behaviors and their academic behaviors. She is vigilant, moving back and forth between these two sets of goals again and again throughout the day. Keeping these boys "on-task," Anne exhibits one of the key components of her craft as a teacher. That is, she finds a way to balance the goals of the curriculum and the needs of the boys; more often than not, the outcome is a completed academic task.

When the two boys finish their own designs, they accept large laminated pages from Anne. On each of these pages is drawn the perimeter of a different shape. In the lower corner is a legend that informs the boys in symbols of how many orange trapezoids, or yellow squares, or red triangles can be used in composing the shape on the laminated page. The boys fall to the task, trying to solve their individual geometric puzzles. Aaron is quick about his and is ready for another challenge within a few minutes. Anne offers him a "harder one" and he accepts it, telling her it is actually an easy one. But within a moment or two he is yelling for her help in his harshest tone of voice.

"GIVE ME HELP!!!"

"Change your tone of voice," she commands him, matter-of-factly. He does, and makes an effort to ask for help with a pleasant tone; she moves in quickly to assist him. Together they solve the immediate problem that frustrated him, and Anne sits beside him as he works on alone, completing his geometric design.

Pedagogical foundations. In this short math period, Anne demonstrated a number of the key components of her overall math curriculum: The boys spent the time manipulating objects in order to begin building firm conceptual foundations for geometry; her instructional groupings shifted from the whole group to pairs; the boys had freedom to make some of their own choices; the activities were fun. But to understand the curriculum as a whole, it is helpful to understand its philosophical underpinnings, the way in which the content is structured, and the means of instruction. This is necessary, in part, because Anne uses Brighton's school-wide math curriculum as her guide in planning instruction. Although she is competent at math herself and enjoys teaching it, it is not something that she feels a natural affinity for, as she does for the reading and literacy-related curriculum. She uses the Brighton curriculum because it makes sense to her and is congruent with her overall goals as a teacher. It has given her a chance for relearning mathematics herself, from its conceptual basis. Her development as a teacher and learner of math is at an earlier stage than her development as a teacher and learner of reading.

The Brighton curriculum is organized around six premises (Table 8.1), which Anne has adopted and translated into action. Given these premises, the curriculum is organized around fundamental topics in mathematics; for Anne's class this means estimation, the meaning of number, place value, patterns, addition, subtraction, multiplication, geometry, time, and even some division. The topics are divided roughly by months, with each month dedicated to a different math concept or group of concepts. It is a spiraling curriculum, with key topics or skill areas cycling back throughout the year. Depending on the topic, the boys are either instructed as a whole group or in smaller groups.

For example, in September and October of the first year of the study, the goals of the curriculum were to "generate interest and excitement in math manipulatives, exploration, and problem solving; introduce the concept of

TABLE 8.1 The six premises of the Brighton mathematics curriculum

·Mathematics should be viewed in its broadest context. Number, time, geometry, measurement, graphing, estimation, computers, and real life situations should be included.

·Students learn math in different ways due to various factors. Many topics and techniques should be used to appeal to different styles of learning.

·Emotionally disturbed students need preparation for mainstream programs. Because public schools usually stress computation, the curriculum works on building a strong conceptual basis for understanding computation.

·Elementary math should stress manipulatives and visual models. Concrete, direct experiences with mathematics are stressed at every level of learning.

·Emotionally disturbed students need opportunities to develop social skills through peer cooperation in math. Shared learning experiences of problem solving and group drill-and-practice are encouraged.

·Math should be fun. Capitalizing on student strengths and interests, and varying math topics will help students find math a useful adventure.

---

estimation; practice writing numbers 0–10; and to create, recognize, reproduce, and extend geometric and numerical patterns." Most of those activities lent themselves to being conducted as large group activities. By mid-October Anne shifted the curriculum emphasis to smaller group activities, beginning with the topic of addition and subtraction with numbers up to 10; in November the concept addressed was place value; in December she circled back to addition and subtraction with numbers up to 20. After the winter break, Anne began whole group activities in time and money, made a segue into small group work doing problem solving with addition and subtraction, and by April was using manipulatives to introduce the concept of multiplication; in May she began a unit of graphing with the whole group.

Anne doesn't use textbooks in math; she draws many of her ideas from resource books on experiential math and from her supervision hour with Alex. Her materials are teacher collected, like buttons and seeds, or, as in the game of *Sea Monster* mentioned previously, the materials are edibles. Many of her materials, like the pattern boards she used in the lesson described above, she has made herself. But commercial manipulatives such as poker chips, Unifix© cubes (plastic cubes that measure an inch and can be connected like pop beads), base 10 blocks (wooden cubes that are divided into single units, groups of tens, and groups of one hundred and one thousand), tangrams, pattern blocks, and shape dominoes play an important part in her teaching as well.

The ultimate goals of math instruction are the same for every boy. Anne wants them to learn what numbers are and how they can be manipulated systematically in addition, subtraction, and beginning multiplication. She says she will be successful in math if the boys end up "carrying around . . . in their heads" a strategy for solving problems that is based on real understanding rather than "just carrying a list of steps" in their heads, as so many people do. She wants to avoid teaching children "to carry when they're not supposed to carry and borrow when they're not supposed to borrow and those kinds of things because they've learned a series of steps without understanding why they're doing it."

Her pedagogy employs games that teach the boys how to manipulate objects for some mathematical purpose, mixed with more conventional drill-and-practice activities. A staple of her pedagogy, and a good example of using manipulatives in general, is the chip-trading game. Actually a group of games, chip-trading uses the same principle as making change, but it is not limited to base 10. Trading games are used to teach place value and regrouping in addition and subtraction. Chip-trading games are the kinds of strategies Anne refers to when she says she wants the boys "to carry around in their heads" strategies for solving problems. In the following quote, Anne describes how she began teaching the interconnected concepts of place value and regrouping by using base 4. This technique is one that she learned form the work of Kathy Richardson (1984), who thinks that, at their level of cognitive development, children find 4 to be an easier amount to comprehend. Anne agrees that using 4 instead of 10 allows the boys to concentrate on the concepts she is teaching rather than trying to comprehend the amount they are manipulating. Comprehending amount is a separate goal of the curriculum, and she doesn't want worrying about number to confuse the boys about regrouping. Further, she wants to avoid using highly technical vocabulary that can confuse them as well; following this technique, she calls groups of 4 *zibs*.

> The way we started is with a place value board that's red on one side and white on the other side. . . . And the first day [I] would introduce the concept . . . when I teach the number 4, [I say] this many is a zib. The game would start with [a zib] plus 1. Every time I say plus 1 you take one cube and put it on your 1 side. There's a 1 side and a zib side, which will eventually become the 1s and the 10s, so the 1 side is always on the right . . . and the zib side [is on the left]. Plus 1 you put one on your 1 side. Plus 1 you put one on your 1 side. Plus 1 you put one on your 1 side. . . . Plus 1 . . . [Then I ask] what do you need to do now? I need to put them together and move it over to the zib side. . . . We throw out the word [regrouping]. "Oh, look, you need to make a new group" or "you need to regroup" or "do you need to regroup?"
>
> An idea that came from the trading curriculum stuff is the idea of

illegal boards, which the kids really like. They think it's funny so I use that a lot with them. If they forget to regroup, I say, "Oh! Look at your board! I see something illegal," and then they fix it and make their board legal. So usually the first day or two is just doing that, and once they're getting the idea and they're automatically making the groups, then I'll vary it a little, so instead of just saying plus 1 all the time I might say plus 2 or plus 3 and have them adding different amounts at a time, but remembering that as soon as they get up to the zib they need to make a zib and move it over to the other side. So . . . for a couple of weeks, without any written-down stuff at all, they're just going to play these games . . . once they're good at adding, then one day [I'll] say, "Okay, well, today we're going to start with 3 zibs on our board and we're going to take away. Well, if it's only 3 zibs that's 3 on our board, we're going to take away 1, take away 1, take away 1, take away 1. I can't. I don't have any 1s. Yeah, but you've got 3 zibs. What can we do?" And ideally, but not always, . . . what they can do is take a zib, break it apart . . . because 4 1s is really the same thing as a zib.

Along with this hands-on approach to teaching math concepts, Anne weaves in traditional computation instruction. The boys learn to write their numbers correctly, but usually in conjunction with a series of hands-on exercises that reinforce the concept of number. For instance, using Unifix© cubes, Anne spent a number of weeks teaching and reinforcing the meaning of the number 10. The cubes are one square inch and can fit together in a chain. Anne played the game "123—POP" with the boys. The boys would hold in their hands 10 cubes fastened together. Anne would count "123—POP," and the boys would break the chain of cubes into two. They would then count up how many cubes were in their left hand, and how many in their right. On a chart before them that was divided into three columns, they would write the correct number in the corresponding column, right and left, and the number 10 in the final column. Some giddy minutes every day with this game led them to recognize the meaning of 10 and the variety of ways it can be composed of smaller numbers, and eventually led to writing rudimentary "number sentences." As the year progressed, Anne used addition flash cards (and later subtraction flash cards) for a few minutes at the beginning of the period to help the boys become more automatic in their calculations. In these ways her math curriculum and pedagogy reflect the eclecticism of the entire classroom curriculum: Hands-on activities address underlying concepts, but they are matched with corresponding conventional teaching strategies.

Diagnostic Results. As I have already mentioned, diagnostic tests of learning are administered to students each June. A brief overview of the results on those tests provides some conventional measures of these students' progress in their ability to understand and apply primary mathematics. Table 8.2 displays a comparison of results on the Key Math–Revised (Connolly, 1988) after the first and second years of instruction for the four students who remained with Anne for both years. The results point to the fact that many of Anne's efforts had paid off.

All four boys saw substantial growth in their scores after 2 years of instruction, with Brian showing the greatest overall growth, and Samuel the least. By June 1990, Brian, Aaron, and Jason had each tested at or near grade level. Given the emphasis that Anne's curriculum places on understanding concepts in math (numeration, place value, and so forth) and in applying them, it is not surprising to see that these two subareas of math show the strongest promise for these boys. Samuel is the exception, and, as these test results reflect, his understanding of mathematical concepts remained static.

TABLE 8.2 A comparison of key math scores for 1989 and 1990

	1989		1990	
	Grade	Age	Grade	Age
Brian		*(6–4)*		*(7–7)*
Basic Concepts	1.3	(6–5)	2.7	(8–1)
Operations	2.1	(7–3)	2.6	(7–8)
Applications	2.0	(7–3)	3.9	(9–1)
Total	1.8	(7–2)	3.1	(8–4)
Aaron		*(7–6)*		*(8–4)*
Basic Concepts	2.7	(8–1)	3.1	(8–4)
Operations	2.3	(7–5)	2.7	(8–1)
Applications	2.7	(8–6)	3.7	(8–11)
Total	2.5	(7–7)	3.1	(8–4)
Jason		*(6–10)*		*(7–10)*
Basic Concepts	K.2	(5–1)	1.9	(7–2)
Operations	2.0	(7–2)	2.5	(7–7)
Applications	2.7	(8–0)	3.1	(8–11)
Total	1.8	(7–2)	2.5	(7–10)
Samuel		*(8–10)*		*(9–10)*
Basic Concepts	K.2	(5–1)	1.9	(7–2)
Operations	2.0	(7–2)	2.5	(7–7)
Applications	2.7	(8–0)	3.1	(8–11)
Total	1.8	(7–2)	2.5	(7–10)

However, when we recall that his neurological disability centers around diffi-culties with integrating sensory data into useful concepts, the gains in his abil-ity to perform operations and to apply his math become noteworthy.

Math has been a successful time for Anne as a teacher as well as for Anne as a learner. Her thinking regarding her math curriculum is at a different de-velopmental stage than her thinking about reading and literacy. Always a good student in math herself, she is a product of traditional mathematics instruc-tion, which emphasized computation and not understanding. Thus, over the past years at Brighton, she has relearned mathematics from a new perspective, using methods and materials that are different from those she had previously experienced. Her pedagogy in math has been growing rapidly, becoming more her own as her experience with the curriculum increases. Her former supervisor, the one who first introduced her to the math curriculum, viewed her teaching math in the final months of the study. He commented that it was remarkable how certain methods and materials that he had first introduced to her 5 years before had been modified over time, customized both to the boys and also to her own way of thinking and doing. He emphasized the point that Anne is curious and open about new ideas; she is motivated to finding ways to apply them in her teaching and learning. This is clearly evident in her efforts with math, and even more so in her curriculum and pedagogy in read-ing, which occupy the next part of her day.

Reading Class

10:00 a.m. Her first reading class of the day commences, and Anne is in her element, academically speaking. For the first half hour Anne instructs Paul, Cathy instructs Aaron, and Karen takes the other three boys outside for recess. During the second half hour, Anne teaches Jason and Brian, Cathy teaches Samuel, and Karen takes Paul and Aaron outdoors for recess. One of the original reasons that three staff members were assigned to every classroom at Brighton was to facilitate small group or tutorial instruction during reading class. Given the widely varying skills that the children have in reading, com-bined with their behavioral difficulties, effective reading instruction, especially in decoding and connected reading, is possible only with such small ratios. Although reading class takes place during the 10–11 period, reading instruc-tion actually goes on throughout the day. I have alluded to the fact that Anne devotes different half-hour periods to different aspects of the literacy enter-prise: While the 10–11 hour is dedicated to instruction in decoding, 11–11:30 is given over to whole language goals; 12–12:30 is devoted to lis-tening comprehension and pleasure reading; 12:30–1 is devoted to writing; and 1–2 is planned for, among other things, reading for information in the content areas. Obviously, reading and literacy are the major emphases of

Anne's academic curriculum; technically, only the half-hour periods for math, recess, and lunch are not focused primarily on reading itself or on literacy goals.

Anne has an extensive set of goals and objectives for her reading program; she also uses a variety of instructional settings and pedagogies to implement this comprehensive approach. But it is in the area of decoding and connected reading, where the boys' skills vary most widely, that her most detailed planning and teaching take place. The period from 10–11 reveals a clearly remedial pedagogy, ordered and sequenced; it is a type of teaching that Anne uses only sometimes in other parts of the day.

On June 8, Paul came to class in what appeared to be a good mood. He had just had fun in math class; in fact he had excelled at the shape domino game and at using the pattern blocks. His transition from math had been a little rough, but that was nothing unusual. Anne began the period by quickly laying out 10 index cards inscribed with familiar words and by asking Paul to put the words "in ABC order." Often the students in Anne's class, regardless of skill level, begin their reading period with some sort of alphabetizing activity using words they already know. The younger boys alphabetize by first letter only; some of the older boys she has taught can alphabetize to the second letter. Paul is still a beginning reader; unbidden, he sings the alphabet song aloud, and he quickly grabs up the cards that say *are, but, came, did,* and *find,* as he passes their initial letters in the song. He fumbles at "k" and "l," skipping right to the letter "m," but, with a reminder from Anne, he self-corrects. When he finishes putting the cards in ABC order, he reads them accurately as Anne flashes them for him, one by one.

"Put a star next to number one," Anne enthuses, referring to the list of activities she has written on his daily reading contract. Most boys have such contracts in reading and math. The contracts help them monitor their own progress, and Anne can use them as behavior management tools as well. Having drawn himself a star for completing his first agenda item, Paul takes the composition book Anne proffers, picks up a pencil, and listens to her as she explains that she is going to give him words with three letters, but with different vowels. Paul has been learning short vowel sounds in the CVC pattern. In the Alphabet Phonics (Cox, 1980) program, students learn that this means "consonant-vowel-consonant." It is the first word pattern they learn after exposure to consonants and some short vowels. Anne dictates the words *fed, tab, pan, cut,* and *mix,* all of which he has encountered before. He writes these words, subvocalizing as he goes, sounding the vowels carefully—and he gets them all correct. He needs help only on the letter *x*.

For Paul, these two activities are drill-and-practice exercises with knowledge and skills he has already learned. Anne has many such exercises that she uses to drill new vowel sounds or phonetic patterns, and Paul can expect to continue in this mode, practicing short vowels in CVC patterns, for some days to come. But on some day soon, Anne will teach a new sound or pattern, in the order and by the method prescribed in the Alphabet Phonics schedule, probably using cards from what are called "sound decks," which use pictures as memory cues for sounds and spellings. Then Anne will extend the learning using various games made with the cards from the decks. In the Alphabet Phonics program, there are three schedules of skills to be taught, and most of the learning disabled students at Brighton finish one per year. Theoretically, when all three schedules have been mastered, a student will have learned all the basic phonics rules to decode fluently at a third-grade level. The program has been used at the school for over 15 years, with undeniable success—the children learn to read.

Paul draws another star on his contract for doing his dictation so well, and he moves on to read his current book, which is all about dragons. He doesn't need any encouragement to open the book and pick up where he left off. Ordinarily, Anne would spend time on a pre-reading activity to introduce the book, its ideas, and its vocabulary. But Paul has been reading his dragon book for a few days now, loves it, and is impatient to finish it today. He reads along, struggling with words as he goes, accepting help once or twice from Anne, but mostly proceeding on his own. For her part, Anne moves her finger along, keeping his place, and praising him for "reading with good expression." She doesn't stop and ask him comprehension questions today, but lets him keep his momentum. When he finishes the book with a flourish, he asks her if he can make a big drawing about the book. Of course, the answer is yes.

As Anne and Paul draw a picture of a castle, moat, knight, and lady (Paul has asked Anne to help with the castle outline and the moat), he begins to talk. He talks about how if he were king, he would use jousting to settle problems; he mentions different ways outlaws could be punished; he informs Anne that he would make only good laws. Anne encourages him to continue discussing these ideas by asking him questions; she answers some of his questions, like one about the use of the stocks in punishing criminals; she provides him with some extended vocabulary. Eventually, the conversation shifts to a discussion about the president of the United States, whether he is a good leader, and how long he can stay president. The conversation reveals the boy's interest in the story just read, shows some of his comprehension of it, and in a rudimentary way extends his knowledge of the subject of leadership. It is 5 minutes of meaningful talk between teacher and student about the subject at hand, and the expression on both their faces is relaxed and happy. Such talk is a mainstay of the classroom pedagogy, and throughout the day as the year progressed, more of these small conversations occurred between adults and between boys as well.

During this first reading period of the day, Anne and Paul moved rapidly through the entire contract. Paul has been learning to read, loves reading, and thrives on the one-to-one attention. He has learned the routines of Alphabet Phonics and usually attempts learning a new sound or pattern with minimal resistance. He likes the games they play and is good at them. After 1 year, his diagnostic testing on the Durrell Test of Reading Ability (Durrell, & Catterson, 1980) substantiated what Anne already knew. From his beginnings as a complete nonreader, he was reading silently at a first-grade level, and his listening comprehension level was at a fourth-grade level.

Second period. During her second period of reading instruction, Brian has been making similar progress, even though he is a full year younger than Paul. He also started at a pre-primer level but does not seem to have the same need for a very structured phonics program. As Anne says, he just "is zooming ahead!" (Indeed, by the end of the first year of instruction, testing indicated that he had assembled his reading readiness skills and had a listening comprehension level of third grade. By the end of the second year of instruction, he was comprehending stories at a fourth-grade level and under optimal conditions was reading silently at a mid-second-grade level. Of course, conditions were not often optimal, and by June 1990 he was mostly reading at a solid first-grade level).

But Brian's group partner Jason is another story. He is a challenge not only behaviorally, but in reading as well. Jason's vocabulary is large; his listening comprehension is superior. But over the year, it became increasingly clear that in reading (and math as well) he is in the minority of children who have consistent difficulty with written symbols. Anne, Alex, and Martha, the reading specialist, have begun to wonder if he will ever be literate.[1] His reading profile says:

> Jason has a very difficult time remembering written symbols and their sounds. He can recite the alphabet in a song and circle the correct letter when given a choice (choices have no reversals). Jason had trouble writing the letters from memory, naming the letters when they were randomly written on paper and identifying letter pairs when reversals were added. Jason scored highest on tasks involving matching beginning and ending sounds using pictures. While [he] was completing the task he named the letter as well as the sound. . . . Jason has serious perceptual difficulties with written symbols.

---

1. The principal and reading specialist at Brighton can count only three children in the past 15 years that they were unable to teach to read because of a specific reading disability, and they are stung by that fact. The names of those boys have been passed down from their predecessors; Jason marks the first boy of their administration whom they have been, as yet, unable to teach.

Anne's teaching goal is to help Jason recognize in written form what he can recognize only auditorily. She uses classic multisensory approaches to help him learn sound-symbol correspondences: sandpaper letters, tracing, clay letters, mnemonics. She is always trying to involve as much of his body as she can in learning to read.

"Today, let's do something special," she tells him as she starts the period. "Let's cut up the bingo board!" Anne is trying to appeal to Jason's love of taking things apart—or destroying them.

"Are you crazy?" Jason asks, even though he has not hesitated in starting the task of carefully dissecting the bingo game. The word bingo boards are made from laminated oak tag and have written in each of 12 cells the different words that Anne has been trying to help Jason recognize: *the, cat, can, see,* and so forth. Once Jason has rendered the board asunder and it becomes a deck of word cards, Anne starts mixing them up to give Jason a sentence to read. *I like the cat.* He reads it with difficulty. *The cat can see me.* He reads it, too.

"Let's try a longer one," Anne challenges him. *I see the blue cat.* He reads it. Now Anne drills him on the words, asking him to point to the one she says. He points to each one in turn. This is the kind of activity that he is able to do consistently, given the auditory cues. "Now you say one that I should point to." Silence. He looks at the array of words. He quickly looks up at the primary alphabet that is stretched above the windows, searching for a hint in those letters. He looks back at the cards. He rubs his eyes. Finally, he looks at her and asks if she would read them so he can point to the right ones; she reads, he points. This is typical. If Jason hears a word like *cat,* he can usually locate it in the array. But if he is asked to read a word without an auditory cue, he often cannot do it. A sound will sometimes connect with a symbol; a symbol rarely, if ever, implies a sound.

Anne moves on. Her overarching goal is to avoid doing anything that could make the boy feel bad about trying to read. The last activity of his reading period is illustrating a story book. In a composition pad, Anne has already written a story using the words Jason is working on. On the bottom of today's page is the sentence *The cat can go to Jason.* Jason reads the sentence slowly and with difficulty. Anne asks him to draw a picture of the sentence he just read. He looks at her blankly.

"I don't understand the whole thing," his voice sounds tired and sad. He has read the words, but they make absolutely no sense to him. Anne reads the sentence aloud for him, and he immediately understands and knows what to draw. This is another aspect of his disability: Even though he can decode some words successfully, he cannot process their meaning.

The dichotomy between his inability to decode and make meaning, and his ability to comprehend auditorily creates a special dilemma for Anne. She is deeply concerned that as the other boys move ahead of Jason, his already low sense of self will plummet further. She says, "Jason already knows that he is behind, and that's going to be another problem: 'Why did Brian . . . have *Explode the Code*? (Hall & Rice, 1978) Why did Brian . . . read more words than me?' So, I am really worried about what I'm going to do with Jason." In the second year of instruction, Anne took Jason into a one-to-one tutorial. Although he made some progress, at the end of a second year of intensive instruction he could read only 10 sight words automatically, could read only 85% of the alphabet correctly, and could not yet write his last name from memory.

There are obvious differences between Paul, Brian, and Jason in their ability to learn to read; they translate into differences in the structure of the goals Anne has for them and the pedagogies she employs to teach them. The instructional period for each requires Anne to have a different plan, to use materials differently, and to have a different set of personal expectations. Aside from those differences, Jason's idiosyncratic differences provide even more dilemmas. The chasm between his ability to comprehend third-grade level stories read to him and his inability to decode anything meaningful even at a primer level creates quandaries around the choice of materials and methods: What will help teach the requisite skills, but not insult his intelligence? What can Anne do about the fact that Jason "has a very low frustration level. He becomes extremely violent very rapidly, throws things, punches, kicks, bites, and he will run out of the room" ?

Anne makes substantial shifts in thinking as she proceeds through a day: She understands and remembers the different skills of each boy, and each half-hour period takes on its own pedagogy; she keeps cognitive, social, and behavioral considerations concurrently active in her thoughts, and notices when she should shift away from an academic effort, like asking Jason to read a word that she could point to, when it threatens her student's self-esteem. She displays self-discipline as a teacher; she takes a professional distance far enough from the boys that she remains a clear thinker, but close enough that she maintains a warm and caring relationship with them.

Big books. Compared with the routinized schedule of reading class, Big Books period, from 11–11:30, seems relatively free and unstructured. In fact, it is structured for different purposes. Big Books are about 3 feet tall, with large text that can be read by a youngster at some distance from the book. They are filled with colorful illustrations. Big Books is actually a set of whole language activities intended to build sight vocabulary and an appreciation of the structure of language through the repetition of favorite stories and the words they contain. The oversized books are filled with vocabulary at a primary level. At first, an adult reads to the boys. But soon, the adult asks the boys to read with her the word that is highlighted throughout the book, say, the word *bear*. Through repetition the boys recognize that word and read it aloud each time it occurs. After several more repetitions of the book, the boys begin to read along in chorus. Eventually, the group may write a story of their own about bears or make up a rap song. The idea is to have fun with stories and vocabulary while patterning the youngsters' language into a coherent structure. Theoretically, that interior structure will manifest itself in their spoken and written language, as well as in their increased ability to read.

For the boys in Anne's class, it is a successful strategy. With the obvious exception of Jason, the boys have learned to read new vocabulary. Words from a Big Book often will show up again as a boy's choice at word time in the morning or in the sentences boys create during writing time. Their sentences reflect the structure of sentences they've played with as well. It is an indication of the success of the whole language approach in Anne's class that, at different times of the day, the boys use language they were taught during other times of the day.

Read-aloud. The material used during Big Books period is aimed at teaching vocabulary and language skills that the boys can use immediately. But most boys can understand stories at a reading level beyond their ability to decode. Read-aloud is the period designed for the boys to listen to, enjoy, and discuss stories that they are capable of understanding, but cannot necessarily read themselves. Anne uses this half-hour period after lunch to expose the boys to new ideas in a relaxed atmosphere. During the year they heard stories about Pilgrims and Native Americans, Chanukah, Christmas, and other holidays. They read stories from books they chose from the library. They read Dr. Seuss books, de Brunhoff's *Babar*, and Milne's *Winnie-the-Pooh* books. E. B. White's *Charlotte's Web*, Roald Dahl's *James and the Giant Peach*, and Berends's *The Case of the Elevator Duck* were all read aloud to the boys. They did a whole unit on stories about giants and another on stories that were centered around the number 3. This period was not in Anne's original schedule for these boys. She had thought, given their youth, they would still need naps at mid-day. But when naptime didn't work, she instituted Read-aloud, a period she had always included in her schedule during other years. When she did this, she opened a door to learning about knights in armor, dinosaurs, crocodiles, and all matters of fantasy and reality that subsequently emerged in the boys' writing, storytelling, conversations, and drawings. Without explicit intention, Anne created one of the consistently successful periods of the day, academically, socially, and behaviorally. But seeing a successful opportunity, she took advantage of it.

Writing time. Read-aloud also primed the boys for writing time. As I discussed previously, their love of books and stories prompted some of the boys to ask for time to write and publish books of their own. The process writing approach that Anne employed was well suited to that desire. This approach was developed by Graves (1985) and is not known for its use with special education populations. The approach follows a four-step process for writing, mirroring the process that most writers go through. Each boy goes through a period of pre-writing, where the author is stimulated by a topic or gathers information for a topic, followed by a period of writing. Once a piece has been composed in a first draft, he edits the piece. Finally, if the piece of writing is truly satisfactory to the author, he illustrates it and publishes it. Throughout the four-step process, the author meets with his teacher for conferences. These are usually short periods where the author reads aloud what he was written and discusses what is good about the piece, improvements that might be made, or extensions of ideas that could be undertaken. When a piece emerges as a published book, the boy becomes the author of the day and gets a chance to read his book to an audience of his peers.

Whereas writing class commenced directly after Read-aloud, often there was no need for Anne to do a specific pre-writing conference with the boys. They would easily find an idea on which to work. Frequent conferences were necessary throughout the writing process, however, usually to assuage the boy's frustrations over tearing a page with an eraser, over not being able to spell a word, or over Anne or another adult not getting to help them immediately. They were used as well to stimulate a boy to write a little more than he had, or to seize the moment and use a boy's writing to teach him about synonyms or remind him about uppercase letters starting sentences and periods ending sentences. Using conferences for these purposes is a diversion from what most primary teachers do during conference. The nature of the boys' disabilities has caused Anne to modify the process writing pedagogy to accommodate those needs.

At the beginning of the first year, Anne planned that by June, Paul, Aaron, and Samuel would all be writing their own short stories and Brian and Jason would be dictating stories. However, all the boys except Jason ended the year writing their own stories, with less dictation taking place as the spring progressed. More than 15 books were published in 6 months time on a wide range of topics—from pet dogs to dinosaurs. Anne wanted the boys to have a highly successful first encounter with writing, to find it pleasurable and rewarding. Although feelings among the boys could run high and behaviors could be widely variable, to a large extent Anne reached her goal.

Content area instruction. The final hour of instruction is reserved for work in the content areas, where reading is undertaken to gather information. Units that Anne entitled "Our Bodies," "Insects," "Around the World," "Martin Luther King," "Transportation," and "Kitchen Chemistry" were presented through the use of storybooks, filmstrips, and especially experimentation and exploration. Although reading and writing were not the primary goals of these units, they played a key role. For instance, a favorite activity for the boys was drawing and captioning their own filmstrips on the subject they were studying. Captioning in general remained a preferred activity for some time. In science, the boys labeled and charted information, posted it on the walls or in scrapbooks, and, with Anne's guidance, would periodically refer to it in subsequent lessons.

Thus, reading and literacy goals stretched throughout the day. In reading class, the goal was to learn to decode and to apply the skills of decoding in connected reading; in Big Books, the goal was to develop an understanding of how language works, and that language is vocabulary and sentences, as well as stories, poems, and songs. Above all, it is a chief way to communicate. In Read-aloud time, Anne taught the boys the pleasure of books and of reading, while at the same time increasing their knowledge of the world, their vocabulary, and their language skills. In writing, the goal was to "value kids' own expression." Anne was adamant that the children leave her class believing that they had something important to say and that they could say it in writing. Finally, in science and social studies, through the use of literature and film, and charting and graphing, Anne taught that reading and writing could be used to gather information as well as transmit it. Perhaps most important, throughout the day the boys and adults talked with each other. There was rarely a silent moment in this class. Even when three boys were working quietly on their own, two were talking about some subject they were being taught, some thoughts they were having, or some feelings that needed expression. Language permeated the day and was both the curriculum and the pedagogy of Anne's class.

TAKEN ALTOGETHER, Anne's academic curriculum is very detailed in both structure and content; there is a very large volume of academic goals for the group and for each student, which Anne keeps current in her head as she teaches. But while she is paying attention to those goals, she is watchful of and responsive to the social and behavioral needs of individuals and the group as well. She is constantly shifting between the different types of goals in an effort to keep the school day on track. We can see this happening in earlier examples. When word time did not succeed as a strategy for sufficiently gathering the group's attention, Anne quickly shifted her group goals and pulled out a favorite book that she knew would draw the boys in. And as soon as she felt the tone in the room was conducive to morning meeting, she began that activity. What we see throughout this chapter is a high degree of what Doyle (1986) calls improvisational teaching, that is, an "understanding of the likely configuration of events in a classroom, and skill in monitoring and guiding activities in light of this information" (p. 424). Anne is a person who quickly perceives a need in the class and is able to respond creatively and decisively, braiding her knowledge of the needs of the boys into strategies that are effective.

CHAPTER 9

CONNECTING ANNE'S THINKING, CURRICULUM, AND PEDAGOGY

An undergraduate student teacher of mine, Monica, began seminar one day before I had even had a chance to say "good afternoon" to my students. "We've gotta talk about Anne!" It was urgent. Monica had read a version of Anne's story that I had assigned the week before, and clearly it had had a strong effect on her. As she began to speak, it was apparent that her thoughts about teaching were running far faster than her ability to express them. She was halfway through her practicum in a resource room at a large urban middle school and day by day was becoming more discouraged because her students seemed able to resist even her best activity ideas and teaching techniques. I had asked Monica and her classmates to read Anne's story to spark a conversation about, among other things, the effort of thought even veteran teachers must make to teach troubled children. Now, Monica was highly animated, as some people get when their ideas are coming together rapidly and their path ahead is finally becoming clear. Speaking with her hands and face almost as much as with her words, Monica listed a number of ways that she identified strongly with Anne's dilemmas. She was fascinated by the ways Anne went about resolving them, but she had many questions. Among other things, she wanted to know how Anne learned to notice what was important or not important in a classroom episode? How did she learn to act decisively and accurately? And most important, how could she, Monica, learn to think like a teacher?

These are crucial questions to ask about Anne and about teaching in general. It is always exciting when novice teachers start asking questions about how they can begin to think like a teacher. At the same time, it is always a quandary how best to respond to those questions. We still know very little about what is entailed in learning to think like a teacher, despite the past 20 years of research into teacher thinking. Most likely one's preservice training plays an important role. But experiences in life and at teaching itself have much to do with how a teacher's knowledge is constructed and thinking is shaped. So, too, do the core values one carries through life and through which knowledge, experience, and training are constantly filtered.

In Anne's case her reasoning abilities, beliefs, personal and professional knowledge, training, and values appeared to work in synchrony to aid her in "thinking like a teacher." Although her thinking is idiosyncratic, the different components that make it up share a fair amount in common with the components of teacher thinking described in the research literature. That research has followed three general strands, with inquiries pursuing an understanding of teachers' information processing abilities, teachers' knowledge of subject matter and pedagogy, or their personal practical knowledge of children, classroom processes, and themselves (Carter, 1990; Clark & Yinger, 1987).

However, Monica had a second burning question. "How," she asked, "is Anne able to keep the kids doing academics given all of their behavioral and social problems?" This question seemed to be the heart of the matter for Monica, as it had been for me when I began studying Anne. Monica went on to say that her greatest disappointment in her own work was that her students were not motivated to do interesting work in reading, math, or social studies; moreover, she was at a loss to find ways to engage them. She was beginning to think that her cooperating teacher was also at a loss for what to do and had settled on giving children work simply to avoid exacerbating their behavioral problems. Indeed, if the children behaved better, that seemed to constitute success, and meaningful work was not an issue. To her mind, that was not what school should be about. She perceived the problem quite clearly but was at a loss as to what to do about it, and she realized that connecting what one thought about a situation to what one did about it was difficult at best. What made Anne's story compelling to Monica was that Anne had been able to translate her thoughts into actions and had addressed the learning needs of the children without succumbing to their behavioral and social difficulties.

Anne's thinking, curriculum, and pedagogy are connected in such a way that children actually learn reading, writing, mathematics, and how to get along with each other. At the center of Anne's thinking are her core values, and they shape much of her teaching and her philosophy. Those values represent a different paradigm of curriculum and teaching from the current paradigm for educating troubled and troubling children. In Anne's thinking and action, we see her emphasize the normalizing power of academic pursuit in learning for troubled youngsters. She insists on meaningful learning experiences and shifts away from applied behavioral curricula so prevalent in standard special education, toward cognitive-developmental curriculum and pedagogy that draw on the work of such thinkers as Bruner (1961), Piaget (1966), and Vygotsky (1978). She also exhibits a respect for disturbed youngsters' intellect and ways of thinking, while negotiating with them the path of learning without a loss of rigor. Her teaching demonstrates the crucial role of teamwork, as well as deep, meaningful, daily discourse about teaching among adults. Importantly, she relies on a strong, shared institutional mission to teach troubled youngsters, without which she would be hard put to teach her students.

Undergirding Anne's paradigm for teaching is a discernible thought process, a strong theory of curriculum and pedagogy, a willingness to take the needed time to develop a learning environment, and a supportive institutional context. These interrelated thoughts and beliefs, and the human ecology Anne creates and in which she participates, work together to help shape her teaching, and together had a substantial, positive effect on what transpired in her class.

How, then, does Anne actually think? And how is it that she reconciles the academic, behavioral, and social learning needs of the students? In the discussion that follows, I do not attempt to mount new theories about how teachers think generally, nor do I corroborate any one existing theory of teacher thinking. Instead, I discuss how Anne constructs and uses knowledge in order to teach, given an understanding grounded in what she said, did, and wrote over 2 years. My effort is not to explain her thinking in terms of existing theory, or even to provide an extensive review of studies in teacher thinking, but to reference studies and theories when her thinking points in those directions.

ANNE AS A THINKER

When Anne met her new class of students, she greeted them not only with her own mixture of warmth and firmness, but with her clinical mind as well. Years of training and experience have shaped within her a distinctive approach to understanding who her students are and what they need to learn. Anne's approach to understanding is an interative process that integrates much of her knowledge of children, subject matter, and methods to shape what she does in her teaching. Generally, it starts with observing and describing individual children's strengths and weaknesses, in situ and over a considerable period of time. She then considers those observations using knowledge from as many as six different domains to find existing, or to shape new, thinking structures with which she can understand the child. Given those thinking structures, she makes preliminary decisions about the nature of the learning needs of the children, and, armed with those decisions, she shapes individual plans for the boys as well as plans for the group as a whole. One cycle of thinking is completed when she has implemented the individual and group plans and she begins again to observe and describe the individual children in response to the plans. Figure 9.1 illustrates the general outline of this thinking process.

It is important to underline the effects of her spiraling thought process and to show that, in every encounter she has with a child or the group, she performs a diagnostic procedure that integrates what she thinks, plus other people's estimations, plus formal testing. These encounters are iterative, and with each iteration she comes away with more data and more knowledge, which then inform each subsequent encounter.

This discussion is meant to uncover Anne's information processing strategies; the chief intention is to describe the broad intellectual context in which Anne reasons as a teacher of troubled children. It is not a model of specific planning or decision-making processes. Previously, information processing has been studied by investigating the pre-active and interactive thoughts and processes of teachers and then modeling decision trees to explain those processes (Clark & Peterson, 1986). Here, the attempt is to model what it is "to think like the teacher who is Anne," to outline her professional mental processes that encompass as well as orient her planning and her interactive thoughts.

FIGURE 9.1 Anne's method of thinking

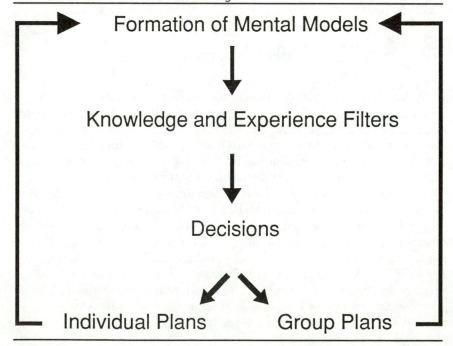

Building Mental Models

At the first step of Anne's coming to understand, she builds mental models for each boy, using data derived from her evaluations of four key domains of his personality: She observes and describes his social, emotional, behavioral, and cognitive strengths and weaknesses. She assesses which domains predominate and then arranges the four domains in relation to one another to form a profile of how the child presents himself in the classroom. Anne does not think of these four domains as mutually exclusive, but she does have the capacity to focus on each in isolation. Thus, she thinks of the social strengths and weaknesses of a child in terms of his abilities to make and sustain relationships with peers and adults. She thinks of his emotionality in terms of his feelings about himself and others, and in terms of the drives that he exhibits. When she thinks about a boy behaviorally, she focuses on his surface behaviors that exhibit self-control or violence, that are provocative or endearing, or that are or are not socially acceptable. Cognitively, she focuses on a boy's abilities to process information presented in school and how he processes information socially; she ponders other neurological considerations, such as his ability to screen out extraneous stimuli, or his ability to control neurologically based impulsive behaviors.

In Figure 9.2, I have drawn a paradigmatic model of Anne's thinking with respect to the relative contributions of the individual domains of personality.

In this model, each circle is equal in size and overlaps evenly with all other personality domains, suggesting that Anne perceives each domain of personality as equally developed and balanced in relation to the others; the equal areas of overlap suggest that each domain is not mutually exclusive, but that she views the interactions between them to be balanced as well. In her actual models for the boys, however, the relative size of each circle changes to reflect the predominant and subordinate role each of the domains takes as she thinks about the child's presentation of himself in class, and his corresponding needs. The areas of overlap change in size as well, reflecting Anne's thinking about the predominant and subordinate interactions between domains in each boy's personality. Brian provides a good example to illuminate this model. Her thinking about him provides good access to how she thinks about each of these personality domains, as well as their relationships to each other.

In her initial reports and assessments of Brian, Anne wrote that, emotionally, he "is a very depressed and needy child with many concerns about trust and personal safety." She perceived him as others had, that is, as a boy easily overwhelmed with feelings of sadness, anger, and fear. He appeared to be a child who needed copious amounts of nurturance, manifested in his de-

FIGURE 9.2 Paradigmatic mental model of individual boys

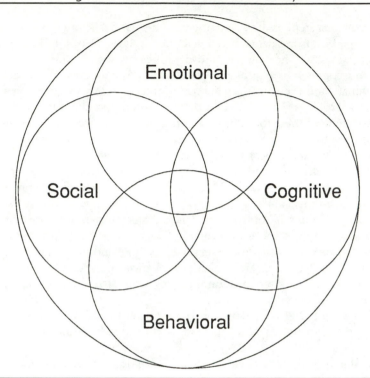

sire to sit in adults' laps as often as possible or to keep them in very close proximity, and his tendency to whine and become baby-like when vulnerable. However, when he was distressed, he would threaten to kill himself or to run away.

Regarding his social difficulties, Anne described a boy who would at-tempt to provoke his peers in sneaky ways by whispering swear words, poking them, or making provocative sexual gestures. When not initiating problems with other children, he was easily drawn into another's difficulties. He was also highly competitive with his peers and quick to respond aggressively to perceived threats. With adults, Brian was engaging and affectionate, but highly demanding of their attention. He would often become loud, rude, or manipulative when he could not get it, saying things like, "I'm just a stupid kid" or "You hate me!"

Behaviorally, Anne saw a boy who was extremely impulsive, who found it hard to sit in a seat, raise his hand, and wait his turn, and to control "his mouth and body in socially appropriate ways." When limits were set on his behavior, he could become extremely rude, using explicitly vulgar and sexual provocations "atypical for a boy his age." When frustrated, he might jump from his seat, storm around the room, knock things off shelves, and kick over chairs.

Cognitively, Anne described him as a bright boy functioning in the normal range of intelligence (an estimation corroborated by the WISC–R, on which he achieved a full-scale score of 95, with a verbal score of 108 and a performance score of 82). He could listen to and comprehend stories at a third-grade level, and she found his receptive and expressive language abilities to be particularly strong. She was presenting, and he was successfully doing, first-grade mathematics. He did not appear to have any major neurologically based impediments to learning. She had some questions about his visual-motor skills, and his fine motor coordination was weak, but his gross motor skills were quite good.

On a day-to-day basis, Anne's writings and discussions reveal her conclusion that Brian's emotional and social needs dominated his profile. Particularly his feelings of distrust and overwhelming concerns for personal safety affected his behavior and often his ability to think or concentrate. Figure 9.3 depicts Anne's overall initial thoughts about Brian.

Both the social and emotional circles are quite large and overlap each other substantially, denoting the recursive effects of his emotions and social weaknesses; in turn, these two larger preoccupations overlap with the cognitive and behavioral circles, denoting how his social and emotional difficulties interact negatively with his cognitive abilities and his behavior. The model also displays the recursive effects between Brian's behavior and his cognition.

Anne knows that the areas of overlap, which depict the interaction of different aspects of a boy's personality, provide the deepest source of potential insight into his needs. She also knows that these interactions are most difficult to untangle. In Brian's case, for instance, Anne came to realize that he was highly distrustful of adults to keep him safe from harm, while simultaneously desperate for their nurturance and protections. Thus, behaviorally he could fluctuate between a pugnacious, self-sufficient roughneck and a powerless little boy. His need for nurturance and adult attention manifested itself socially as well, in his competitiveness with peers to win adult attention and his intense manipulations of adults when their attention was not forthcoming. Anne applied her mental models to describe these interactions, but it is at her second step of thinking that she came to understand them. It is there that she formulated them as quandaries, weighing various interpretations for the behavior she saw exhibited within the context of her own knowledge.

But before turning to her second step of thinking, it is important to note that Anne developed these largely descriptive mental models for each of the

FIGURE 9.3 Anne's mental model for Brian

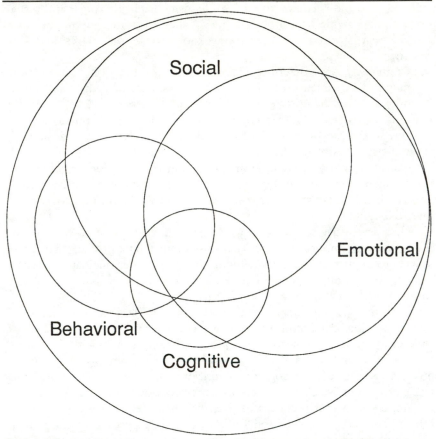

five children, with each having a somewhat different profile and different patterns of interaction. Her mental models for Jason and Paul were dominated by behavioral concerns; the cognitive aspects of Samuel's difficulties dominated a significant portion of Anne's mental model for him; quite different cognitive concerns dominated her model of Aaron.

Knowledge and Experience Filters

At the second step of Anne's thinking, she considers her mental models for the boys and their ongoing behaviors, using some or all of six knowledge and experience filters. In an effort to interpret the children's needs and to prepare adequate interventions, she weighs the data about the boys, using her knowledge of and experiences with (1) normal childhood development; (2) childhood emotional disturbance; (3) primary reading, mathematics, and writing curriculum and pedagogy, as well as other subject areas in the elementary curriculum; (4) the behavior of groups; (5) behavioral management; and (6) her personal beliefs, tolerances, strengths, and weaknesses. The bases of these knowledge and experience filters can be traced to a variety of sources, such as her formal education, her previous experiences with children, and her collaborations with other professionals at Brighton. But, before demonstrating how these filters are put to use, it is instructive to review what researchers consider to be teacher knowledge, and to examine how Anne's knowledge and experience filters articulate or complicate that view.

Generally, researchers have argued that the knowledge base of teaching can be divided into subject-matter knowledge, pedagogical knowledge, and personal practical knowledge. Subject-matter knowledge involves the substance of a discipline, that is, the ideas, concepts, and facts of a field, and the ways they are interrelated (Wilson, Shulman, & Richert, 1987). Thus, the fields of reading, mathematics, social studies, and the like each have their own substance and syntax, and the effective teacher is one who has a firm grasp of both.

Pedagogical knowledge is closely related to subject-matter knowledge, insofar as it is the knowledge a teacher has of organizing learning experiences and translating subject matter into learning opportunities for students (Carter, 1990). Wilson, Shulman, and Richert (1987) include in this category of knowledge "theories and principles of teaching and learning, knowledge of learners, and knowledge of principles and techniques of classroom behavior and management" (p. 118). Subject-matter and pedagogical knowledge can be construed as propositional knowledge, that is, substantive, factual, conceptual, or skill-based knowledge—the "know what" of teaching. But, particularly in the case of pedagogical knowledge, there is also a strong element of "know how" involved. Often, the ways in which knowledge is translated by a teacher into pedagogical action are a function of the teachers personal practical knowledge.

Personal practical knowledge differs from the previous two in that it is not knowledge that can be codified into a set of skills. Rather, it is experiential knowledge that grows from what Schön (1983) refers to as "reflection in action." Personal practical knowledge is created through the character of the teacher herself in response to the challenges of practice. Thus, researchers have explained it in terms of the personal theories, values, and beliefs that teachers use to weigh options and decisions (Elbaz, 1987; Janesick, 1977), the "rules of practice," "practical principles," and "images" that they use to meet the demands of their daily work (Elbaz, 1983), the dilemmas that teachers must negotiate daily (Lampert, 1985/1987), and "core constructs" that teachers build that direct and shape thought toward action (Freeman, 1990).

As Anne tries to understand what and how to teach her students, there is ample evidence that she actively draws on all three kinds of knowledge. However, Anne accesses subject matter knowledge and pedagogical knowledge derived from domains that most classroom teachers do not ordinarily use. For instance, Anne daily uses her extensive knowledge of deviations in human development, as well as her deep understanding of behavioral difficulties, to inform her work. Although such knowledge has been characterized by some as pedagogical knowledge (Wilson, Shulman, & Richert, 1987), it is important to see that such knowledge is, for the teacher of troubled children, a kind of subject matter knowledge as well. There are deep conceptual bases of such knowledge that have been developed in the fields of sociology and psychology, and that, put to use in the context of a classroom, add a specific dimension of social and behavioral teaching that ordinarily is not seen in such depth in most regular classes. Because Anne construes social and behavioral growth in children as the equivalent of subject areas, she has developed the knowledge base to address them. This has, in turn, made a fundamental difference in what she thinks about, how the curriculum is designed, and how the pedagogy gets implemented.

Knowledge of child development and disturbance.   Brian again provides a good example to explicate Anne's use of each of her knowledge and experience filters. Anne used her knowledge of normal childhood development as well as her knowledge of emotional disturbance to comprehend much of his needy behavior. For example, she was cautious not to mistakenly conclude that Brian's need to sit on her lap was predominantly troubled behavior; he was, after all, only 5½ years old and she knew that even untroubled young children continue to need the physical warmth and protection of adults. On the other hand, the severity and amount of his demanding behaviors, his tendency to manipulate adults by invoking their pity, or his threats of self-abuse when he could not command their full attention prompted her to draw on her considerable knowledge of emotional disturbance. She came to associate these latter behaviors with Brian's troubled personality; he was a child whose neglect and abandonment during the first years of life had left him fearful of an unpredictable world. It took some time and considerable effort of thought before she was able to differentiate the babyish behaviors that she considered within normal developmental parameters from those that were regressions into primitive, self-defensive, or manipulative behaviors, and to make her pedagogical decisions accordingly.

Knowledge of behavior management.   Using her behavioral management knowledge, Anne knew from experience that she had ample and appropriate strategies in her repertoire for handling Brian's behaviors: She found, for instance, that in day-to-day circumstances his competitive streak could be used to keep him on-task largely because he was so motivated to have an adult's attention. Standard techniques for positive reinforcement worked well. For instance, if other boys were sitting quietly in their seats, but Brian was whispering obscenities under his breath, she found that giving clear praise to the other boys for sitting correctly, while ignoring Brian's whispering, often worked to redirect his attention. Her behavioral techniques worked less well when he was under emotional stress. She needed to use her filters around emotional disturbance in stressful situations such as visits from his mother or state social worker, or during incidents such as the sex play between Jason and Aaron. Yet even in those circumstances, she felt confident that he presented few behaviors that she did not have ready responses for provided that the group behavior was under sufficient control for her to spend the necessary time. (In contrast, she did not feel as confident about Paul, whose violence and physical strength left her feeling unprepared to manage his behavior regardless of the circumstances.)

Knowledge of group behavior.   By viewing Brian in light of her group behavior knowledge, Anne recognized that he was particularly vulnerable in the group. His immature responses to other boys' provocative stimuli, his pugnacious attitude toward adult authority, his high level of impulsive activity, and his overly competitive orientation toward his peers (an attitude hat I've shown she could sometime manipulate to positive ends) were just a few of his characteristic behaviors that Anne knew from experience could increase the likelihood of problematic group behaviors. In fact, as I have already described, all of the boys exhibited some variation of those behaviors, making group behavior problems the major preoccupation of the first 6 months of school. During those months, Anne used this particular thinking filter unceasingly.

Anne's knowledge of group behavior is particularly complex because "group behavior" is, of course, highly social. So, although it was imperative that she manage the surface behaviors of the group to guarantee basic safety, she knew such surface management was not sufficient to address the driving cause of the behavior. Clearly, her students were severely stressed when they had to work in groups, and her thoughts necessarily turned to the underlying social causes of the difficulties. Thus, her group behavior filter does more than sift information about the surface behaviors she sees manifested; it also seeks to gain insight into what the sources of the behavior might be.

This specific effort is a crucial factor in her thinking and demonstrates how her pedagogical knowledge applied to group behavior differs from that of many of her special education counterparts. Special education, as a field, draws heavily upon applied behaviorism, and teachers of disturbed children ordinarily are trained to address only the surface behaviors of students so as to minimize disruption and maximize academic, on-task behaviors. Teachers are exhorted to avoid interpreting student behaviors and thereby playing "junior psychologist" (Hewett & Taylor, 1980; also see Cambone, 1990; Mastropieri & Scruggs, 1987; Stephens, 1977 for extensive discussions of limiting teachers' roles in interpreting student behavior). Anne does not subscribe to this school of thought. Indeed, interpretation of underlying social stressors played a central role in her thinking and planning for her students and in reconciling the needs of the children and the social expectations of school. Ultimately, those interpretations played a key role in instituting an academic classroom environment.

Knowledge of curriculum and pedagogy. Her academic knowledge played a major role as well. As I have already pointed out, she knows that by "pushing" the students to do academics, she probably creates more behavioral difficulties in the short term. Yet, she is adamant about retaining academics as the central activity of her classroom, employing her knowledge about learning and cognition to develop an academic curriculum and pedagogy.

It is in her rigorous approach to academics that we see another example of her thought, as well as the ways those thoughts stretch the definition of subject-matter knowledge. Anne is a well-trained teacher in the variety of disciplines necessary for success in a primary classroom for disturbed and learning disabled children. She is trained in educational diagnostic methods; she is an accomplished curriculum developer with a very strong philosophical inclination toward whole language curriculum in language arts and experience-based instruction in mathematics and science; and she has nearly 10 years of instructional experience with learning disabled and emotionally disturbed children. At the beginning steps of her thinking about any group of students, she draws upon her training as an academic diagnostician by conducting a full battery of formal tests, seeking insights into the students' skills. Given these initial insights, she conducts informal assessments designed to ascertain the accuracy of the formal tests in predicting the performance levels of the children. In this regard, she pays particular attention to which methods students respond best to: How do they respond in groups of five to a teacher presentation? To a whole group participation exercise? To working alone or in pairs doing experiential curricula in math? To highly structured tutorials? Throughout this process, Anne attempts to find the learning situation that allows the students to consistently perform with the greatest possible hope of success.

Studies of the pedagogical content knowledge of teachers have focused on the ways in which academic subjects of mathematics, social studies, reading, or English are organized in the mind of the teacher and carried out in practice (Carter, 1990). Traditionally, special education teachers have focused less on the content knowledge of the subject they teach, and more on the pedagogical approach that will help facilitate student learning. The goal is often less to help develop the conceptual basis of student learning in, say, social studies, and more on remediating the students' deficits in order to help them catch up with other students. Thus, there has emerged a dichotomy between those teachers who teach what is to be known, and those who specialize in translating that knowledge base so it is comprehensible to learning disabled or behaviorally disordered students. Anne has bridged those two knowledge bases in her academic work.

In the case of Brian for instance, Anne coupled her subject-matter knowledge of emergent reading and math, her psychological knowledge of Brian, and her pedagogical knowledge to form an academic learning situation. She was hesitant to use his extremely poor performance on initial diagnostic tests to assign any labels about his learning abilities or style because he was so young. With the exception of his underdeveloped fine motor skills, Anne could perceive in Brian's classroom performance no neurologically based impediments to his learning. She attributed his poor initial performance on tests to his lack of early learning experiences; the motor skill deficit Anne also considered a by-product of his age and immaturity. She began by teaching him reading in a two-to-one tutorial session and found that he was very enthusiastic and capable of moving along at a rapid pace except when he was distracted by his peer. In math, the story was the same. He did well in two-to-one situations, and even better when he was alone. Anne concluded that he was a student who had a very good chance of reaching and staying at age-expected levels in key subjects if she could find a way to attenuate the effects of his poor socialization skills with peers. She also saw that Brian liked learning, took real pleasure in conquering a new sound in phonics or finishing an "I Can Read Book," and he loved being read to. He had academic strengths, and she reasoned that her expectations for sound academic progress should play a major role in her thinking about Brian. She concentrated on blending his love of stories with her desire to have him read and write.

Personal Knowledge.   The final filter through which Anne passes the data about her students is a personal filter. As I have discussed earlier, Anne is highly self-critical. One of the questions she asks herself consistently is whether some aspect of her experience, personality, or personal preferences is altering her judgments of the students and their needs. In the present case, Anne came to see that some of the difficulty she was having with her students arose because she was planning her lessons with previous students in mind. For instance, while talking over one failed lesson she said, "I forgot how much younger, more impulsive, and unable to sit still and listen these guys are than even the group I had last year." She had to struggle with herself to aim her activities at more preschool-type activities, admitting that she liked first- or second-grade activities much more. She had to tolerate being less product-oriented and eventually she had to rethink the overall structure of her school day—something she had never considered doing before. Anne's personal filter acts as a self-monitoring system for her method of thinking. It is the means by which she asks herself for honesty about whether her choices are inadvertently self-serving or self-protecting. It is the filter through which she passes her own behavior and analyzes it to ensure she is acting as effectively as she can.

In Figure 9.4, I have added to Anne's first step of thinking, her mental model of Brian, the second step in the model of her thinking about Brian, her knowledge and experience filters. I have drawn each filter a different size to display its relative importance in the early period of Anne's attempts to understand Brian. The relationships that emerge between his behaviors observed at Step One and the importance Anne places on those behaviors at Step Two provide insight into her curricular and pedagogical reasoning regarding Brian.

Using Figure 9.4, there are some one-to-one correspondences between the predominant domains in Anne's mental model of Brian at Step One and the attention given those domains at Step Two. For instance, the social difficulties observed for Brian at Step One and the amount of effort Anne gave to thinking about his effects on the group's behavior at Step Two are balanced. Yet, in what appears to be a paradox, she gave little weight to thinking about managing his personal behavior, even though his observed behavioral difficulties were comparatively large in her original model. This was because when Brian was alone he was relatively easy to manage; it was only in a group that his social difficulties exacerbated an already difficult group behavioral situation.

In a related paradox, Brian's cognitive needs played a relatively small role in Anne's mental model for him, yet she strongly invoked her academic filters to understand him. In initial observations, his cognitive abilities were almost obscured by his other difficulties, particularly his poor school behavior. In fact, the professionals at his former school pointed to his difficult behavior in school as an indication that he might be a learning disabled child. However, when Anne sifted his cognitive abilities through her academic filters, she found them to be quite solid. She concluded there were few indicators of learning disabilities; rather, his behavior was seriously affected by his feelings of self-doubt and his explosive peer interactions. She also found that he enjoyed learning.

Anne was already convinced that she could handle his individual behaviors, and that he learned best when the social pressures were minimized, so she wondered if she should emphasize Brian's cognitive strengths by teaching

FIGURE 9.4 Steps One and Two of Anne's method of thinking using Brian as an example

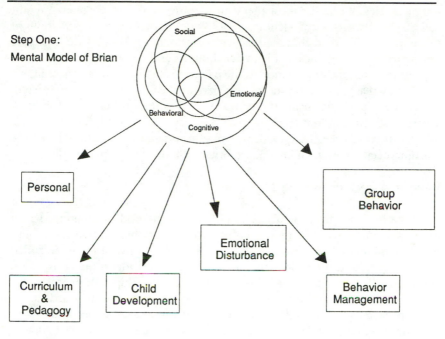

Step One:
Mental Model of Brian

Step Two:
Knowledge and Experience Filters

him in very small tutorial sessions, at least at the start. She reasoned that Brian's observed behavioral difficulties were less problematic than they had originally appeared, while his cognitive abilities were actually of major concern. He was a bright child whose behavior masked his intellectual abilities. Therefore, her subsequent planning focused more on shaping learning episodes in small tutorials with very stimulating but nevertheless average activities, rather than on specialized pedagogical means (i.e., carefully ordered, incremental learning, usually used to address children with learning disabilities). As her time with him progressed, she introduced him to larger groups and consequently more social difficulties. In sum, the relationship between the child's descriptive needs and the emphasis Anne gave to any one of them was largely affected by the knowledge and experience through which she filtered the observation. But most of all, her decision was informed by her personal practical knowledge of teaching. Shaping her thoughts was the belief that finding some way to stimulate Brian's intellect would constitute the most therapeutic means for dealing with him. This notion, that "teaching skills and competencies can be the most therapeutic thing of all," is what some might call an "implicit theory" (Janesick, 1977) or "core construct" of thought (Freeman, 1990) that guides a teacher's decisions. In Anne's case, this core construct plays a significant role in her thought and decisions.

Anne sifted the mental models she had for each boy through these filters; had I chosen any other boy, the relative sizes of the filters would have differed. To gain an appreciation for the complexity of Anne's thinking at this step, envision all five children configured in this way, each with different profiles. We can begin to see the quandaries Anne pondered as she thought of the learning needs of each child concurrently, while distilling a group plan.

Reflecting Decision Making

Until this point in my discussion of Anne's method of thinking, I have attempted to discuss it in a linear fashion. But clearly her thinking is not linear. When a model of her thinking is arrayed with all five students included in the display, and the various interactions between students are considered, the model becomes more web-like. Multiple relationships are processed simultaneously and rapidly. But for the purposes of discussing the third step in her approach to understanding, reflective decision making, I continue to simplify her thinking process by controlling multiple elements in order to adequately focus on single elements. It is not unlike what Anne herself did when dealing with the voluminous stimuli produced by her students. When all five children were present in her class, she often had to slow her thinking down and focus only on the salient classroom happenings.

Her reflective decision-making process was often apparent during writing class. The early success of this class played a significant role in engaging the students in schoolwork. During one class, the five boys were divided between Anne and her assistant teacher, Cathy, sitting at tables on different sides of the room, composing stories of their own. The period was progressing relatively well, insofar as most of the boys were engaged and the group behavior seemed under control. Anne was working with Aaron, Paul, and Samuel, and each boy was involved in a different stage of his story. At various points in the 20-minute period, Aaron was trying to dictate parts of his story to Anne, Paul was trying to write his on his own, and Samuel was illustrating his story about his pet dog, Sunshine. Each boy was asking for attention from Anne, and she was on the move constantly between them, answering questions, redirecting them to the work, retrieving paper, crayons, and pencils.

Samuel was in an ebullient mood, interacting freely and loudly with the dog in his story, alternating his talk with the chanting of a phrase or word that another boy had just said. Paul seemed gleeful as well; he was in perpetual motion, first with his leg up on the table, leaning over his composition pad with a pencil in his mouth trying to remember how to spell "to," then jumping up to see Samuel's picture-in-progress, then running to the window to see when the train went by on the tracks out back, then dashing back to his story about firefighters. Throughout the following incident, each of them needed Anne's attention periodically. Aaron, of all three, was the least physically active, but he appeared to be having the most difficulty behaviorally and academically.

Anne sat beside Aaron and they talked about what was going to come next in the story he had begun the day before. It was a sentence about what the protagonist of the story, Karen, was going to do next. Cheerfully, Anne pointed out to Aaron that she didn't need to spell Karen for him because he already had written it a number of times in his story and could just copy it. He didn't like that idea, became demanding, and growled at her, "No! You write 'Karen'!" She ignored the behavior and asked, "What are you and Karen doing?" He began to tell her, "Me and Karen like to go to the farm." "To the farm, that's a good sentence." At that moment, Anne was distracted momentarily by Samuel. Paul began to talk with Aaron, and Aaron began calling Paul a "Pussy!" Anne seemed to ignore this at first, but he continued to use the word three more times in quick succession, and finally she quietly put her hand on his arm and pointed to his bench, and he walked there to begin what turned out to be a 1-minute time-out. No words were spoken between them; he understood her silent cue completely.

Very soon after, she brought him back to the writing table. Characteristically, she picked up where she had left off without saying anything about the behavior that had gotten him sent from the table. She asked him enthusiastically about what he and Karen were doing, letting him know that he could find the spelling for Karen somewhere in the existing text. On a strip of paper she wrote, vertically and in order, the words he had dictated for his sentence, except for the words that she knew he could spell. For those, she drew a line instead. This was a method she borrowed from *Doing Words* by Katie Johnson (1987). She had recently introduced the technique to the boys to help them progress fluidly with their writing. As she wrote the words, Aaron watched and then began writing his sentence in his book. He made a mistake. "DAMN," he yelled. Very calmly she said, "That's okay, let's . . . ." As she replied, he tried to erase and tore the paper. "FUCKING PAPER!!" he screamed. Again, she calmly said, "You know what, this is a very thin kind of paper." She suggested to Aaron that he write underneath where the paper tore. In an angry and impatient voice he told her no and commanded her to get the tape and fix it. She assured him she'd get the tape, but that it would still be hard to write over the tape, and so he should write in another spot just the same. "I hate you. I'm going to stab you," he said through clenched teeth. For the next few moments, Aaron became progressively more frustrated with his work, demanding that Anne read it for him, calling her names, blaming her for any possible problem that might arise: "You messed me up by being a jerk," he told her as he went to erase again. "See, if I rip it it'll be your fault." For her part, Anne continued to ignore his outbursts and to talk only about the lesson itself. She also gave the other two boys positive attention, smiling, giving hugs when they came to her, responding quickly to their requests. All the while, she gradually moved closer to Aaron physically, put her arm around his shoulder as he railed against her, and finally drew him onto her lap. Ultimately, he finished the job with her body wrapped around his.

Anne reflected on the situation directly afterward while watching the videotape of the lesson. In what she said we can hear her grappling with the variety of inputs she considered as she came to a decision about how best to handle Aaron, and we hear her invoking nearly all her areas of knowledge. Characteristically, she began her reflection by conceding that she wasn't sure why he was behaving as he was, and she did a review of possible explanations.

> I'm not sure what's happening with Aaron. I'm not sure. Aaron is really frustrated. Whether he is frustrated because he really doesn't understand what he is supposed to be doing or whether he is really frustrated because Aaron has been having to go home part time for the past couple of weeks and is just frustrated at life in general, I'm not sure. Since this is a new task, I am having a really hard time figuring out if the task is too hard for him—if he doesn't understand what to do with these words that I am writing. I think that he does. I think that it is not really too hard for him, and that he is being cranky and that is why he is getting so frustrated.

Anne found she could quickly generate three plausible explanations for his behavior: First, she thought about his academic and cognitive abilities. He might be confused by the new task, that is, the use of the strip of unknown words listed with lines as placeholders for known words. Second, she wondered if he was easily frustrated because he was emotionally tired, "frustrated at life" as a result of his recent attempts to visit home. In this instance, she used her knowledge of both normal development and emotional disturbance. After all, she seemed to think, wouldn't even a well-balanced boy feel vulnerable and angry at these trial visits home? How much more so for Aaron? Finally, she wondered if the behavior was part and parcel of his typically obstinate behavior. She didn't know and was in a quandary about it.

Moreover, she wasn't convinced she could figure out the cause of Aaron's behavior well enough to form an effective intervention, given the energy it was taking to manage the high activity of the other two boys. She explained this as she continued.

> Part of the reason I am so wishy-washy about setting limits on how rude he is being is because I am trying to juggle everybody. He is saying he hates me and that I am a fucking bitch, but I'm trying to ignore it and trying to go back and forth with everybody else. And part of it is because I am really not sure about where it is coming from.

She wondered about the best way to manage the group behavior. Juggling everybody left her feeling "wishy-washy" about Aaron, but keeping the group balanced appeared to take precedence. She thought about a means for behavior management: Ignoring the behavior might actually cause it to recede, she thought. Anne often ignores behavior as her first tool of behavior management. But the real reason she was so indecisive here stemmed from the fact that she could not determine the root of Aaron's behavior. For Anne, that meant that if she were to act with insufficient knowledge, she would not be acting therapeutically. A therapeutic intervention requires that she aim at the cause of behavior, not the symptomatic behavior itself.

At a loss to find a discernible cause for Aaron's behavior, she turned to herself and critically analyzed her expectations and behavior to see if she might be the cause. As she continued to ruminate, she was critical about her choice to ignore his rudeness but decided it was a "toss up."

> What I think I am saying . . . is [I wonder] whether it is my fault that he is getting too frustrated because I am asking him to do something that really is too hard for him. Not that that makes it okay for him to be that rude. I think I am letting him be too rude without doing anything about it, other than ignoring him. . . . I am really not sure about the task. It is definitely hard for him. I don't think it is too hard for him. But part of me is thinking maybe I needed to go back a step. . . . It is not really okay to let him be rude, but . . . it is sort of a toss up.

Anne seemed to be saying that she would not feel justified giving him a consequence if his rudeness actually was caused by a mistake of her own, by the fact that she had not adequately taught the skill he needed to do the task. She concluded that ignoring him was doing something about the behavior, but it probably was not enough. Nevertheless, she continued to emphasize the productive, positive behavior of the others, while ignoring Aaron's negative behaviors, but at the same time moving closer to him physically. In some respects, she wanted to enjoy the other boys and how well the group was doing. She was a little disgusted with having to worry about the group being affected by Aaron's behavior, when she said:

I didn't have time to deal with it right now. . . . He is being rude, he's not bothering anyone else; he's sitting there being really rude to me. The best response might have been a time-out. But instead I am just going to ignore it. I am certainly not going to help him . . . I'm not going to respond to his demands to "erase this damn you!" and "give me the words," I will just ignore it and deal with the others.

She knew that sending him to time-out could have erupted into a major scene, as it so often did. Such a disruption would have ruined the period for the other boys. This decision is an example of how she "saves her battles," choosing to directly address only those incidents from which she believes she can reap the maximum benefit.

In this situation, her decision to keep the group together was a kind of compromise. Ignoring the worst of Aaron's behavior, and emphasizing the best of it, resulted in all boys finishing their assignments. True, Aaron finished the last sentence of his story on her lap. But he had a product that was his own, and Anne believed that Aaron's memory of a finished product would last far longer than his memory of his bad mood. Given the choice to address his rudeness, an opportunity that most assuredly would recur, or to work toward a successful academic experience, something that was still a rare occurrence, Anne chose the latter.

Anne was pulled in three directions by three boys, but I have narrowed Anne's thinking to her thoughts about Aaron only and have slowed that thinking down considerably. Thus, it is only one small portion of what she was thinking. My purpose is to draw attention to both the components of her reflectiveness and how consciously reflective she is in her practice. In this example, Anne explicitly searches for a source of Aaron's behavior by posing quandaries drawn from her knowledge of his life and activities; she juxtaposes the task demands against the abilities of Aaron-in-the-moment; she weighs a variety of possible responses to his behavior; she considers the effect of her actions with one boy on the behavior of the whole group; she weighs the potential cost of upsetting the group against the benefit of marking Aaron's behavior; she thinks about whether Aaron has a greater need to have his behavior marked or to finish his story. Eventually she makes a decision that she admits may not be "the best" response to Aaron's behavior, but is one that saves a battle so she can win a war. That is, she opts for finishing an academic product that will hopefully begin to build the boy's self-esteem.

Lampert (1985/1987) has written that "who the teacher is has a great deal to do with both how she defines problems and what can and will be done about them" (p. 108). She writes of teaching "dilemmas," those times where choices are borne of an internal "argument between opposing tendencies with oneself in which neither side can come out the winner" (p. 110). Perhaps, she argues, it is such dilemmas that drive a teacher's thinking. In the vignette of Anne and Aaron above, we get a flavor of a no-win dilemma that nevertheless must be resolved by the teacher. But we also see Anne's decision mediated, at least in part, by her knowledge of Aaron and his needs, as well as the belief that these same problems will undoubtedly repeat themselves. Because her goals for his learning are long-term goals, she can wait to address what in the present situation is closed to her. Putnam (1984) has argued that a teacher's long-term goals for a student or a group of students may help to form a central construct that mediates both her planning and her decision making in interactive situations. That is, interactive decisions become somewhat clearer if a teacher has a clearly reasoned direction in mind for a student. Indeed, Anne appears to use such a central construct—her ultimate learning goals for Aaron—as she reflects upon what she will do when facing her teaching dilemmas.

When I first began observing Anne work with the children, these components of her reflectiveness were not always readily apparent. I would often wonder why a particular boy's behavior might draw a response from Anne while the same behavior would be overlooked when exhibited by another boy. Others who have observed her teaching for brief episodes have also questioned her decisions, wondering what her motivation could be, for instance, in allowing Aaron to use such abusive language toward an adult. Anne has said that she does not believe that her work can be understood from a brief observation alone, that her method is not clearly observable except over time. Indeed, only after observing for some time does a clear pattern of decisions emerge that display certain heuristics for responding to the boys. Consider these: Given the choice between a potential problem or a potential success, choose success if it is at all possible. Consistently and predictably treat the boys differently to address their individual strengths and needs in the group; they will eventually come to realize that there is greater fairness in this approach than in arbitrarily treating everyone the same. To redirect one boy's negative behavior, reward another boy's positive behavior with adult attention. If a direct confrontation with a boy is called for, be sure you have reflected upon and located a probable root of the problem. A confrontation must be accurate to be instructive. Thus, be willing and able to work through the potential outburst and on to a satisfactory closure.

Anne's decisions are affected strongly by the complexity of the goals she has for the students and are guided by the belief that she must take time to work on those goals: Aaron will be abusive again, and she will have ample opportunity to address that behavior. But because the goals are complex and will take time to reach, her planning becomes all the more important in organizing her knowledge of the children. At the fourth step in her method of thinking, Anne develops plans for teaching the individual boys in each of their personality domains and plans for the group in each of those domains as well. These plans become not only the outcome of her decisions, but also the basis for a renewed cycle of thinking. To borrow the medical terminology so prevalent in special education, her plans are both prescriptive as well as diagnostic.

Individual and Group Planning

The goal of Anne's formal planning is to come to know a child's needs in such detail that she is entirely prepared to respond "in the moment." In the situation described above, Anne could make a decision to pass over Aaron's negative behavior because she knew her goals for him and had them prioritized in her mind. Her decision was drawn, at least in part, from her plan to increase Aaron's self-esteem by increasing his sense of accomplishment. Yet, this plan competed with her other, equally important plan to help him limit his negative and obstinate stance toward the world. She had to choose between the two—all while she was attempting to carry out plans for the other two boys and for the whole group. To understand how this was possible, we must look at what enables Anne to synthesize her copious data on the children into a cohesive blueprint for action in the classroom. To do this, two questions must be answered: How does she generate her multiple, yet concurrent plans? And how does she organize them?

To answer the first question, I must introduce the influence on her thinking of other professionals at Brighton. My reason is simple: Anne does not work alone in designing the overall plan for the children in her care. The constant teamwork and face-to-face interactions among Brighton staff regarding the children strongly affect Anne's knowledge, and it is that knowledge she brings to bear on her planning and subsequent actions. Although staff interaction around children is constant, the influence of other professionals on Anne's thinking and planning can best be seen in three specific venues where staff share information and plan for the children's education: periodic treatment team meetings, weekly classroom team meetings, and weekly individual supervision.

The treatment team comprises people both inside and outside of Brighton: staff social workers, residential workers, specialists, teachers, parents, and outside social service and school personnel. This team meets at approximately three-month intervals and addresses the child's needs within the broadest social context. At these meetings, staff and parents divide up both planning and programming responsibilities. Anne has responsibility for the hours of school, but the sharing of information is invaluable to her for planning schooltime. It is at team meetings, for instance, that Anne might learn more about Samuel's sensory integration difficulties from listening to an outside specialist; she may gain insight into Aaron's behavior by hearing about difficulties on the weekends from his mother and father; she might deepen her understanding of why Jason lies from listening to the consulting psychologist. The effect on her knowledge, and consequently on her planning, is significant.

The classroom team meeting is the second important venue for planning. The team focuses their weekly discussions on the school hours of the day. The teacher, intern teacher, and child-care worker share information that not all of them could see, or were present for; they collaborate on planning how certain behaviors will be managed; they talk about the techniques they will all share with a boy so they can present a united front; they plan a field trip or a pizza party to reward a week-long effort to minimize violence in the class. Much of Anne's planning for the organization of the day and the ways in which the team will work to manage behavior emanates from these sessions.

The third planning venue is weekly supervision. For usually an hour a week, sometimes longer, Anne meets with Alex, the school principal. Together they discuss teaching or managing individual children or groups; they critique her current curricula and generate new curriculum ideas, often collaborating in gathering materials or writing parts of the new curriculum. At times, they discuss Anne's frustrations and disappointments. This is a crucial time for Anne, one where her concerns about her teaching and her students are paramount.

To understand the planning needs of her class, Anne combines the knowledge she gains in these three collaborations with her own experiences with the children. She is able then to generate the multiple plans she has for individuals and the group, and she organizes her curriculum by laying out a careful infrastructure using the myriad goals and objectives for the individual children. Upon that network of interrelated objectives, she plans and builds original academic curricula that are thematic in nature. These plans are meant to create situations that allow her to manage multiple one-to-one learning relationships.

The organization of this infrastructure is partially determined by the federal- and state-mandated Individual Education Plan (IEP) each child must have. The IEPs require teachers (and other professionals) to set yearly terminal goals for student learning and to perform a task analysis of those goals. Each task in the task analysis must be turned into a formal behavioral objective (or group of related objectives) and laid out in some logical sequence for instruction. Then, at each quarter, the teacher must account for the progress of the student in meeting those objectives.

Anne does not find the IEP to be a completely accurate representation of what children really need to learn, even when the IEP is thoughtful and well written. As a teacher who organizes her academic learning to be thematic and highly experiential, she believes that much of what she tries to teach children is hard, if not impossible, to control and measure in quarter-year chunks of behavioral objectives. Despite her objections to IEPs, she has come to use her IEP writing time to gather her thoughts together about a child's needs; the way she organizes the final document reflects the way she categorizes curriculum components in her mind, and demonstrates the priority she places on each. Thus, when Anne thinks about planning for a child's needs, she breaks those plans into such categories as classroom behavior, peer relationships, adult relationships, basic care and hygiene, fine motor skills, reading, mathematics, written language, science, social studies, and computer. In her IEPs, these main categories are laid out in order of priority to meet the boy's needs, and the objectives within each category are prioritized as well.

The IEP goals and objectives provide the intellectual infrastructure for Anne's larger, most creative planning effort, what she calls "the neat curriculum." She does not follow the objectives in rigid sequence; rather, she plans the topics she wishes to cover in each academic area and proceeds to design the curriculum thematically. She does not use basals or predesigned and packaged curricula, with the single exception of phonics instruction. Thus, for each academic class she chooses the themes to be taught, plans the scope and sequence, and chooses or makes the materials. She aims to design and plan learning situations that address the objectives of multiple children but use the same core activity, building a cohesive group among the boys, yet addressing their individual needs simultaneously.

A good example is one activity she was observed using in math: With a chart for recording data in front of each of three boys, they played dice, with each boy rolling two dice. The math objective of one of the boys was working on counting, and he used his chart to write down the total he had counted on the dice. Another boy was able to count aloud and say the number he had counted. But he had significant difficulty reading or writing numerals and then remembering how many that numeral represented. His objective was to read an abstract symbol for a number and to demonstrate how much that symbol represented. Thus, he rolled and counted, then tried to remember what numeral to write. Later in the period, he played a game with Anne, trying to read from his chart how many 6s he rolled or how many 8s. The third boy's objective was to learn the various combinations that could make up a number, that is, that 2 and 5 made 7—but so did 3 and 4. He rolled the dice to see how many different combinations he could find that added up to 10, 3, 7, and so on, and then used his chart to write down "number sentences." Thus, three boys with three different objectives could participate in the same activity. The objectives provided the infrastructure for Anne's planning, and the group activity was fashioned around them.

Clearly, Anne's planning process is not something that she does alone at a desk. Rather, it is a dynamic process influenced by the observations and knowledge of other professionals as well as her own. It is a process that takes place with various groups to address various purposes: With the treatment team, Anne plans with a boy's ecological concerns in mind; at classroom team meetings, she plans with the concerns of her classroom as a whole; in her supervision, she works to critique her work and to generate sound ideas to implement in her instruction of the individual boys. Finally, when Anne does sit to plan instruction, it is thematic and experiential in content and method, but is built on a stable infrastructure composed of each child's learning objectives.

In Figure 9.5, the completed paradigmatic model of Anne's method of thinking is displayed. Both the third step, decisions, and the fourth step, planning, have been added to the model, as well as mental models to represent all five students. Notice the interaction between her individual planning and group planning, as discussed above. Also, notice the addition of recursive lines leading from Step Four back to Step One. This recursive function of her thinking is most important; it denotes her constant reference to the boys and how they are changed by her curriculum and teaching efforts, which are, in turn, changed by the boys.

THE EFFORT OF THOUGHT

Describing Anne's overall thinking process does not answer fully the question of what propels her thought into action. Doubtless, Anne's systematic, structured way of thinking enables her to understand the often chaotic behavior and widely varying psychological needs of her students, and to delineate the lessons, skills, and attitudes they need to learn to function, if not successfully, at least neutrally, in the larger society. To recognize the factors that assist in integrating her thinking and driving her action, we must turn to what Freeman (1990) refers to as the *mediating conception* of teaching thinking. He argues that teachers may reason through a core construct that is an amalgamation of their beliefs about the matters or subjects at hand, their values regarding those matters, and the long-term goals they hold for students.

What appears to drive Anne's action is a core construct that attempts to reconcile the needs of the children she teaches with what she perceives to be the requirements of the society she is preparing those children to function within. John Dewey (1902), in his book *The Child and the Curriculum*, writes that this reconciliation embodies, for the teacher, the greatest effort of thought.

> The fundamental factors in the educative process are an immature, undeveloped being; and certain social aims, meanings, values incarnate in the matured experi-

FIGURE 9.5 Anne's method of thinking—elaborated

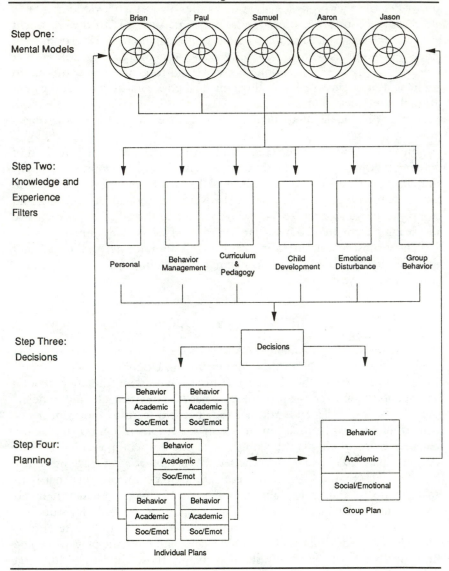

Step One:
Mental Models

Step Two:
Knowledge and
Experience
Filters

Step Three:
Decisions

Step Four:
Planning

ence of the adult. The educative process is the due interaction of these forces. . . .
But here comes the effort of thought. It is easier to see the conditions in their
separateness, to insist upon one at the expense of the other, to make antagonists
of them, than to discover a reality to which each belongs. (p. 4)

Anne, at work with her students, appears to be of the same mind: The
"educative process" resides in reconciling the needs of children with certain
of the aims, meanings, and values that adults have come to understand and
incorporate. In her teaching situation, however, the gap between those two
end points stretches well beyond Dewey's intention, and the "effort of
thought" required "to discover a reality to which each belongs" is formidable.
Anne recognizes without hesitation that the children she teaches are emphati-
cally immature and undeveloped beings. Yet simultaneously she values much
of what schooling can offer them. Particularly, she has a desire for her students
to reach the social aims she believes are implied in understanding mathematics, reading, social studies, and science; she wants to encourage meaningful
and significant emotional health; and she hopes to assist children in valuing
self-control, physical and emotional safety, effort in their undertakings, and
motivation for success. These are the values, aims, and meanings worth developing in her students if they are to be even marginally successful members of
society. As Dewey suggests, it would be easier for her to think separately about
the two conditions, disturbed child and social expectation, thereby avoiding the intellectual and emotional tension their interaction creates. That is
not the case: Anne's distinctiveness of thought resides in her ability to negotiate these disparate elements simultaneously, to keep the needs of both the
child and the society in constant intellectual tension and at the core of her
thinking.
     We see her tolerating this core tension at every step in what I have theo-
rized to be her approach to understanding: She begins by forming mental
models of the boys, filters those models through her knowledge and experience, makes preliminary decisions about those needs, then shapes both individual and group plans—only to begin the process again. Although her inves-
tigatory focus is on the boys, she introduces the core tension with society
from the initial moments of her encounter with a boy. As she forms a mental
model of a boy, she is already working to delineate his social and behavioral
needs in relation to his individual cognitive and emotional needs. From the
first, her question is not only: Who is this boy? but also: Who is he in relationship with others? At her second stage of thinking, when she invokes her
knowledge and experience to understand him, Anne weighs his unique presenting difficulties, strengths, and personality against considerations of norma-
tive child development, academic growth, and group behavior. In doing so,
her thinking shifts from purely descriptive conceptualizations of the boy to
evaluations of him in the context of the larger society.

Her decisions, at the third step, are about what immediate and intermediate actions to take in planning or caring for a boy; those decisions are usually based on a balance of group and individual needs, a social reconciliation.
But, in what I consider a truly distinct aspect of her thinking, her decisions
have implications for the future; by increments, she insists, the child will be
brought into line with the society. "It wouldn't be worth doing," she says, "if
they were always going to be at a place like Brighton for their whole lives.
Like *who cares* how much socially appropriate behavior they learn, and if they
learn how to read and do math. . . . Always in the back of my head is the
thought and hope that at some point down the road they're gonna go to
some more normal setting."

Finally, her classroom planning is a distillation of the aims of society, academically and socially, and the needs of the boy, emotionally and cognitively.
Not only will the boys learn to read, write, and do mathematics, but they
will do it as a group, valuing the cooperative work they do, recognizing the
accomplishments of others, while at the same time attributing their successes
to their own hard work. Thus, at each step in her thinking, Anne keeps the
core tension alive, intentionally juxtaposing the needs of the child to what
she believes are the aims of society. Eventually she finds the "reality to which
each belongs," not only in her thoughts about teaching, but in the curriculum
and pedagogy that she subsequently carries out.

A theory of Anne's thinking is useful; it provides us with the skeletal material for understanding how she processes the complexities inherent in teaching. But given this particular story, the severe difficulties of the boys and the
ways Anne responds, there is something bloodless about such theorizing. In
some important ways, atomizing her thinking as I have done distances us
from the quickness and the passion of her thoughts; it does not reveal her
tenacity and determination of thought. Those qualities of her personality
must be woven into her method of thinking if a fuller portrait of Anne as a
vital thinker is to emerge.

Anne's identity and purpose are closely related to her sense of herself as
an intelligent teacher. She is aware of herself as a powerful catalyst for change
in the lives of troubled children. She knows she is insightful, able to "see the
really neat, hidden inner parts of these kids." She is confident; she knows that
she can understand and design the means for change in the lives of children,
as well as carry them out. She manifests an authority that is based on knowledge, for she has worked diligently over the years studying children, teaching,
and disturbance both in theory and in practice. She has studied herself as
well, and continues to learn more about her capacities, her tolerances, and
her shortcomings. In some important ways, teaching troubled children helps
to unify her past and her present: From the shy, sensitive girl, "nerdy" and
"labeled," unsure of the meaning and utility of her intellect, she has grown

to a confident helper of another generation of labeled children. Her life, past and present, has meaning and purpose partly because she is a teacher.

Perhaps that is why she stubbornly insists on pursuing normalizing school activities with her students. She is unusually tenacious as she holds constant the academic pursuits of her classroom in the face of extreme behavioral and social challenges. When a boy is in emotional turmoil over the conditions of his life, she is tempted to put a rudimentary phonics lesson aside, for instance, and to reach out in sympathy instead. But she realizes that continually doing so will not teach the boy adaptive behaviors for managing stress; she is aware that over time such well-intentioned sympathy will positively reinforce the sense of helplessness that attends his emotional distress and will reinforce the avoidance of work as well. She focuses her thinking on what a boy can do, even while she is aware of what he is unable to do. Such stubbornness could result in inflexibility of thought and, at the extreme, an inability to comprehend the very real emotional, behavioral, and psychological impediments to learning. As we have seen, with Anne that is not the case. Her pursuit of normalizing activity is tempered by her deep comprehension of her students' psychological and behavioral impediments, and by her ability to flexibly shift her therapeutic focus onto them when they disrupt the flow of an activity, and off them when the issue is resolved. Anne has said that she concentrates so strongly that as she works with the boys her thoughts rarely wander and her attention is rarely diverted from the work at hand.

It is not surprising that Anne thinks that whatever success she has with the boys will result from her hard work and that her failures with them are no one's fault but her own. These attributions are an important part of her thinking style, revealing both her tendency to be strong and decisive about an assessment of a boy and his needs, and, simultaneously, her willingness to be wrong and to "go back to the drawing board" in an effort to teach the boy. Anne's thinking is iterative, and with each interation, she works to draw more information in from wherever she can get it. Even, for instance, when the information or insight comes from a co-worker with whom she is at odds on a case, she tries not to be defensive and discount the information, but to see as the other sees. She knows that a boy's problems are much more complex than she alone can comprehend. However, once she has decided on a course of action, it is rare to hear her attribute the success or failure of her effort to anyone but herself.

Her attributions of success or failure are closely linked to her ability to find problems that are solvable. She knows how to look for the problems hampering her students' success, and she knows where to look for them. Through the process of assessing, planning, implementing, and reassessing, Anne conducts what might be referred to as formative evaluation. Such a process allows her to realign her teaching in intermediate steps while keeping her terminal goals in mind. But more important than how she finds the problems to solve, is where she looks for them: When she asks why a child is having difficulty learning, her investigative focus is on more than just the boy. She looks for problems in the group interactions; she asks questions about what the boy is being asked to do; she assesses the class schedule, the order of activities within a given period; she monitors the choice, timing, and quality of her own interventions. In short, if a boy is having difficulty, she looks for sources of the problem in the ecology of the class.

Anne's strategy echoes the work of Doyle (1986). Classroom management is actually management of the classroom ecology, he writes, and can be thought of on four dimensions: the patterns for arranging students (e.g., small group vs. whole group); the resources and sources of information available for use; the roles and responsibilities for carrying out actions and events (in academic terms); and the rules of appropriateness. By arranging and rearranging the classroom ecology to meet the demands of academic work, teachers shape *programs of action* within the classroom. In turn, these programs of action help to shape order in the class. In the final analysis, he writes, "classroom management is fundamentally a process of solving the problem of *order* in classrooms rather than the problem of misbehavior. . . . The teacher's management task is primarily one of establishing and maintaining work systems for classroom groups rather than spotting and punishing misbehavior, remediating behavioral disorders, or maximizing the engagement of individual students" (p. 423). Anne has found that by focusing her efforts on solving the problem of order, rather than the problems of the individual child, she is more successful at managing her class. She thinks in terms of the interrelatedness of factors that are affecting her programs of action, and hence learning in the classroom, and makes moves to adjust those factors ecologically.

Perhaps her ecological strategies are a key to understanding the connection between her knowledge and her practice, between what others might refer to as her *know what* and her *know how*. For it is clear that what Anne knows is impressive. She knows much about many different aspects of curriculum, pedagogy, cognition, emotional disturbance, behavior management, the normal psychological development of children, treatment planning, teamwork in teaching, and more. But she also knows how to relate these various aspects of the teaching–learning enterprise into a plan of action. She does this as she listens, observes, reflects, and draws on her various sources of knowledge, before she forms and tests her hypotheses about the boys and their learning.

A THEORY OF CURRICULUM AND PEDAGOGY

Anne's curriculum blueprint reflects the constituent parts of her ecological thinking. As we've seen, she divides her curriculum into three distinct domains, the academic, the social, and the behavioral. Each has a unique set of goals, but Anne addresses those goals through the single activity structure of academics. Her interactive curriculum and pedagogy clearly manifest her interactive thinking. Her theory of curriculum and pedagogy reflects a shift from traditional special education practice toward a teaching paradigm that is not ordinarily associated with teaching disturbed children.

Table 9.1 summarizes the curriculum and pedagogy in each of the three domains. The table begins with academics because they are central to the classroom activities. Displayed in this way, we can see how ambitious the academic curriculum is, particularly when we take into consideration how troubled the students actually are.

It is common practice in the special education of disturbed children to reduce the amount of stress in their lives by reducing the amount of academic work they are required to do, and then carefully sequencing what remains of the traditional school curriculum into easily accomplished steps (Cambone, 1990). Anne's curriculum is different; it does not reduce the expectations for learning academic content as a result of the students' troubling behavior. Instead, it is comprehensive in its coverage of primary school learning goals. Moreover, her academic curriculum is grounded in a different paradigm from that of the traditional special education curriculum. It does not reconstitute the traditional curriculum into easily accomplished sequences, but is designed to approach the academic goals from a cognitive-developmental perspective. In mathematics, for instance, her curriculum is not restricted to drill and practice of basic computation, but involves working with the boys until they successfully build the cognitive structures necessary to understand what numbers actually are and how they can be manipulated. In reading, she not only includes goals for students to learn to decode and comprehend, but goals for consciously building language through writing, sustained silent reading time, and enrichment activities such as word time and Big Books.

The paradigm shift is particularly evident in her pedagogy. Although she has analyzed the learning needs of her students, her methods, with the exception of instruction in decoding, do not reflect the carefully sequenced, remedial methods so prevalent in special education. She uses constructivist methods, grounded in the following notions: Students can be trusted to learn and learn well if the work they are asked to do is meaningful and adapted to their developmental levels; learning must be active; different children use different cognitive strategies to learn, and accommodation must be made for them. Her methods emphasize learning by doing, and they intentionally include content that is tantamount to method.

TABLE 9.1   A summary of Anne's curriculum and pedagogy

Curriculum	Pedagogy
Academic	

Curriculum	Pedagogy
·Reading and Language	·Reading and Language
·Decoding	·Phonics
·Whole Language	·Data-driven grouping
·Listening comprehension	·World time
·Pleasure reading	·Multi-modal activities
·Writing	·Big books, Read-aloud
·Reading for	·Process writing approach
·Mathematics	·Mathematics
·Estimation	·Concrete, direct experience
·Numeration	·Manipulation of objects
·Place value and re-grouping	·Emphasis on games
·Patterns and geometry	·Traditional drill
·Addition	·Spiraling activities
·Subtraction	
·Multiplication	
·Money	
·Content Areas	·Content Areas
·Time orientation	·Graphing, charting
·Civics	·Use of multiple media
·Science basics	·Experiments and field trips

Behavioral	
·Tolerate proximity to others	·Behavioral management system
·Move from activity to activity	·point system
·Share adult attention	·contracts
·Raise hands for attention	·target behaviors
·Stay in seat	·Consistently treat boys differently
·Ask for help	·Read the *tone,* and act accordingly
·Accept limits	·Divide and conquer
·No violence	·Isolate for violence
·Additional, individual goals	·Make safety the first priority
	·Re-order the schedule
	·Plan for pre-school behavior

TABLE 9.1 Continued

Social

·Do what is social, be social	·Use group lessons as social stimulus
·Achieve "groupishness"	·Use activities that hold interest
·focus on others	·Model behaviors
·learn from others	·Model social language
·cooperate and share	·label
·Learning is rewarding	·limit alternatives
·delay gratification	·means to an end
·maintain focus	·prompt reflection
·resist displacement of frustration	·Reward pro-social behavior
·trust adults	
·"Language between impulse and action"	
·do the right thing	
·do good ignoring, waiting	
·be a good friend, audience	
·don't set up	

Some of the key writers in the constructivist tradition who have either directly or indirectly shaped Anne's curriculum have been mentioned in earlier discussions of her work, but they bear reiteration here. Anne's work in mathematics and science, for instance, has been influenced highly by the writings of Piaget, particularly in the ways his work has been interpreted by Eleanor Duckworth (1987). As the curriculum in math was being rebuilt at Brighton during the mid-1980s, Duckworth's notions about how teachers can help individual children construct mathematical knowledge in their own ways played an important role. As a result, staff came to emphasize conceptual understanding instead of just algorithmic math. Anne has read and used the pedagogical ideas of Baratta-Lorton (1976) in *Mathematics Their Way* and of *Developing Number Concepts Using Unifix© Cubes*, by Kathy Richardson (1984). Each has contributed immeasurably to Anne's understanding of constructivist curriculum and pedagogy in math. In the area of science, reading the essays of David Hawkins (1974) on teaching and learning helped shaped the hands-on, experimental approach that is used in building knowledge in the children about the physical world. The writings of Sylvia Ashton-Warner (1963) on Language Experience, Donald Graves (1985) on Process Writing, and Katie Johnson (1987) on *Doing Words* functioned together to stimulate the growth of Anne's constructivist pedagogy in language and writing. In the area of social development, the work of Vygotsky (1978) and his ideas about the internalization of social understandings are evident in Anne's work. And throughout her pedagogy, we see careful attention to co-constructing knowledge with children by scaffolding their learning within their zone of proximal development.

Each of these writers and curricular developers played some role in Anne's developing sense of herself as a developmentally oriented teacher, as did her training at Tufts. But it was Anne herself who blended her knowledge of development with that of disturbance, and it was she who developed her unique theory of curriculum and pedagogy.

What makes Anne's theory of curriculum and teaching so compelling is that she is doing it with children other teachers might think are unlikely candidates for such methods; but more important, it is compelling because of the crucial connection she makes among all three curricular domains: The academic curricula are useful, in fact crucial, to Anne's reaching her behavioral and social curriculum goals. This is because the content acts as a catalyst for bringing about desired behaviors, or bringing out the behaviors that the boys need to change. Watching a caterpillar become a butterfly, for instance, does not teach about metamorphosis alone; it becomes the catalyst for a successful discussion where "it's not even occurring to anyone to set each other up or to have a problem," but where boys listen to each other and take turns talking—clearly desired social behaviors that Anne wants taught.

But the content and activities can act as a catalyst for bringing out the boys' negative behaviors as well. When playing the game of *Sea Monster,* for instance, Brian could not contain his impulsivity and jammed all the edible goldfish into his mouth, spitting them out on others and ending the game badly. But his behavior did not result in Anne's reducing the activity to something less stimulating. She was convinced, given her analysis of his needs and abilities, that it was the appropriate academic activity for Brian, in both content and method. What she needed to do was address Brian's propensity for inappropriately acting out his high level of stimulation.

We've heard Anne say that she knows her methods exacerbate the boys' behavioral difficulties—but that is part of her method of teaching. It is in their active engagement with the real-world dilemmas of the classroom that these boys have their greatest troubles; and it is at that intersection where Anne can do her most effective work. Therefore, she creates an environment where the intersection becomes inevitable, but she also creates a curriculum that can address the resulting behavioral problems. The central task of her behavioral curriculum is teaching the boys the skills necessary to maintain a basic level of safety and order in the face of real learning challenges. This area of curriculum and pedagogy is perhaps the most familiar to special education teachers; they often expend extraordinary energy designing humane behavioral management systems that help limit dangerous or inappropriate behaviors and that attempt to teach new behaviors—all without squashing the spirit of the children. Usually, managing and controlling students' behavior is the extent of behavioral teaching in classes for troubled students (Cambone, 1990). Anne's curriculum goes beyond controlling student behavior. The curriculum includes a behavioral management system as a crucial element, but the curriculum extends beyond the system itself, incorporating it into an overall behavioral pedagogy. That pedagogy manages the ecology of the classroom by redirecting the influences on student behavior. This constitutes another paradigm shift in curriculum and pedagogy for troubled children.

We have seen, for instance, that Anne uses a behavioral management system to reward behaviors, that she verbally and nonverbally marks and rewards desirable behaviors as they occur, and that she uses contracts to help boys manage their own work behaviors. But those classic behavioral techniques are part and parcel of an overall strategy based on redirecting the boys' energy away from negative interactions and onto the work at hand. Beyond controlling the boys, she is concerned with such ecological factors as the tone of the room, with reading tone accurately so she can redirect it if it turns negative or "shaky"; she uses her technique of divide and conquer, separating boys by space, by different activities, and sometimes by having an adult sit between them to minimize their influences on each other; she works hard to avoid an impending occasion of behavioral difficulty by quickly shifting the activity to, say, reading a storybook for a few minutes and then returning to the original task; she ignores minor infractions of behavioral rules in an effort to redirect attention to the important academic work at hand; she praises boys who are doing well in order to redirect a boy who is not. Her ecological management is particularly apparent in the changes she wrought in the classroom schedule. Because the boys felt bridled by it, she altered her day to be in tandem with them and their needs, thereby redirecting their increasing agitation with the daily rhythm she had created for them.

In these examples, we can see that Anne's pedagogy is concerned with management of the classroom beyond directly rewarding and punishing the boys' behaviors. She certainly confronts the boys directly about their behavior, marking both the appropriate and inappropriate behaviors as they emerge; but she works hard to avoid struggles over the boys' behaviors that would result in negativity dominating the classroom. When all redirection has failed, or the behavior is beyond the point of safety, we see her move intrusively and decisively to manage the behavior of a boy.

Anne perceives most of the boys' behavioral difficulties through a social lens. Whereas the behavioral curriculum addresses the manifest behavioral difficulties of the boys, the social curriculum aims at the underpinnings of the behavior. Her social curriculum actively intervenes in the emotional and social growth of the boys, and consequently it is her most subtle curriculum effort: Her goal is to shape a classroom culture, a social milieu that will emphasize not only doing what is social, but being social. But although it is subtle, it is not a "hidden curriculum" (Jackson, 1968) where social values are taught but not seen. Indeed, she puts her curriculum forth strongly and centrally. Her values are clear—she believes in the worth of schooling and intellectual stimulation, and in the necessity of working in groups; of cooperation, compassion, and fairness; and of friendship. Her class is organized around this set of values in much the same way as her academic curriculum is organized around a clear set of intellectual activities.

These values are grouped within the three goals of her social curriculum and teaching. These goals are complex; because they are social goals, they embody what is known, as well as what is done. Thus, they are both the content and the pedagogy. For instance, the first goal is to provide schoolwork that is salient and developmentally appropriate so that she can teach the boys that work can be meaningful and rewarding in itself. This is important content for her social curriculum, and communicating that idea is no small feat with boys who ordinarily shun all occasions that might demonstrate their lack of skill or knowledge. At the same time, salient work provides a pedagogical tool: It provides a means for grabbing and holding a boy's interest; it is practical and useful in diverting his attention away from his negative impulses and into positive, productive behavior. Ultimately, she hopes the boys will know the meaning of work, as well as know how to work.

Her second goal is to teach as much as possible in groups. She wants to teach "groupishness" because she believes that the ability to work in groups is a key element of a normal life. As a teacher, she is most concerned about working in groups in math, in reading, and in all other academic activities. It is the content of her social curriculum. But it is also a cornerstone of her pedagogy. Anne uses groups to intentionally exacerbate the social difficulties of the boys. She wants to address their social problems, particularly their school-related social problems, in situ. Again, she teaches both the value of groups and the way to be in the group successfully.

Third, her goal is to teach the boys language that will help to shape social thinking. Language is intended to interpose "thought between impulse and action." No other aspect of her teaching is more clearly both content and method. Anne constantly uses language to label the boys' appropriate and inappropriate social behaviors, to structure the social alternatives they have open to them, to explain what they need to do in order to get what they want or need, and, most important, to think about what they are doing or saying. The goal is to use language as a primary social tool; she reaches that goal by using language in increasingly complex ways.

Language provides connecting links to every other curriculum area. It permeates the room, and its intentional use provides one of the most potent means for teaching. Whether it is in math group or reading tutorial, Anne uses carefully selected language to braid the social goals and objectives with the academic goals: Aaron demands help in writing class, and Anne tells him she won't offer help until he "does good waiting"; Paul continues doing his writing even though Aaron is taunting him, and Anne teaches Paul that he's "doing good ignoring" and, moreover, that ignoring Aaron is "the right thing."

The three curriculum domains can and must be braided together into one activity structure—academics. By keeping academics central to the purpose of school, Anne acknowledges that school is the place where young boys normally spend their days; her troubled students can be fortified by the knowledge that they are doing as others their age do. Further, by creating a predominantly academic classroom, she brings her students, by successive approximations, closer to the day when they can participate in a regular classroom. But by braiding the social and behavioral curriculum together with the academic, she can keep the needs of each child central as well. No theory of curriculum would seem to satisfy Anne unless it could reflect the core tension of her thinking as a teacher. Thus, in Anne's theory, three kinds of content are taught concomitantly, and three pedagogies are braided into each instructional episode. Each strand of the braid is unique but intimately related to the other two. Anne's academic curriculum provides the central structure for what students do in the class; her behavioral curriculum provides the structure for how to proceed in an orderly and safe fashion; and her social curriculum binds the entire teaching–learning enterprise together by providing the boys, and herself, with the reason why they should be learning at all.

THE ROLE OF TIME AND PATIENCE

A chief dimension of Anne's teaching is the role of time and patience. Her job was to socialize into school a group of boys who had had very little experience being socialized. The social, as well as academic, and behavioral growth of this group, and of each of the boys within the group, was painfully slow. Establishing order and routine, a process that might take a regular classroom teacher a few weeks to accomplish, took months in this class. At the start of the year and for many months, Anne was often unable to conduct a complete lesson. The wild, panicked violence of the boys did not subside until well past the new year. Carefully planned interventions would begin to take effect, only to be dashed on the rocks of a group-wide regression. It was hard for Anne to know what constituted success with this group of boys. Without some sense of successful accomplishment, it was hard to face the next, seemingly insurmountable problem that would inevitably present itself.

Yet, even when her patience and hope were at their lowest, Anne knew that the task she had been given would take time. This is an important aspect of her success as a teacher of troubled children. She knew there were absolutely no quick fixes for the kinds of long-standing, deep-seated problems that these boys had. At the same time, she believed she was not impotent in the face of those problems. She gave herself the permission and encouragement she needed to mentally process the vast amount of data the boys presented, to organize it in her own mind, and to administer an appropriate plan. When the plan was laid, it included short-, intermediate-, and long-term goals that were flexible enough to help her respond to the unexpected events of the class, yet stable enough to help her keep her equilibrium and reach her ultimate goals. It was a plan unique to this particular group; a new group of boys would require a completely new curricular plan.

Thus, we can see in the narrative of her teaching a methodical uncovering of the layers of her curriculum. It was over time that she mentally processed the behavior of the boys, the social underpinnings of their behavior, and the relationship that each had to the boys' academic success. And over time we saw her thinking become manifest in her actions: Each domain of thought had its time to be called to the forefront of her work as a teacher, refined into an individual curricular structure, and subsequently braided with the other two goal structures. Ultimately, Anne was able to balance all three curricula in her thoughts and her actions, but it took time and patience: time to make sense of the data, time to develop a plan of action, time to institute it, and time for the boys to learn, and to learn deeply.

THE INSTITUTIONAL CONTEXT

Finally, our discussion must turn to the effects of the institutional context on Anne's thinking and teaching. There is little doubt that Brighton provides a high level of quality support for Anne and her colleagues. There is a strong tradition of academic curriculum at Brighton that provides a foundation for Anne's classroom curriculum. She shares with her colleagues a reason for working with these students, that is, to give emotionally disturbed and learning disabled children maximum intellectual stimulation through the use of progressive academic curricula and teaching strategies. This community of shared values is important to Anne, especially because of the many intellectual, emotional, and physical risks she must take in the course of any workday. Anne feels safe to try something new and to make mistakes because, as she says, she knows she's "going down the same track" with her colleagues. Without the worry of being at variance with the community, Anne's mind is freed to concentrate on her work, and she is able to use her best efforts on her job.

It is also important that her continuing work is supported by the institutional commitment to the careful study of the children. So much of Brighton's resources are spent on deepening practitioner understanding and building practitioners' competencies. Anne's thinking is stimulated by the constant flow of information from formal and informal assessments, and by the daily opportunities for listening to other staff members and their theories about a child's behavior or learning needs. Her work is strengthened by the ties that the institution makes with parents and community resources. She is but one part of a network of resources devoted to understanding children and their needs.

Brighton's resources of time, dollars, and personnel are aimed at developing appropriate learning environments in each classroom as well. Anne's work is enhanced by having the space and materials she needs to teach, the staff needed to do the work, and the time to think and plan. But perhaps most important, the institution provides opportunity for an ongoing dialogue with a supervisor. Without this intellectual and emotional support, Anne says, her work would be too difficult to do.

Institutional support manifests itself at Brighton through the ways in which teachers are assisted in keeping a deep focus on their students and what they are learning; through the strong commitment of resources of time, dollars, and personnel to the teaching–learning process; and through an equally strong emphasis on working in interdisciplinary teams that include parents, guardians, and key community agencies. But most important for those who teach, there is deep and daily discourse among adults about the work, the students, and the self, all in an effort to do the best possible job at teaching students.

CHAPTER 10

IMPLICATIONS FOR PRACTICE
AND POLICY

The results of a single study of one teacher's thinking and action are not generalizable to the wider practice of special education with troubled children. However, the dimensions of Anne's practice provide compelling points of departure for a discussion of what might constitute best practice with troubled children. In Anne's case, we see a teacher who thinks and behaves in substantially different ways from the ways we would expect from teachers in classes for emotionally disturbed children—given what we know of current educational philosophy, teacher training, and service delivery models.

The various dimensions of Anne's practice discussed in the previous chapter are compelling in their own right; they are made more so because her students grew substantially in their academic, social, and behavioral understandings and abilities. What can be yielded when Anne's practice is juxtaposed to current practice, and what are the implications of such a comparison for best practice?

RETHINKING HOW WE THINK ABOUT TROUBLED CHILDREN

To begin, Anne's practice encourages us to rethink who troubled children are and to realize that they are people with many more facets than the children we see reflected in the research literature or, for that matter, in federal and state regulations. Those troubled children are too often described solely in terms of their deficiencies and not in terms of the strengths they frequently possess. Until now, our entire educational effort has been aimed at remediating those perceived deficiencies, but rarely have we dwelled on educating these youngsters for their possibilities. Indeed, based on the language we use to describe them, our damning assessments of their intellectual capabilities, and the reductionistic curriculum we currently offer them in schools, one could conclude that beneath our veneer of concern we're not convinced that our students actually have viable social possibilities at all.

Change the Language of Deficits

If our language is any reflection of our thoughts, then our thoughts about troubled children and their place in society are decidedly constricted. Research articles, textbooks, and even college course syllabi define them using language focused almost exclusively on student deficiency in ability and achievement, their passivity in learning situations, their resistance to control and conformity, and their need for extensive remediation. We repeatedly use words such as *disordered, impaired, maladaptive, deficient,* and *deviant* to describe our students; we argue that there is a clear need to *remediate, manage,* and *train* them (Cambone, 1990).

Of course, given the behavior of many of these children, these are logical appellations. But equally logical are labels such as *resourceful, resilient, clever, creative,* and *tenacious,* especially when we consider how many of these students continue to function in difficult living situations, or, for instance, how they can often talk or work their way out of a jam, or how they can deftly manipulate the classroom behavioral system. We don't readily consider these strengths, because they are too often mustered toward unhealthy ends. Yet, they are strengths nonetheless and, with an effort of thought on our part, can be redirected toward healthier ends. We can choose to educate our students instead of simply remediating their weaknesses or training them to conform.

There are but a few writers who have focused on the strengths of troubled students as a means to assist their growth. Vorrath and Brendtro (1985) and their associates are proponents of developing what they call a *positive peer culture* among troubled young people, particularly those considered to be delinquents.

> Preoccupation with the negative, the disturbance, with the weakness of troubled young people blinds one to the reality that many are immensely adaptable, resilient, and resourceful. . . . It is a great mistake to assume that difficult children are inadequate. In many ways they have learned to be stronger than youngsters with a more tranquil life experience. Think of the strength it must take to be able to stand in defiance of parents, principals, police. . . . If only our schools and youth organizations could figure out how to turn the strength of troubled youth around, but instead the typical response is to kick them out. (Brendtro & Ness, 1983, p. 73)

These teachers have taken the notion of student deficiency and turned it on its ear. In a positive peer culture with troubled adolescents, teachers acknowledge that the peer group is considerably more powerful than the adult society in shaping the behavior of its members. They further acknowledge that many troubled young people, in a struggle to find a sense of belonging, identity, and self-esteem, often manipulate their power over peers, adults, or social expectations, and engage in behavior that is maladaptive and deviant. To be negatively powerful is to be good.

Instead of wresting power from these young people, teacher effort is aimed at exploiting what seems to be maladaptive through "re-educating" the peer group by "reversing the valence of certain behaviors so that helping is seen as strong, mature, and powerful, while hurting and dishonesty is appropriately seen as inadequate and immature" (Brendtro & Ness, 1983, p. 208). Teachers relabel negative behaviors that students have distorted into acceptable behaviors; they teach the peer group to help its members recognize and face their difficulties; and they conduct highly structured group meetings where peers teach each other that the only powerful behavior is positive behavior. The emphasis is taken off adults remediating student deficiencies and is placed on educating students to recognize and use their own strengths, in this case their power, to overcome obstacles to success.

Emphasize Students' Potential

Most practitioners and researchers find it difficult to focus on the potential of troubled children. Particularly insidious is how it has become commonplace to typify the intellectual capabilities of our students as deficient. In the oft-cited studies of troubled student IQ, Kauffman (1985; Kauffman, Cullinnan, & Epstein, 1987) showed that these students most often scored in the low-average range on tests of intelligence. But Mastropieri and Scruggs, two influential researchers in the field of behavioral disorders, summarized 25 available studies on the intellectual, academic, and psychosocial functioning of behaviorally disordered children and also found that they perform in the low-average range. They conclude, erroneously, that these students "consistently have been seen to exhibit academic and intellectual deficiencies . . . and the need for academic remediation in this population is as great as the need for behavior management and social skills training" (Mastropieri & Scruggs 1985, pp. 100–101).

Although I would agree that academics ought to take their rightful place in the school lives of troubled children, I nevertheless find the assertion of intellectual deficiency to be distinctly problematic. Mastropieri and Scruggs are not alone in this inference of intellectual deficiency. Out students are typified as such throughout the literature (see D'Alonzo, 1983; Hewett & Taylor, 1980; Mastropieri & Scruggs, 1987; Stephens, 1977; Wang & Walberg, 1985). Although it is undeniable that troubled students, taken together, fail in public schools, it is mistaken to conclude that academic failure is due to their intellectual deficiencies. Even if one accepts the use of IQ tests as true indicators of intellectual capacity (which, in light of recent reconceptualizations of intelligence, such as those by Howard Gardner, 1983, appears more unlikely), these students are not deficient—they are low average. And if IQ is a good indicator of school success, then these students ought to be doing low-average work and achieving at it. They are not. In fact, they are failing and dropping out in disproportionate numbers (Knitzer, Steinberg, & Fleisch, 1990). Clearly, other factors are at work beyond student intelligence or lack thereof.

Our preoccupation with student intellectual deficiencies is masking other important reasons our students are failing in school. There is ample evidence that their perceived deficiencies could actually be a result of the misalignment of students' cognitive, social, emotional, and cultural needs with the misguided requirements of our classrooms. Indeed, our students' difficult behaviors and poor achievement may be, to a large extent, the results of our cultural and racial biases (Kugelmass, 1987; Sigmon, 1987), our misunderstanding of cognitive differences (Ashman & Conway, 1987), and barometers of our own failed curriclum and pedagogy (Cambone, 1990). Steinberg and Knitzer (1992), in describing their national investigation into classes for behaviorally disordered students, write of the impoverished learning environment so many of our children experience.

> We witnessed a depressing lack of intellectual content: concepts and challenges were few. Worksheets and workbooks filled the six hours of the school day. Classrooms were sparse with the most clearly displayed objects in each classroom being the commendation cards the children got when they reached a new "level" in the point and level systems which were the spine of the management systems. (p. 147).

Unfortunately, such classrooms are all too prevalent, and student misbehavior may actually be a nearly sane rejection of our reductionistic, patronizing, and debilitating curricula.

Reconceptualize Student Performance

If we define our students' intellectual strengths and weaknesses in relationship to the demands of the tasks we put before them, but the tasks themselves are not engaging or worthwhile, we can hardly claim that the children are intellectually deficient when they fail at the tasks. Yet, that is exactly what we seem to have concluded. Such a conceptualization has resulted in a cycle of ever-lowering expectation of success, which results in reduced student performance, which results in lowered expectation of success. Somehow, we still consider this a failure of the student. Howard and Hammond (1985) refer to this phenomenon in their discussion of minority student failure, especially African-American males, a group that comprises a disproportionate percentage of the labeled population (Kugelmass, 1987; Office of Civil Rights, 1986;

Sigmon, 1987). They point out that there is a "rumor of inferiority" that students begin to hear about themselves. That rumor is rarely spoken aloud, but it pervades the society, the atmosphere of school and community; the rumor is present in what students are asked to do, and what they are not asked to do, and in the way they are stigmatized. It is inevitable that many students would begin to believe the rumor about themselves, and that adults do as well.

Troubled students display sociological characteristics similar to those of other minority populations. Marginalized and distrusted socially, considered dangerous and incomprehensible in their behavior by the adults around them, subjected to prolonged segregation in schools and hospitals, and served up boring and reductionistic school work that repeatedly whispers—indeed shouts—the rumor of their inferiority, troubled students would have to be truly without any intelligence to miss the point that they are considered inferior.

Erving Goffman (1963) said it well when he wrote: "By definition, of course, we believe the person with a stigma is not quite human." While an untold amount of ink is spilled to explain student deficiencies, the literature is bereft of studies or stories about helping troubled students to discover their gifts, to exploit their strengths, and to develop their intellectual interests. Of course, there is little doubt that children like those in Anne's class are disturbed or disordered in some aspects of their personalities or behavior. And there is little doubt that for some children the difficulties are pervasive. However, most of these children are, like everyone else, more than the sum of their troubles. Nonetheless, their troubles have become our constructs for them, schemata that are hard to change. A "disturbed" or "disordered" child is thus, and we cannot comprehend him otherwise.

Undoubtedly there are those who would say that my argument to reconceptualize who troubled students are ignores the key facts: These children are massively difficult to manage and to teach; they present themselves to the world in ways that often make them difficult to even like, much less to engage in any depth; and the chances of them improving to the point of self-sufficiency are slim. Of course, those facts are compelling. However, we must reconcile them with the equally compelling fact that troubled children can and do have strengths and possibilities. This requires an effort of thought. It is that effort that Anne has undertaken, and one that other teachers—and the field as a whole—must undertake as well.

Stress Academic and Intellectual Pursuits

A main implication of Anne's story is that intellectual and academic pursuits can and should be moved to a central position in our conceptualization of troubled children and should be braided closely with our behavioral, social, and emotional teaching efforts. For too long we have kept social and behavioral considerations uppermost with these children, compartmentalizing our work with them and inadvertently denying them the power of their intellects. We can no longer ignore that when our students are engaged at an appropriate intellectual level and with reference to their complete developmental profiles, they can be trusted to learn in active and participatory ways. Clearly, that learning will proceed with difficulties and setbacks, but it can proceed nonetheless.

In Anne's work we see a teacher who models her efforts around students' proficiencies, and not just their deficiencies. Anne works with her troubled students as though they were people with possibilities, with intellects that can be stimulated and directed toward productive ends. Of course, they need a reason to learn and to make meaning out of the learning—but they can be trusted to engage. She does not deny that they are extraordinarily difficult to teach, given their behaviors. But her effort of thought is to shift her focus, and her students' focus as well, away from their weaknesses and onto their strengths, to help students put their weaknesses in the context of themselves as whole persons. In Anne's classroom, her students are encouraged to do more than avoid punishment or seek rewards from adults; they are taught to seek the inherent rewards of successful socialization and of intellectual stimulation.

Knitzer, Steinberg, and Fleisch (1990), in their critique of the education practices in classes for disturbed children, argue that the curricula put too much emphasis on controlling children and not enough on teaching children to control themselves. However, in Anne's practice we see that she places importance on developing a child's curiosity about the empirical world, which eventually brings the child to where he is willing to learn new ways of behaving, new reasons for self-control, in order to continue his investigation. The child chooses to behave so that he can get something positive for himself. In an essay entitled *I, Thou, and It,* David Hawkins (1974) writes of this phenomenon when he argues that some children have turned their attention to manipulating other people. But, he says, manipulating objects or ideas, and not people, is the truly liberating activity and ought to be the goal of education.

> One thing such a child cannot do is to get wholeheartedly involved in anything else; he has to be watching all the time to see what the adults and the other children think about it. But if you can set enough traps for him, if you can keep exposing him to temptations, if he sees other children involved and not paying any attention to the teacher, he is left out in the cold. So the temptations of bubbles or clay or sand or whatever it is are reinforced by the fact that other

children aren't playing his kind of game. If such a child once forgets his game, because he *does* get involved in shaping some inanimate raw material, in something that's just there to be explored, played with, investigated, tried out, then he has had an experience which is liberating, that can free him from the kind of game-playing he's got so expert at. He comes, after all, from a species that is called *homo faber.* If he doesn't get free of manipulating persons somewhere in his life, that life is going to be a sad one. In the extreme case perhaps it will even be a psychotic one. Children of this extreme sort are a special case, but being extreme, in a way they tell us a lot about what is involved in the three-cornered relationship of my title. They seek to get and to keep, but cannot yet even begin to give. For the verb *to give* has two objects and only the indirect one is personal. The direct object must be something treasured which is not I, and not Thou. (p. 61)

Hawkins's words evoke our memory of Anne discussing her students huddled around a jar with a butterfly, watching the process of metamorphosis, and forgetting to get into trouble. His words accurately capture the essence of Anne's thinking about her students and about the kind of curriculum and pedagogy that best suit their needs. Anne thinks that by engaging her students' minds, she intervenes in their social and behavioral difficulties. Moreover, she believes that because they are part of the species, disturbed children can come to actually choose learning—if they are given the opportunity.

This conceptualization of our students, what they know and what they can do, implies a parallel change in our concept of ourselves as teachers—our purpose, the knowledge we need to meet that purpose, and the intellectual means we must employ in daily practice.

If our students are to engage in intellectual pursuits, it follows that our purpose can no longer be merely "to deliver instruction" from preformed packages of information, as is the current practice. Instead, teachers must work to create and enliven learning contexts that provide the opportunity for student interests to be piqued and their learning needs to emerge. We must find fresh, innovative, and appropriate ways to reconcile those learning needs with the requirements of society—and not just those that call for behavioral and social control and conformity. In a classroom that respects individuals for their intellect and strengths, our purpose must be to avoid the reduction of our troubled students to the sum of their problems.

Develop Professional Knowledge

To address the needs of our students in their complexity, we need to develop our professional knowledge in at least three general areas: our knowledge of child development, our content knowledge, and our pedagogical knowledge. Looking at Anne's case, we see how deep and detailed that knowledge can be. She has developed, through her formal education and through supervised clinical experience, knowledge of normal child development, emotional disturbance, group behavior, ecological theory, family systems, and behavioral management. For her, this is knowledge that she must use every day to locate and address the problems her students experience. It is knowledge that her superiors expect her to have and to continue to develop. That is why they hired her.

But she is also expected to have considerable content knowledge in reading, mathematics, science, social studies, and language development. That knowledge must be deep as well, because she is asked to put it to use in a variety of situations for children with different ways of learning. Anne and her colleagues are in the business of teaching children who, almost by definition, display the complete variety of thinking and learning styles of children. Teachers must be able to call upon knowledge from a variety of sources and perspectives if they are to have any hope of understanding, first, what their students need to learn and, second, what constitutes a best approach for teaching. Teachers of troubled children must become voracious seekers of knowledge, eschewing exhortations to adhere completely to particular schools of instruction. They are called upon to teach the Jasons of the world, whose reading disabilities require a teacher to conduct a task analysis, form a sequence of behavioral objectives, and carry out a direct teaching problem in reading. But they are also called upon to teach the Brians, necessitating that they cross over into the usual domain of progressive elementary educators and use innovative practices for deepening student understanding of the world through experiential mathematics, process writing, and whole language. Teacher knowledge must be deep, broad, and flexible. The job calls for nothing less.

Build Collaborative Support

It is a tall order, and virtually impossible to fill without a high degree of support. At the very least, teachers need a high degree of daily collaboration and extended discourse with respected colleagues that undergirds a strong problem-finding and problem-solving skill set. In Anne's case, for instance, we see a woman who has a strongly developed method for thinking through the problems of practice. She is intellectually focused and surefooted as she treads through the data on individual and group learning needs, builds curricula, and tests them. But as rigorous as her method of thinking is, she could not sustain the intensity of thought or work without collaborating with other teachers in her classroom, with members of her various teams, and in her one-to-one supervision. Such support is not a luxury; it is a requirement if a teacher of troubled children is to do her best work.

Let me take a moment, then, to re-define support in the special education context. *Support* is the input into a teacher's thought processes and class-room life that enables her to continually and effectively find and solve curricu-lar and pedagogical problems in her classroom. This is different from support in current special education service delivery models, where *support* is defined as the ancillary services provided by specialists. Psychological, reading, lan-guage, vocational, and occupational specialists are all part of the services of-fered to troubled children. These support services are entirely necessary for the care and education of troubled youngsters. Unfortunately, in many situa-tions those services take place entirely outside the classroom. Aside from re-moving the difficult student for a time, these services seem to do little that supports teachers' solving the problems of teaching and learning within their classes. Indeed, teachers seem to be increasingly dependent on these special-ized services; teachers have become deskilled (Apple, 1983), believing that they as teachers do not possess the ability to solve the problems specialists can. To a certain extent, for certain problems and children, this is probably true. No one can know all there is to know, or do all that is necessary, to teach troubled children. Nevertheless, it would seem wiser to muster our resources to strengthen the classroom environment and thereby increase a teacher's sense of efficacy in addressing students' behavioral, social, and academic needs.

In Anne's situation, we see that kind of support at work. For instance, reading specialists help her to understand student reading needs and to de-velop innovative methods for teaching. Staff is used to shrink the teacher–student ratio during instructional periods. Crisis personnel are trained to facilitate solving behavioral problems within the classroom. Language special-ists provide extensive consultation on shaping classroom environments that facilitate language development. Teams meet weekly to process events, deepen understandings, strategize for new efforts, and coordinate them. Most important, staff are provided the opportunity to work individually with a supervisor whose job it is to help teachers improve their efficacy in class-rooms. A full description and analysis of these, and other, supports at Brigh-ton could fill a second volume.

Schools are places where students should be recognized for their poten-tial, and every effort must be made for them to reach that potential. This is no less true for troubled students than it is for those whose development has been more placid. Schools are also places where teachers work and learn, and efforts must be made for them to reach their potential as well. We must think again about how we define troubled students, recognizing their strengths as well as their problems. In doing so, we also must necessarily rethink who their teachers are. They too are people of intellect and purpose who, if supported effectively, will help us meet the challenge of teaching troubled children.

EXPANDING OUR THEORY OF CURRICULUM AND PEDAGOGY

A change in our conceptualization of troubled students requires a re-examination of our theory of curriculum and pedagogy. There is little doubt that our current theories must be expanded to incorporate new and innovative notions about teaching. Unfortunately, applied behavioralism, with its admittedly effective methods for both managing and reshaping student behavior, has become the de facto curriculum in classes for disturbed children. Absent in these classes is a sense of exploration of the empirical world or an emphasis on building knowledge. Steinberg and Knitzer (1992) have delineated this problem clearly.

> Curriculum and behavior management, most often in the form of behavior modification, have become merged. . . . This merging . . . into what we call the curriculum of control has many negative educational consequences. It strongly influences what information teachers try to help children absorb by putting a premium on isolated responses and behaviors rather than patterns and concepts and making connections between concepts. It affects how teachers teach by concentrating on product rather than on process and on forms of learning (academic and social) that are easily measurable. It causes teachers not to give priority to helping students think out issues and problems. It defines and delimits the relationship between teacher and child by assuming that all questions have right or wrong answers and making the teacher the arbiter and reward-giver. It narrows the range of peer relationships by distrusting interactions between peers, assuming that they are by definition disruptive and in need of containment. (p. 148)

Our behaviorist approaches are clearly geared toward controlling children's learning and teaching them to conform to teacher expectations. Indeed, the investigation of real phenomena is often considered dangerous with hard-to-control children (Latus, 1988), and it is considered better to reduce stimulation rather than enhance it. By controlling the information children are exposed to, and by teaching objectives incrementally, teachers are supposed to manage planning, instruction, and testing more efficiently. But these assertions are flawed.

Consider the teaching model suggested by Mastropieri and Scruggs (1987), who have given considerable attention to what they consider to be the academic needs of hard-to-control children. This curricular approach relies heavily on controlling student behavior and is based entirely on their interpretation of the variables that have resulted from so-called teacher-effectiveness research. For instance, that research has indicated that behaviorally disordered students have fallen behind their cohorts in covering the school curriculum; therefore, the authors assert, it is important that the content of the curriculum be covered quickly. Otherwise, the students will have no hope of ever being mainstreamed, which is the most important goal of special education.

According to these authors, the first thing that every teacher must do is adopt the district curriculum scope and sequence, and edit it for any objectives that will not appear on competency tests. Second, the teacher should analyze the objectives to determine which *types of learning* the objectives require of the students: Will they be learning to *discriminate*, or will they need to learn *facts, rules, procedures*, or *concepts*? Once each objective is determined for type, the teacher should analyze the objectives for *levels of learning*. The authors maintain that there are six levels of learning: *identification, production, acquisition, fluency, application*, and *generalization*. When the types and levels have been determined, the teacher is to organize the objectives into sequential lessons and to deliver those lessons as quickly and efficiently as possible. Finally, the authors point out that research has indicated that to maximize the amount of learning that takes place, every lesson *must* include the following: daily review; presentation by a teacher; guided practice; corrective feedback; independent practice; weekly and monthly reviews; and formative evaluation. No mention is made of exploration or investigation of phenomena, or of the discussion of ideas.

These authors developed the effective teaching variables into model lesson plans, one of which I include in Table 10.1 to provide a comparison with the ways in which Anne conceives her lessons.

Mastropieri and Scruggs warn a teacher delivering such a lesson not to engage in any discussion with students that is outside the objectives of the lesson. Teacher off-task behavior is defined as unnecessary digressions such as talking about personal experiences or about such things as "different kinds of cars during the solving of miles per hour word problems" (1987, p. 7). These warnings are disconcerting. Obviously, sustained digressions and unclear language are not conducive to learning. But there is no reason to believe that personal experience and interesting digressions used wisely might not enhance the interest and engagement of students, not to mention build more meaningful human relationships. But such is the curriculum of control and conformity—it reduces students to subjects and teachers to technicians.

Besides the dehumanizing aspects of these curricula, critics of current special education practices point out that these curricula and methods, used to the exclusion of other methods and curricula, needlessly reduce learning to facts and rules (Heshusius, 1984, 1986a, 1986b, 1988) and probably preclude learning critical thinking skills (Bickel & Bickel, 1986). I have already argued here that rubrics such as these may negatively affect troubled students' self-esteem. Students can perceive in such treatment an undue emphasis on what they cannot do well and often a complete absence of opportunity to do

TABLE 10.1   An example of the Mastropieri and Scruggs method

Sample Lesson to Teach the Main Idea

Review	T: Remember all last week and yesterday we practiced identifying the main ideas from stories after we read them? Who can tell me what the main idea is? [Signal]. S: The main idea is a summary statement of the story
Goal statement and teacher	T: That's right, the main tells us in one sentence what the story is about. The main ideas we identified yesterday were selected from multiple choice items. Today we are going to practice coming up with the main ideas on our own. First, watch how I do this example. [Reads paragraph out loud while students follow along silently]. Now the main idea of that paragraph is [states main idea] because it tells us in one sentence what that paragraph is about. Remember, the main idea is not simply a fact or detail from the story. The main idea tells more of the general idea of the whole story. Let's read the second paragraph together. [Signal, everyone reads]. Now, what would be a good main idea statement? S: [States main idea].
Summary and review	Let's review the answers to the examples you just completed. [Reviews answers]. Today we practiced writing the main idea after we read passages. Remember the main idea is a summary statement telling us what the passage (or paragraph) is about.
Formative evaluation	T: [Distributes sheets]. Now will give you a 5 minute quiz. Please read the next three paragraphs silently. After each paragraph write the main idea. Any questions? Ready? Begin.

Source: Mastropieri and Scruggs (1987), *Effective Instruction in Special Education*, p. 151.

what they can do. There is also a subtle implication that to be troubled means that one is of a lesser ability and in need of less intellectual stimulation.

When we compare Anne's curriculum and pedagogy with those of Mastropieri and Scruggs, we can see important differences in what students ought to learn, how they ought to learn, and the role the teacher ought to take in the teaching–learning enterprise. Because Anne respects her students' intellect and expects that by developing their minds they will increase their chances for a better life, she takes a holistic approach in her teaching. She encourages students to encounter whole problems and ideas, and does not mete out the parts of an idea in carefully sequenced patterns. She is interested in how the individual student is developing cognitively and socially, and not just in what the students might need for success in public school. Therefore, the content she teaches is gathered from neither published taxonomies nor district sequences, but is based on carefully inciting students' interests in words, stories, numbers, and patterns—and then negotiating with the boys the subsequent path of their learning. In Anne's pedagogy, students learn by doing work within the subject, using the methods of the subject: The child learns to do math by doing math; to read by reading; to write by writing. The facts, rules, and procedures of math are learned not didactically, as in the Mastropieri and Scruggs model, but in the context of boys solving mathematics problems.

In a refreshing development, more recent writings of Scruggs and Mastropieri (1993) have suggested that discovery- and activities-based curricula in science might be conducive to learning in students with disabilities. They point out that activities-oriented curricula de-emphasize reading from texts, provide beneficial concrete experiences, and may heighten attention, motivation, and social skills of students with disabilities. They warn against the use of materials that might be used inappropriately by troubled students, but appear to have become more open to the possibilities of alternative methods to direct teaching only.

Anne's curriculum does not atomize what students are to learn; nor does she atomize her pedagogy. She does not reduce the learning context to easily managed and compartmentalized areas of space or time. In fact, she places the boys in the midst of intellectually stimulating situations, thereby causing behavioral problems to arise and exacerbating social difficulties. She wants to teach the boys how to manage problems in the context of real classroom pressures. She does not think one can teach behavioral and socialization skills in the abstract, as do Mastropieri and Scruggs and other researchers. They script social skills lessons that are identical in form to the lesson plan presented earlier, thereby taking socialization out of context—when socialization is, by definition, highly contextualized learning. Anne seeks and solves problems that are decidedly complex and interactive. In her pedagogy, academic, behavioral, and social teaching are braided together in each lesson, and for each boy as well as for the group taken as a whole. Anne's pedagogy engages complexity rather than artificially reducing and avoiding it, as in behaviorist curricula.

The curriculum of control and conformity has accustomed us as teachers, administrators, and policy makers to a false sense of security. We've allowed ourselves to believe that we can account for student learning if behavioral objective sequences are followed and then checked "mastered" or "addressed" in our equally carefully constructed Individual Education Plans. Although applied behavioral curricula have helped us to successfully teach our students many crucial skills, it is foolish to assert that we have accomplished what is both necessary and sufficient for the full education of our youngsters. We need to find alternatives. In Anne's case we can see an existence proof of one effective way of conceptualizing curriculum and pedagogy that honors troubled children as whole persons and works on the assumption that they are more than their pasts predict. Such a case is not something we have previously had access to, and more cases like it are needed to enrich our understanding.

SEEKING A COMMON UNDERSTANDING

Not only does this study raise questions about who these students are, and how they should be educated; it also raises questions about where these students could be educated, and who will be able to do it. Proponents of the General Education Initiative have suggested that many, if not all, special education children be brought into regular classes. This proposal appears to overlook some important facts clearly illuminated through this study: There are children such as those in Anne's classroom, who are unlikely candidates for reintegration into any public school, at least for now. As democratic as the idea of a unitary educational system is, the needs of some children go well beyond the scope and ability of a public system that is already under attack for being unable to control its student populations and get them to learn. A moderately learning disabled child with no significant behavioral problems might benefit from being educated in a well-prepared public school classroom. But there is little doubt that a child like Paul would suffer badly in the current educational system; there is little doubt that his classmates would suffer as well. Long before Jason, Paul, Aaron, Brian, or Samuel could be even minimally successful in a public classroom, fundamental changes in the organization, staffing, curriculum, and pedagogy of American schools would need to take place.

Special Teacher versus Regular Teacher

The central players in such a change are teachers. We have learned enough from past efforts at school change to know that, without their tacit or explicit support for the GEI, it is doomed to failure (Gersten & Woodward, 1990). Long before any successful, full-scale integration project could be implemented, change would need to be wrought in the minds of the teachers who would be asked to teach such students alongside other boys and girls of less troubling propensities. Attention must be paid to the well-documented dissatisfactions and difficulties that "regular" teachers have teaching emotionally disturbed children (Braaten et al., 1988). Researchers have shown that a child's placement in emotionally disturbed classes results as much from his or her regular school teacher's tolerance for the child's behavior as it does from the child's needs (Hewett & Taylor, 1980; Knitzer et al., 1990). When Horne (1985) reviewed 20 years of research on teachers' perspectives on children with special needs, she concluded that teachers rate emotionally disturbed students as their least favored group. Such dislike, she said, resulted in large measure from teachers' feelings of helplessness. Expressions of exhaustion and powerlessness pervade teacher accounts of working with emotionally disturbed children (Latus, 1988; Martin, 1988). And once a difficult child is removed, teachers do not usually welcome the student's return. The research accents widespread bias among regular school personnel against reintegrating emotionally disturbed students, despite the Least Restrictive Environment mandate of EHA, because teachers believe that emotionally disturbed students are a drain on teacher resources and a threat to regular students (Latus, 1989).

As we have seen through Anne's story, emotionally disturbed children are extraordinarily difficult to understand and to teach. Davis (1989) points out that, as far as special education teachers are concerned, many regular classroom teachers have not yet developed the understanding, skills, or tolerances to mainstream and educate students with disabilities. In the case of emotionally disturbed students, many don't want to. Until now, very little advocacy for the GEI has come from teachers; almost all support has come from the research and policy-making community. These facts alone militate against dismantling the system. But if the GEI is to succeed, regular teachers will need to find new ways of arranging curricula, pedagogy, and classroom behavioral management to effectively teach these children.

The integration of troubled children into public schools is not a mission that regular teachers are, as yet, able to share. It is possible that they could come to share such a mission. However, it would require a much stronger alliance between special and regular education colleagues to deepen understandings about alternative, positive ways of conceptualizing troubled children and teaching them. In effect, regular teachers would need to adopt the social and behavioral mission of special education. Conversely, special educators would need to adopt the academic mission of regular public education. This is as problematic for special educators as it is for regular teachers. Paul (1985) has written that teachers of emotionally disturbed students have demonstrated a greater affinity for the psychological, sociological, and philosophical foundations of teaching emotional disturbed children than have mainstream educators. However, he concludes regrettably that, as a whole, teachers of troubled children have been unable to integrate their knowledge into discussions of pedagogy and curriculum. We have, then, regular teachers who haven't the tolerance for the psychology and behavior of troubled students, but have a strong affinity for curriculum; and we have special educators who haven't developed the necessary understanding of curriculum and academic pedagogy, yet deeply understand the troubled child. And each group is somewhat suspicious of the other.

Glatthorn (1990) speculates about four distinct aspects of this conflict between special and regular teachers. First, it would appear that special education teachers conceptualize their role differently than regular education teachers conceptualize it. A study by Dugoff, Ives, and Shotel (1985) suggests that resource room teachers see their role in assessment, consultation, and instruction to be much greater than regular education teachers believe it to be. Second, it would seem that these groups of teachers view teaching and learning differently. Special education teachers focus on individualizing instruction and developing social or behavioral skills. In contrast, regular education teachers focus more on group achievement and academic skills. Third, he points out that there are substantial language differences between the two groups, and jargon used in special education can be particularly off-putting to regular education teachers. Most important, there are differences of opinion as to which group is more effective in working with students, with each group maintaining that the other is not as effective as it is.

This antagonism is unfortunate. It is not just special education practice that would be improved by a collaboration between regular and special educators. Indeed, children of all skills and propensities would benefit from schools where teachers blended deep psychological, sociological, and philosophical understandings with developmentally appropriate and rigorous academic curricula and pedagogy. This antagonism is also unnecessary. With the effort of thought that Dewey suggests, special and regular educators could begin to share their knowledge and skills to create curricula and pedagogy that serve the greater good for all students.

Bridging the Gap

A number of researchers have suggested new avenues for developing better communication between these groups of teachers. Glatthorn (1990) suggests that a program of *cooperative professional development* be adopted that encourages small teams of experienced special and regular education teachers to set personal professional development agenda. Four different activities could be implemented. First, teams would engage in such activities as professional dialogues, where teachers meet regularly to discuss topics of common interest, in particular, teaching. This is a recommendation echoed by Miller (1990), who suggests that the development of common vocabulary is essential for discussing students, teaching, and learning, and for breaking down barriers and increasing cooperative schooling efforts.

Second, collaborative curriculum development efforts could be mounted, where not only curriculum modifications are considered, but the "big questions" of learning are explored as well. Miller (1990) writes:

> Teams can profitably focus on such curricular issues as the following: What are the long-term goals of the social studies program? How much knowledge should be emphasized? What enrichment can be provided . . . so that the curriculum for this group does not become a neverending concern with "basics," "fundamentals," and "survival skills"? (p. 32)

A third activity for teams would be peer supervision, where each teacher observes another and collects data-based observations in preparation for extended conversations about effective practice. Such a practice, carefully constructed between trusting pairs of people, could provide a rich avenue for teacher growth.

Finally, Glatthorn writes that teams could participate in peer coaching to learn particular new methods or programs. The peer coaching strategy for staff development has been developed by Joyce and Showers (1982), in part to combat the tendency of school change to crumble under the weight of teacher isolation. This strategy changes the work conditions of teachers and thereby decreases isolation and increases cooperative learning among them. Over a considerable period of time, teachers are given training in new methods, practice with peers, and subsequent mutual observation and coaching to improve and solidify learning. Showers (1990) writes that in one school with a preponderance of failing students, a peer coaching program brought together special and regular teachers to learn cooperative learning strategies on how to teach mnemonic strategies, inductive thinking, and concept attainment. After 2 years of training, the school saw student promotions based on merit increase from 34% to 95%.

In the final analysis, I maintain that teachers need exemplars whom they can analyze and discuss. We know that the literature on special education is full of suggestions for curricula that can control troubled children's behaviors on the one hand, and suggestions for optimal service delivery schemes on the other. Yet, teachers are in need of stories about people and situations that mirror their own lives. Unfortunately, scant literature exists documenting and analyzing what actually happens, academically or otherwise, in classes for troubled youngsters. This discontinuity—between what is known about actual practice and what policy makers and researchers suggest should be practice with troubled students—is deeply troublesome, particularly for those teachers who are being asked to change their practice to accommodate some of the nation's most troubling students.

It is teachers like Anne who deserve study. In her, we see a teacher whose affinity for the foundations of teaching is strongly matched by her skill and depth of knowledge of progressive curriculum and pedagogy; she has bridged the gap between what until now have been two distinct fields. Thus, Anne's story provides fresh insight into how teachers would need to think and what kinds of skills they would need to develop in order to experience success with such children. Her story is encouraging because it demonstrates that a teacher can successfully teach troubled children *academics*—something so many mainstream and special educators have been unable to imagine doing with them.

Currently in many states the dismantling of special education services for these children is being seriously contemplated, based on incomplete research. Long before educational policy makers begin making changes to the existing system of service delivery, it is imperative that they develop deeper insights into the complex problems that face teachers of troubled children. We must delineate the understandings, skills, and tolerances that both special and mainstream teachers need to work effectively with these children. Studies such as this, which unearth the dilemmas and strategies of exceptional teachers, provide a promising but sadly underused path toward that badly needed knowledge.

CODA

As I write this note, Samuel, Paul, Aaron, Jason, and Brian are all still at Brighton, nearly 5 years after they first arrived. Each has now stayed in treatment longer than most Brighton students do, and with the exception of Paul, all will be staying for at least another year. Staff had been right at the start, it seems, when they had said that these particular boys presented some of the most difficult behaviors and challenging social and emotional needs that any staff had previously experienced. In the 3 years since the end of my study, each of these five boys has lived several lifetimes of challenge, pain, and growth.

True to Brighton's mission, their parents, guardians, teachers, social workers, and child care workers have engaged those challenges, and along with the boys they have struggled through as a team, supported each other one step forward at a time, and worked unceasingly to find a better way. On this clear and mild summer day, as I make the rounds of conversations with social workers, principal, and teachers, I am struck by the pride each takes in the boys and their accomplishments, and I realize how tightly the boys have been woven into the lives of the staff. These boys are already part of the rich lore of the school and stories of their exploits abound. They have fashioned a special place in Brighton's collective memory. And as one staff member shows me photos that she has kept of Paul at rest and play, and as another reads the "best" of Jason's writing and shows me his "published" report, and as yet another vividly relates a particularly painful episode between Brian and his mother, I begin to hear in their voices and see in their eyes that these staff truly love the boys who have been entrusted to their care.

Evaluating progress is a difficult thing with children such as these. They neither began nor do they live their lives on a level playing field with others; and the social, emotional, and bodily trauma, not to mention the genetic package they were handed, comingle to handicap their growth toward self-sufficiency. The milestones for growth that educators and laypersons alike often try to superimpose over the lives of all children—measures that aggregate and therefore cheapen the inherent differences among children—simply fail to reflect the truth of childrens' lives. To see growth authentically, we must look closely to discover if the threads of a whole life are being joined where once they were torn. We must ask if a child is safe in the protection and care of loved ones. We look to see if he is respected for his gifts and not just noticed for his troubles. We search for evidence that he is finding meaning in his own work and accomplishments without belittling himself. We look for increased self-control, a budding sense of power to meet the demands of childhood, and an interest in making and sustaining relationships. Above all, we look to see if his dignity has been restored to him.

Perhaps Paul and his family have experienced the kind of success that one could hope for with these troubling boys. For the past 2 years he has been a day student, and in August of 1993 he will be leaving Brighton to attend a substantially separated sixth grade classroom in public school. His mother and family, homeless when Paul first came to Brighton, have had a home for 3 years now, and his mother has a permanent job. They were aided in this endeavor by an agency outside of Brighton, especially by one social worker who also happened to be the spouse of Brighton's executive director. A strong web of interagency—and personal—support helped to stabilize this family, and it is the kind of support all these children and families need.

Paul's homelife, judging by all reports, is going relatively well. He has been successful in his neighborhood and seems to get along adequately with his siblings and neighborhood peers. At nearly 12 years old, he remains a highly anxious and impulsive child in need of tremendous adult support and attention. When it was suggested he attempt a transition to public school in the fall of 1992, his anxiety overwhelmed him, and before long he was attempting to jump out windows and was climbing onto the roofs of buildings. The team pulled back from the plan and decided for one more year at Brighton. Almost immediately, he calmed; and as part of a new transitional plan that lasted throughout the spring of 1993, a staff member picked him up at home one morning a week and brought him to the public school and classroom it was hoped he would attend. Once there, the two of them participated in a full morning of classes; gradually, as the spring wore on and Paul became acclimated, the staff member withdrew from the class. Paul remains anxious about his impending move, but he is also ready.

Paul currently is reading and doing math at a solid third grade level, and is being taught at a highly supported fourth grade level. His fund of general knowledge, though, is that of a late fifth grader. He participates in learning with vigor when he is at peace, and in a whiny and infantile way when he feels unsure or frustrated. All of his teachers' reports continue to emphasize his enthusiasm for learning, as well as his incredibly high need for adult structure, clear expectations, and small groups in order to keep his anxieties in check. They also discuss how he can be negatively impacted by his peer group. They talk, too, about how caring he is, and how he is able to lead his classmates in important and deep discussions, and how there is a touch of the poet in him.

Samuel's growth is of a more subtle nature. He is nearly 13 years old and remains a highly atypical child whose sensory integration difficulties make it hard for him to screen out extraneous stimuli. The last 3 years have been a behavioral roller-coaster for Samuel, with periods of relative quiescence and extended periods of bizarre, out-of-control behavior that often left staff at a loss for what to do. Twice during the past years he has been sexually molested, first by a teenage boy in his neighborhood, and once by his bus driver. He has begun to occasionally expose himself and to sexualize inanimate objects, such as furniture. He has an unexplainable and violent fear of balloons; certain words, such as *eggs*, *pyramid*, and *hurricane*, cause him to become loud and silly.

Samuel's parents are his great friends and advocates, and have shown a remarkable fortitude in having Samuel live at home with them as a family. It is in this arena, his family life, where the greatest measures of success lay. Samuel is an active Boy Scout because his father takes him to every meeting and on sporadic overnight camping trips. He knows his way around his community because his mother includes Samuel in all her plans, and he is an integral part of everyday life. His mother has also come to treat Brighton as she would any other elementary school, helping out her son's teachers with trips or events. Brighton staff put a good deal of energy into supporting these parents so they can, in turn, continue to support their son.

In school, Samuel enjoys reading books, and is reading slightly below his age level. His teachers write that he is drawn to real and interesting characters, that he empathizes with them, and enjoys discussing them in class and forming his own opinions regarding their worth as people. Not surprisingly, he has a great memory for details, but much less ability to infer meaning or understanding causal relationships. His work in mathematics has stagnated at a second or third grade level, and a curriculum in life skills for math is being initiated for him. As always, he is very easily frustrated and is often resistive to doing that which he does not want to do. He is a challenge for all who interact with him, but they care deeply about him nonetheless. Most of all, it is his therapist who finds him fascinating and always enjoys her time with him. In another era, Samuel may have been institutionalized for life, left unstimulated and overlooked. But through the efforts of many people he leads an enriched social and academic life for a boy of his limitations; a year from now he will be moving on, probably to a vocationally-oriented school for adolescents.

Brian's mother was never able to care for him adequately even though the state courts and social service department insisted she have the opportunity to try. Brian began spending weekends and holidays with her in 1991, but her relationship with him was indifferent and neglectful at best and, at times, mildly abusive. A handful of abuse or neglect allegations were made by Brian's pediatrician and staff at Brighton regarding his mother and her boyfriend.

Finally, with startling maturity and insight, Brian himself voiced his great unhappiness, and asked if he could stop visiting his mother. Once again, he became a 7-day student at Brighton and a virtual orphan, although he lives in the group home and not on campus. However, his mother still will not relinquish her rights to him and free him for adoption; Brighton staff are advocating strongly that D.S.S. sue for custody. D.S.S. is ambivalent because their policy is to always reunify families.

Brian has continued to learn in school, and remains very invested and motivated. He loves novels and chapter books, and thrives with one-to-one attention. At age 10, he is doing all of his school work on or just below his expected grade level. He is an incredibly expressive child both in speech and in writing. One of his best stories from writing class goes on for 15 pages and tells the story of two friends who go to a scary movie. Most of the story is told through dialogue—with quotations, indentations, and elipses all used correctly. Not surprisingly, he remains a child whose behavior varies with his mood, and when faced with a new or tough task, is easily frustrated and overwhelmed. He remains very motivated by peer approval, but his social skills are poor, as he is frequently manipulative, provocative, or teasing.

Brian is strongly connected to staff and to Brighton because it has been his home for half of his life. He feels ownership of the place and is thankful for it in his way. He has begun a campaign to collect and redeem refundable bottles and cans, and he has been turning the money over to Alex to apply toward a new playground. He wants to contribute his allowance, too, but Alex won't let him. Such an attachment is as troubling as it is touching. He is a bright and lovable boy who needs and deserves a family and home; but he has fallen victim to a social service system that currently advocates family reunification regardless of the recommendations of those closest to the case. Brian's case is in limbo, and no one is willing to venture a guess at its outcome.

Similar issues with D.S.S. policies regarding family reunification have bedeviled Aaron and his family. Over the past 3 years, his compulsive and oppositional behavior, incredible mood swings, self-endangering episodes, and violent lashing-out increased to the point where he was briefly hospitalized twice. In an odd and illogical series of events, his adoptive parents, overwhelmed and confused about how they could raise this boy, were pressured by D.S.S. to decide if Aaron could come home to live. If he could not, social services suggested, then perhaps the family should give him up for adoption—which would mean, in effect, unadopting him. Brighton staff and other advocates were able to make the case that Aaron was an unlikely candidate for a second adoption, and that his best chances for a family remained with the one he already had. However, it was clear that the most he or his family could manage was one overnight visit and several day visits each week. This is how the case stands now, and although it is likely that Aaron will be raised in some sort of group care setting, his parents are committed to remaining closely tied to him. Currently, he is living in a Brighton group home and not on campus.

Aaron is now 11 years old, and possesses a fair amount of intellectual ability. He reads good books and does math at an age-appropriate level, and he has developed an abiding interest in ecology and the natural environment. He has begun a poster campaign at the school that encourages a range of means for protecting our natural habitat. When conditions are right, he is quite successful in classroom situations. But he remains competitive for adult attention, and is often disruptive to the flow of group activities, using his substantial verbal prowess to control other boys and be mean to them. He has immense difficulty working on sustained tasks without eventually becoming oppositional, rude, and demanding. Nevertheless, staff are hopeful that he might eventually attend a public school classroom, even though he will be returning at night to some sort of group care facility.

It seems that everyone I speak with about Jason begins with a long sigh. Perhaps of all the boys, his progress has been the most dramatic, beginning as he did as a near feral child; at the same time, he is the child least likely to lead anything approximating a normal life. In the last 3 years, his mother has been released from prison, but she and her son have yet to meet each other because neither could muster what it took to do so. She would not show for preliminary meetings; he threw a tantrum wildly at the thought of an encounter.

Jason, at 10, has begun to verbalize his intense feelings of confusion and rage instead of acting them out against people. Over the years, his vicious attacks have been many: he has kicked the broken arm of a staff member in an attempt to break the cast; in a calculated move, he has kicked a pregnant staff member in the stomach. Everyone points with pride to his movement away from violence against people, and considers it as one of two major accomplishments of 6 years of intensive treatment. How one measures progress with a child like Jason is charged with irony: It happens that he was told recently that he will be moving to an off-campus residence. This is a sign of progress to the children and something Jason has worked hard to achieve in the last 8 months. But it also happens that last night, after he moved back into his newly renovated on-campus bedroom, he gouged the words FUCK YOU in huge letters into the just dried plaster wall. Jason himself connects his actions with fear and anxiety over the impending change. Alex exhales loudly as he tells me it's progress because Jason, in his rage, didn't hurt anyone; the executive director rolls his eyes and shakes his head, angry and exasperated— and tells me it's progress; a clinical worker close to Jason laughs and says the same thing. And it is indeed progress.

After 3 more years of intensive one-to-one reading instruction, 1 year of which was spent with two half-hour sessions a day, Jason is reading on a first grade level. Staff rejoice with him over this second great accomplishment, display with pride the stories he has now written on his own, and encourage him to push onward. He remains bright and verbal, with a huge fund of general knowledge and a great sense of humor. He loves to listen to books written at a fifth grade level. But for all of his strengths he remains short-tempered, demanding, argumentative, and sometimes threatening in the extreme. He still requires a very specialized system to manage his behavior. Staff offer a bleak prognosis for his adulthood, and some see him ending up in jail. Yet, they point to the years he has been at Brighton as positive and stabilizing for a boy whom no other institution or family would take for any amount of money. Each person I speak with calls this a success, and they are probably right.

Anne is now the supervisor of the lower school classes at Brighton. In that role she still teaches tutorials and small groups, and has primary responsibility for the support and development of the teachers, curriculum, and pedagogy in those classrooms. As I write this she is at home for the summer, getting to know her newborn son, a child whose birth seems to me to be a particularly profound sign of hope.

July 1, 1993

APPENDIX: METHODOLOGY

Anne's is the youngest of six classes with the smallest number of students at Brighton. I selected Brighton and Anne's class for a number of reasons. First, for 14 years I had taught youngsters of junior high and high school age who were in some sort of separate setting as a result of behavioral or emotional difficulties, and I had, and continue to have, a strong interest in learning how troubled students can be successfully schooled. For the last 6 of those years, I worked at Brighton School. During the first 3, I was the teacher in the oldest classroom, teaching 12- and 13-year-old boys. For the next 3 years, I was a program director with primary responsibility for the older three of the six classes. Additionally, I was the coordinator of special education services and acted as liaison with the public schools. I have not worked at the school since 1988, except to consult with my successor during the first 2 years of transition. Thus, I had the benefit of knowing the institution—what it is like to teach at the school, to design and implement curricula, to be part of a treatment team, and to handle children's crises. I also had the benefit of knowing the institution from a management perspective, and have an understanding of the school's internal workings and its position in the large community. As a researcher, I was able to be a fully acclimated participant-observer at Brighton.

My second reason for choosing Anne's class was that, for all my experience within the institution, I had had limited contact with her personally, except around certain administrative business, namely, the IEP conferences that I chaired. I approached her for this study, in part, because I observed the respect given her at IEP conferences by her students' parents as well as her professional colleagues. Additionally, the children in her class made academic progress, a fact that was my job to verify as coordinator of special education. Finally, her supervisor, who was my colleague, had high regard for her skill as a practitioner. Such universal regard, combined with her documented success in academics, suggested that she was a good candidate for my study.

My third reason was that I was a teacher of adolescents and preadolescents and had little expertise in the teaching of young children. Therefore, I believed I would not be encumbered by my own biases about pedagogy. Although I knew little of what Anne did or how, I knew that both she and the children recognized me from the larger school community and that probably I would not be distracting as a participant-observer. Originally, I negotiated entry to Brighton and to Anne's class for a 1-year pilot study. When that fieldwork proved fruitful in shaping research questions, and because Anne was scheduled to teach the same group of boys, except for one, for a second academic year, I successfully negotiated the continuation of my fieldwork for a second year. I reasoned that this classroom provided a rare opportunity to conduct longitudinal research where the same teacher and students worked together for 2 academic years.

Fourth, the children who attend Brighton come from a wide geographical area and are considered by the professionals who have placed them there to be among the most challenging youngsters to teach. Fifty-four boys ages 5 through 12 attended the school in 1988, some staying for as short as 1 year and others as long as 5. At the time, the children came from 32 different towns in Massachusetts. There was a wide variability of family background, social status, and income. Boys come to Brighton through one of three routes: recommendation of a Special Education evaluation at the local school level because of pervasive emotional and learning problems; the Department of Social Services because they are in need of care and protection; or the recommendation of both agencies. At the beginning of the study, the five boys in Anne's class were diverse racially, socioeconomically, and in the troubling behaviors they presented. The class had one African-American and four white students. One boy was homeless, two were wards of the state, one was adopted at birth and, like the fifth boy, was living with his parents in an upper middle class, suburban home. In some important ways, the boys' characteristics represented a microcosm of those that many teachers of emotionally disturbed and so-called normal children have in their classes.

Fifth, and finally, because I was known to the school administration as well as students' parents, I was able to negotiate permission to access all data on the children in this class. These data included written reports from school, social work, and child-care personnel, as well as crisis reports. I was also given permission to attend meetings with parents, social service agency personnel, and school personnel.

I used four strategies to collect data for this inquiry: videotaped, ethnographic observations; taped conversations with Anne elicited from watching the videotape together; semistructured interviews conducted with Anne and other key informants; and document review.

I used a hand-held video camera as my primary means of collecting observational data in Anne's class, but I also used conventional fieldnote recording. I chose to emphasize videotaping over collecting fieldnotes because it enabled me to capture far more accurately the rapid talk of the boys and teacher, the quickly shifting goals of the teacher, and the frequent behavioral

outbursts of the boys. After each session, I viewed the videotape and transcribed it into fieldnotes. This transcription enabled me to analyze and code
the observational data very finely.

During the first year of study, I videotaped Anne's class once and sometimes twice every month throughout the school year in 30-minute sessions,
usually, but not always, during writing class. Twice during that year, I conducted two 2-hour conventional field visits as well. During the second year,
1989–90, I videotaped Anne teaching in 2-hour segments once every month.
These segments covered all reading and mathematics instruction, as well as
oral language time. During the final months of the study (May and June
1990), I videotaped 2 full days in Anne's class. The object of full-day observations was to experience the classroom activity as an integrated day. During
those observations, I gathered data particularly on the movement of students
from activity to activity and Anne's transitions in curricular and pedagogical
style as she moved between subjects. It gave me the opportunity to observe
the boys doing such things as going to the library and at play, which I had
not been able to do until then. Additional observations were conducted of
Anne in supervision meetings with the school principal, while in a supervision
meeting with her teaching intern, and while she was conducting individual
year-end, academic testing with one boy.

After each videotaped class, Anne and I viewed the taped lessons together. During these sessions, I stopped the tape often to ask questions about
what she was saying or doing in the lesson, if she recalled what she was thinking, and what she was thinking or feeling as we watched. Anne also would
stop the tape when thoughts occurred to her. My goal was to locate the recurring themes in her thinking, the salient emotional and cognitive aspects of
her as a practitioner. Those discussions of immediate, concrete feelings and
thoughts invariably led to discussions of larger, more abstract philosophical
and practical thoughts in teaching and learning with disturbed children.
When an idea was spent, we returned to watching the tape. All of those conversations were audiotaped and subsequently transcribed.

During the first year, watching videotapes together elicited 10 hours of
audiotaped conversation with Anne about the boys, the curriculum, and her
pedagogy. In the 1989–90 year, the videotaped lessons elicited 5 more hours
of taped conversation. These elicited conversations, combined with the videotaped lessons, constitute the largest portion of data to be collected for this
study.

In addition to elicited conversations, I conducted three additional semistructured, open-ended interviews to investigate Anne's personal history, her
perceptions of her place in the Brighton institution as a whole, her professional relationships, and her philosophy of teaching.

Brighton is rich in written report data. I received permission to investi-

gate three classes of documents written about the students over the 2 years
of the study. The first class of documents included (1) the narrative reports,
or what Brighton teachers call "Student Profiles," written by Anne and other
educational personnel as the result of periodic academic testing; (2) narrative
quarterly and yearly summation reports on academic and behavioral progress;
(3) Anne's accumulated unit plans; and (4) the permanent products of students' work that Anne had saved. These longitudinal data assisted me in
tracking Anne's thinking on paper about her students and then cross-
checking it with her thinking gleaned from elicited conversations and my observations of her teaching.

The second class of documents included reports on behavioral crises that
transpired during the academic day. These data were helpful insofar as they
tracked the daily reasons and length of time students were out of class for
behavioral problems. The third class of documents included the "Conference
Reports" on Anne's students written by noneducational team members.
These documents are not academic in nature; they are written by therapists,
social workers, and child-care workers. But they assisted me in checking the
validity of Anne's social and emotional assessments of particular boys.

I analyzed these data in four stages. In the first stage, I tested two
hypotheses that I had drawn from sustained observation: first that Anne was
involved in three general types of instruction—behavioral, academic, and
social/emotional; second that over time her academic utterances increased,
and her behavioral talk decreased. To conduct this analysis, I used the transcribed videotaped observations from the first 6 months of fieldwork. I coded
every utterance of Anne's where she initiated some instructional move with
the boys as *Behavior*, *Academic*, or *Social*. Analysis revealed that there were
three areas of instructional talk, although behavioral and academic talk far
exceeded social/emotional talk. Additionally, although the number of academic and behavioral utterances numbered approximately the same at the
start, the number of behavioral utterances decreased while academic utterances remained relatively constant.

At the second stage of analysis, I reasoned that teacher utterances in a
particular category of instruction might denote thought in that category. To
test this hypothesis, I analyzed the conversations that were elicited from
watching the videotapes. As I've mentioned, as Anne watched a tape she
would comment on what she was thinking as she watched, and what she recalled thinking at the time of the episode on the tape. I, on the other hand,
asked her to explain why she had said something to a boy, or what she was
trying to accomplish with a given action. I coded all interviews for the first 6
months of the study using the three existing coding categories, and I matched
the videotaped lessons of the first analysis with their corresponding conversations. This coding and matching strategy yielded evidence that corroborated
my earlier findings, that is, that three areas of instruction/thinking were sa-

lient for Anne. However, it also revealed that, although academic and behavioral teaching was evident in *what* she talked about with the children, social teaching was evident in *how* she talked with them and in how she structured the environment. In other words, in elicited conversation, Anne described how she was approaching social and emotional issues implicitly, something that was less obvious in her explicit talk with the students.

At the third stage of analysis, I conducted a cross-sectional analysis of the interview data, coding all of the interviews for the 2 years by category of instruction. Analysis of Anne's conversations revealed that, over time, there was a shift in her focus among the categories. That shift corresponded roughly to the shift in teacher utterances found in stage one of the analysis: Behavioral utterances during teaching episodes, and her preoccupation with talking about student behavior as we watched the tapes, both decreased in frequency, while academic teaching utterances and talk remained constant. Furthermore, coding and sorting of the interviews revealed that an increase in her comments about the social goals of the class coincided with the decrease in her behavioral comments. This longitudinal analysis led me to divide the data into three overlapping intervals corresponding with her periods of manifest preoccupation with behavioral concerns, social/emotional concerns, or academic concerns.

In a second pass through the interview data, I analyzed each of these three categories of instruction more specifically, coding each for curriculum as well as pedagogy. I then divided the academic category of instruction into its constituent subject areas (reading, math, and writing) and coded for curriculum and pedagogy in each subject area. This cross-sectional strategy enabled me to analyze the data in each instructional category more finely. Furthermore, I coded across interviews in other categories, including Anne's overall thinking, her background, and her stories about individual boys.

Finally, having determined (1) that there were three distinct, albeit overlapping, stages of teacher thinking and action in class; (2) that each stage had an instructional preoccupation (although all three areas of instruction were clearly evident at every stage); and (3) that each instructional category revealed substantial and salient content, I divided the data temporally into each of the three intervals and conducted the final analysis. In what was largely an inductive analysis, I used the videotaped data to create as objective a narrative of the class events as I could. I paid careful attention to verbatim transcription of the boys' and the adults' talk, as well as the movement in the class and the activities that were carried out. In parallel, I worked to capture Anne's subjective experience of those same class events. I did this by listening to her talk about the events, observing her physical responses to them, and using clinical interviewing techniques in our extended discussions to understand her understanding of the class phenomenon. I then placed one description next to the other—my attempt at objective description of observable phenomena

and my transliteration of Anne's subjective experience of those same phenomena—and proceeded to analyze the relationship between the two, looking for
recurring patterns, as well as obvious discontinuties, in Anne's thought and
action. It is this final analytic stage that yielded the bulk of the information
used in writing this book.

Because I am a special education teacher and a former staff member at
Brighton, I was particularly careful to safeguard against bias throughout the
study. I have been trained in the jargon and ways of thinking used in my field,
as well as in the particular jargon and ideology of Brighton. As a result, I was
concerned that I would overlook data that I simply took for granted, that I
would under- or overinterpret particular events or discussions of significance,
or that I would fail to notice and critique aspects of the school culture that I,
as a former staff member, had once made my own. To address those validity
threats, I engaged an independent researcher to conduct the data analysis
described in stage one of my data analysis. Using the videotapes, she conducted tests of my coding system, and then together we refined the coding
and analysis strategy. I also engaged a graduate student trained in videotape
analysis, who was involved in research into the language development of autistic children, to view videotaped sessions that I transcribed and analyzed.
She critiqued my analyses of Anne's use of language, looking particularly for
unexamined data and assumptions.

A second threat to validity concerned my remaining objective about
Anne and her teaching. After working together for 2 years collecting data on
her practice, we had developed a friendly acquaintance. Although this acquaintance facilitated our deepening discourse, I took pains to remain objective and critical about her work with the children, using memos to explore
my potential biases.

Finally, because I was the major instrument of data analysis and interpretation, I guarded against erroneously interpreting Anne. On two occasions
after data collection had been completed, I shared written analyses with Anne
in order that she might discuss them and correct or verify my interpretations.
After the first completed draft of the book was prepared, she read the entire
document and offered thoughtful critiques of my analyses of her thinking,
made some minor corrections on such things as dates of events, authors of
curriculum materials, and facts about the students.

It is important to underline the fact that in doing this project I had wide
access to the private information of five children and families, as well as to
Anne's classroom practice. I assured the boys, their parents or guardians, and
the school's executive director that I would use only pseudonyms for the participants and the school. Thus, the name of the school as well as all the names
of children and adults have been changed in this document.

REFERENCES

Apple, M. (1983). Curricular form and the logic of technical control. In M. Apple & L. Weiss (Eds.), *Ideology and practice in schooling*. Philadelphia: Temple University Press.

Apter, S. J. (1984). *Childhood behavior disorders and emotional disturbance: An introduction to teaching troubled children*. Englewood Cliffs, NJ: Prentice-Hall.

Ashman, A. F., & Conway, R. N. F. (1987). *Cognitive strategies for special education*. New York: Routledge.

Ashton-Warner, S. (1963). *Teacher.* New York: Simon & Schuster.

Avery, S. (1985). *Secondary levels curriculum handbook: Program for emotionally handicapped students*. Pinellas County School Board, Clearwater, FL.

Baratta-Lorton, M. (1976). *Mathematics their way*. Menlo Park, CA: Addison-Wesley.

Berends, P. B. (1973). *The case of the elevator duck*. New York: Random House.

Bickel, W. E., & Bickel, D. D. (1986). Effective schools, classrooms, and instruction: Implications for special education. *Exceptional Children, 52,* 489–500.

Braaten, S., Kauffman, J. M., Braaten, B., Polsgrove, L., & Nelson, C. M. (1988). The regular education initiative: Patent medicine for behavioral disorders. *Exceptional Children, 55,* 21–27.

Brendtro, L. K., & Ness, A. (1983). *Re-educating troubled youth: Environments for teaching and treatment*. New York: Aldine.

Bruner, J. S. (1960). *The process of education*. Cambridge, MA: Harvard University Press.

Bruner, J. S. (1961). The act of discovery. *Harvard Educational Review, 31,* 21–32.

Cambone, J. (1990). *A review of the literature on academic curricula for emotionally disturbed children*. Qualifying paper, Harvard University, Graduate School of Education.

Carter, K. (1990). Teachers' knowledge and learning to teach. In W. R. Huston (Ed.), *Handbook of research on teacher education* (pp. 291–310). New York: Macmillan.

Clark, C. M., & Peterson, P. (1986). Teachers' thought processes. In M. Wittrock (Ed.), *Handbook of research on teaching* (3rd ed.; pp. 255–296). New York: Macmillan.

Clark, C. M., & Yinger, R. J. (1987). Teacher planning. In J. Calderhead (Ed.), *Exploring teachers' thinking*. London: Cassell Educational Limited.

Cohen, D. K. (1988). *Teaching practice: Plus ça change . . .* (Issue Paper 88–3). East Lansing: Michigan State University, Institute for Research on Teaching.

Cole, J. D., Dodge, K. A., & Kupersmidt, J. (1989). Peer group behavior and social status. In S. R. Asher & J. D. Cole (Eds.), *Peer rejection in childhood: Origins, consequences, and interventions*. New York: Cambridge University Press.

Connolly, A. J. (1988). *Key math—revised: A diagnostic inventory of essential mathematics*. Circle Pines, MN: American Guidance Service.

Cox, A. R. (1980). *Alphabet phonics*. Cambridge, MA: Educational Publishing Service.

Cutler, C., & Stone, E. (1988). A whole language approach: Teaching reading and writing to behaviorally disordered children. *Teaching: Behaviorally Disordered Youth, 3,* 31–39.

Dahl, R. (1961). *James and the giant peach*. New York: Knopf.

D'Alonzo, B. J. (1983). *Educating adolescents with learning and behavior problems*. Rockville, MD: Aspen Publications.

Davis, W. E. (1989). The regular education initiative debate: Its promises and problems. *Exceptional Children, 55,* 440–446.

Davis, W., & McCaul, E. (1989). *New perspectives on education: A review of the issues and implications of the regular education initiative*. Orono, ME: Institute for Research and Policy Analysis on the Education of Students with Learning and Adjustment Problems.

Dewey, J. (1902). *The Child and the curriculum*. Chicago: University of Chicago Press.

Doyle, W. (1986). Classroom organization and management. In M. Wittrock (Ed.), *Handbook of research on teaching* (3rd ed.; pp. 392–331). New York: Macmillan.

Duckworth, E. (1987). *The having of wonderful ideas and other essays on teaching and learning*. New York: Teachers College Press.

Dugoff, S. K., Ives, R. K., & Shotel, J. R. (1985). Public school and university staff perceptions of the role of the resource teacher. *Teacher Education and Special Education, 8*(2), 75–82.

Durrell, F. G., & Catterson, J. H. (1980). *Durrell analysis of reading difficulty* (3rd ed.). San Antonio, TX: The Psychological Corporation.

Education for All Handicapped Act (EHA). (1975). (PL 94–142), 20 U.S.C. Sec. 1401.

Edwards, L. L., & O'Toole, B. (1985). Application of the self-control curriculum with behavior disordered students. *Focus on Exceptional Children, 17,* 1–8.

Elbaz, F. (1987). *Teacher thinking: A study of practical knowledge*. New York: Nichols.

Federal Register. (1977). Vol. 42, No. 163, p. 42478.

Freeman, D. (1990). *"Thoughtful work": Reconceptualizing the research literature on teacher thinking*. Qualifying paper, Harvard University, Graduate School of Education.

Fuchs, D., & Fuchs, L. (1988). Evaluation of the adaptive learning environments model. *Exceptional Children, 55,* 115–127.

Gable, R. A., Hendrickson, J. M., & Young, C. C. (1985). Materials selection and adaptation: Strategies for combating curriculum casualties among the behaviorally disordered. *Severe Behavior Disorders of Children and Youth, 8,* 70–85.

Gable, R. A., McConnell, S. R., & Nelson, C. M. (1985). The learning-to-fail phenomenon as an obstacle to mainstreaming children with behavioral disorders. *Severe Behavior Disorders of Children and Youth, 8,* 19–25.

Gardner, H. (1983). *Frames of mind*. New York: Basic Books.

Gartner, A., & Lipsky, D. (1987). Beyond special education: Toward a quality system for all students. *Harvard Educational Review, 57,* 367–395.

Gersten, R., & Woodward, J. (1990). Rethinking the regular education initiative: Focus on the classroom teacher. *Remedial and Special Education, 11* (3), 7–16.

Glatthorn, A. A. (1990). Cooperative professional development: Facilitating the growth of the special education teacher and the classroom teacher. *Remedial and Special Education, 11* (3), 29–54.

Goffman, E. (1963). *Stigma: Notes on the management of spoiled identities.* Englewood Cliffs, NJ: Prentice-Hall.

Graves, D. (1985). *Write from the start.* New York: Dutton.

Hall, N., & Rice, R. (1978). *Explode the code.* Cambridge, MA: Educational Publishing Service.

Hawkins, D. (1974). *The informed vision.* New York: Agathon Press.

Heshusius, L. (1984). Why would they and I want to do it? A phenomenological-theoretical view of special education. *Learning Disability Quarterly, 7,* 363–368.

Heshusius, L. (1986a). Paradigm shifts and special education: A response to Ulman and Rosenberg. *Exceptional Children, 52,* 461–465.

Heshusius, L. (1986b). Pedagogy, special education, and the lives of young children: A critical and futuristic perspective. *Journal of Education, 168,* 25–38.

Heshusius, L. (1988). The arts, science, and the study of exceptionality. *Exceptional Children, 55,* 60–65.

Hewett, F. M., & Taylor, F. D. (1980). *The emotionally disturbed child in the classroom* (2nd ed.). Boston: Allyn & Bacon.

Hobbs, N. (1975). *The futures of children: Categories, labels, and their consequences.* San Francisco: Jossey-Bass.

Horne, M. (1985). *Attitudes toward handicapped students: Professional, peer, and parent reactions.* Hillsdale, NJ: Lawrence Erlbaum.

Howard, J., & Hammond, R. (1985, September 9). The hidden obstacles to black success: Rumors of inferiority. *The New Republic,* 17–21.

Jackson, P. W. (1968). *Life in classrooms.* New York: Holt, Rinehart and Winston.

Janesick, V. (1977). *An ethnographic study of a teacher's classroom perspective.* Unpublished doctoral dissertation, Michigan State University, East Lansing.

Johnson, A. (1987). Attitudes toward mainstreaming: Implications for inservice training and teaching the handicapped. *Education, 107,* 229–233.

Johnson, K. (1987). *Doing words.* Boston: Houghton Mifflin.

Joyce, B., & Showers, B. (1982). The coaching of teaching. *Educational Leadership, 40,* 4–10.

Karlsen, B. (1976). *The Stanford diagnostic test.* San Antonio, TX: The Psychological Corporation.

Kauffman, J. M. (1985). *Characteristics of children's behavior disorders* (3rd ed.). Columbus, OH: Merrill.

Kauffman, J. M., Cullinan, D., & Epstein, M. (1987). Characteristics of students placed in special programs for the seriously emotionally disturbed. *Behavioral Disorders, 12,* 175–184.

Knitzer, A. (1982). *Unclaimed children.* Washington, DC: Children's Defense Fund.

Knitzer, J., Steinberg, Z., & Fleisch, B. (1990). *At the schoolhouse door: An examination of programs and policies for children with behavioral and emotional problems.* New York: Bank Street College of Education.

Kugelmass, J. (1987). *Behavior, bias, and handicaps: Labeling the emotionally disturbed child*. New Brunswick, NJ: Transaction Books.

Lampert, M. (1985/1987). How do teachers manage to teach? Perspectives on problems in practice. In M. Okazawa-Rey, J. Anderson, & R. Traver (Eds.), *Teachers, teaching and teacher education* (pp. 106–123). Cambridge, MA: Harvard Educational Review.

Larson, S. C., & Hammill, D. D. (1986). *Test of written spelling*. Austin, TX: Pro-Ed.

Latus, T. (1988). I, Sam, and science. *Teaching and Learning: The Journal of Natural Inquiry, 3*, 3–11.

Latus, T. (1989). *The classroom teacher's role in mainstreaming emotionally disturbed students*. Qualifying paper, Harvard University, Graduate School of Education.

Lytle, J. H. (1988/1992). Is special education serving minority students? A response to Singer and Butler. In T. Hehir & T. Latus (Eds.), *Special education at the century's end: Evolution of theory and practice since 1970*. Cambridge, MA: Harvard Educational Review.

Maddux, C. D., & Candler, A. (1986). Readability, interest, and coverage of 28 textbooks on education of children with behavioral disorders. *Behavioral Disorders, 11*, 124–130.

Marr, M. B. (1982, December). *Teaching reading to behaviorally disordered students: An alternative approach*. Paper presented at the Eastern Regional Conference of the International Reading Association, Boston.

Martin, A. (1988). Screening, early intervention, and remediation: Obscuring children's potential. *Harvard Educational Review, 58*, 488–501.

Mastropieri, M. A., Jenkins, V., & Scruggs, T. E. (1985). Academic and intellectual characteristics of behaviorally disordered children and youth [Monograph]. *Severe Behavior Disorders, 8*, 86–103.

Mastropieri, M. A., & Scruggs, T. E. (1987). *Effective instruction for special education*. Boston: Little, Brown.

McCauley, R. (1984). Alternative school programming for behavior disordered children. In J. Grosenick (Ed.), *Positive alternatives to the disciplinary exclusion of behaviorally disordered students. National needs analysis in behavior disorders* (pp. 89–113). (ERIC Document Reproduction Service No. ED 249 670)

Miller, L. (1990). The regular education initiative and school reform: Lessons from the mainstream. *Remedial and Special Education, 11(3)*, 17–22.

Milne, A. A. (1926). *Winnie-the-pooh*. New York: E. P. Dutton.

Morse, W. C. (1985). *The education of socio-emotionally impaired children and youth*. Syracuse, NY: Syracuse University Press.

Morse, W. C., Cutler, R., & Fink, A. (1964). *Public school classes for the emotionally handicapped: A research analysis*. Washington, DC: Council for Exceptional Children.

Morsink, C. V., Soar, R. S., Soar, R. M., & Thomas, R. (1986). Research on teaching: Opening the door to special education classrooms. *Exceptional Children, 53*, 32–40.

Office of Civil Rights. (1986). *Elementary and secondary civil rights survey, 1984: National summaries*. Washington, DC: U.S. Department of Education.

Office of Special Education and Rehabilitative Services (OSERS). (1979). *First annual report to Congress on the implementation of the Education of the Handicapped Act*. Washington, DC: U.S. Department of Education.

Office of Special Education and Rehabilitative Services (OSERS). (1988). *Tenth annual report to Congress on the implementation of the Education of the Handicapped Act*. Washington, DC: U.S. Department of Education.

Paul, J. (1985). Where are we in the education of emotionally disturbed children? *Behavioral Disorders, 10,* 145–151.

Paris, S. G. & Winograd, P. (1990). Promoting metacognition and motivation of exceptional children. *Remedial and Special Education, 11*(6), 7–15.

Peterson, P. L. (1988). Alternatives to student retention: New images of the learner, the teacher, and classroom learning. In L. A. Shepard & M. L. Smith (Eds.), *Flunking grades: Research and policies on retention* (pp. 174–201). New York: Falmer Press.

Petty, R. (1989). Managing disruptive students. *Educational Leadership, 20,* 26–28.

Piaget, J. (1966). *The origins of intelligence in children.* New York: International Universities Press.

Putnam, J. (1984). *One exceptional teacher's systematic decision-making model* (Research Series No. 136). East Lansing: Michigan State University, Institute for Research on Teaching.

Richardson, K. (1984). *Developing number concepts using unifix cubes.* Reading, MA: Addison-Wesley.

Rosewell, F. G., & Chall, J. S. (1978). *Rosewell–Chall diagnostic reading test of word analysis skills* (rev. and ext.). La Jolla, CA: Essay Press.

Ruhl, K. L., & Berlinghoff, D. H. (1992). Research on improving behaviorally disordered students' academic performance: A review of the literature. *Behavioral Disorders, 17,* 178–190.

Sarason, S. (1971). *The culture of schools and the problem of change.* Boston: Allyn & Bacon.

Schön, D. (1983). *The reflective practitioner.* New York: Basic Books.

Scruggs, T. E., & Mastropieri, M. A. (1993). Current approaches to science education: Implications for mainstream instruction of students with disabilities. *Remedial and Special Education, 14*(1), 15–24.

Shepard, L. A. (1987). The new push for excellence: Widening the schism between regular and special education. *Exceptional Children, 53,* 327–329.

Showers, B. (1990). Aiming for superior classroom instruction for all children: A comprehensive staff development model. *Remedial and Special Education, 11*(3), 35–39.

Sigmon, S. (1987). *Radical analysis of special education.* New York: Falmer Press.

Singer, J., & Butler, J. (1987). The Education for All Handicapped Act: Schools as agents of social reform. *Harvard Educational Review, 57,* 125–152.

Singer, J., Butler, J., Palfrey, J., & Walker, D. (1986). Characteristics of special education placements: Findings from probability samples in five metropolitan school districts. *The Journal of Special Education, 20,* 319–337.

Small, R., Kennedy, K., & Bender, B. (1991). Critical issues for practice in residential treatment: The view from within. *American Journal of Orthopsychiatry, 61*(3), 327–338.

Stainback, W., & Stainback, S. (1984). A rationale for the merger of special and regular education. *Exceptional Children, 51,* 102–111.

Steinberg, Z., & Knitzer, J. (1992). Classrooms for emotionally and behaviorally disturbed students: Facing the challenge. *Behavioral Disorders, 17*(2), 145–156.

Stephens, T. M. (1977). *Teaching skills to children with learning and behavior disorders.* Columbus, OH: Merrill.

Viadero, D. (1990, April 25). Schools falling short in aiding emotionally disturbed, study says. *Education Week.*

Vorrath, H. H., & Brendtro, L. K. (1985). *Positive peer culture.* New York: Aldine.

Vygotsky, L. (1978). *Mind and society.* Cambridge, MA: Harvard University Press.

Walker, D., Singer, J., Palfrey, J., Orza, M., Wenger, M., & Butler, J. (1988). Who leaves and who stays in special education? A 2-year follow up study. *Exceptional Children, 54,* 393–402.

Wang, M. C. (1980). Adaptive instruction: Building on diversity. *Theory into Practice, 19,* 122–128.

Wang, M. C., & Walberg, H. J. (1985). *Adapting instruction to individual differences.* Berkeley, CA: McCutchen Publishing Corporation.

Wang, M. C., & Walberg, H. J. (1988). Four fallacies of segregation. *Exceptional Children, 55,* 128–137.

White, E. B. (1952). *Charlotte's web.* New York: Harper & Row.

White, R., Beattie, J., & Rose, T. (1985). A survey of state definitions of behavioral disorder: Implications for adolescent programming. *Programming for Adolescents with Behavioral Disorders, 2,* 118–126.

Will, M. C. (1986). *Educating children with learning problems: A shared responsibility. A report to the Secretary.* Washington, DC: U.S. Department of Education.

Wilson, S., Shulman, L., & Richert, A. (1987). 150 ways of knowing: Representations of knowledge in teaching. In J. Calderhead (Ed.), *Exploring teachers' thinking.* London: Cassell Educational Limited.

Ysseldyke, J. E. (1987a). *Instructional tasks used by mentally retarded, learning disabled, emotionally disturbed, and non-handicapped elementary students* (Instructional Alternatives Project: Report No. 2). Washington, DC: Office of Special Education and Rehabilitative Services.

Ysseldyke, J. E. (1987b). *Instructional grouping arrangements used with mentally retarded, learning disabled, emotionally disturbed, and non-handicapped elementary students* (Instructional Alternatives Project: Report No. 3). Washington, DC: Office of Special Education and Rehabilitative Services.

Ysseldyke, J. E. (1987c). *Academic engagement and active responding of mentally retarded, learning disabled, emotionally disturbed, and non-handicapped elementary students* (Instructional Alternatives Project: Report No. 4). Washington, DC: Office of Special Education and Rehabilitative Services.

Index

teacher knowledge of, 135, 138–139
teacher's theory of, 157–163
Curriculum theory, 7, 157–163, 175–179
Cutler, C., 7
Cutler, R., 2

Dahl, Roald, 123
D'Alonzo, B. J., 6, 95, 168
Davis, W. E., 8, 180
Decision making, by teacher, 25–26, 142–148, 153, 154
Decoding, 125
Developing Number Concepts Using Unifix Cubes (Richardson), 159
Developmental theory, 7, 136, 172–173
Dewey, John, 151–153, 181
Dodge, K. A., 9
Doing Words (Johnson), 143, 159
Doyle, W., 125–126, 156
Duckworth, Eleanor, 7, 27, 159
Dugoff, S. K., 181
Durrell, F. G., 24, 120
Durrell Analysis of Reading Difficulty, 24
Durrell Test of Reading Ability, 120

Education for All Handicapped Children Act (EHA; 1975), 1, 5, 8, 9, 180
Edwards, L. L., 5
Effective Instruction in Special Education (Mastropieri & Scruggs), 177
Effective teaching and learning, 10
Elbaz, F., 135
Emotionally Disturbed (ED), 1–4
Epstein, M., 168
Expectations
  of teacher for self, 30, 41–42, 45–47, 60–61, 69, 139–140, 155–156
  of teacher for students, 38–40, 45–46, 56–58, 60–61, 69, 155–156
Experience-based instruction, 138
Expert teachers
  classroom practice of, 11–13
  defined, 10
  study of, need for, 10–11
Explode the Code (Hall & Rice), 122

Fetal alcohol syndrome, 4
Fink, A., 2
Fleisch, B., 5, 6, 169, 171

Freeman, D., 136, 142, 151
Friendly behavior, 85–86
Frightening behavior, 3
Fuchs, D., 5
Fuchs, L., 5

Gable, R. A., 6, 9
Games, 85, 98–99, 160
  mathematics, 109–111, 113–115
Gardner, H., 168–169
Gartner, A., 5, 8
General Education Initiative (GEI), 8–9, 10, 179, 180
Gersten, R., 180
Glatthorn, A. A., 181–182
Goffman, Erving, 170
Graves, Donald, 7, 124, 159
Group behavior dynamics, 56–58
  and games, 85, 98–99, 109–111, 113–115, 160
  importance of understanding, 44–47
  language of, 84–91
  primacy of group in, 91–95
  and reading activities, 95–97
  and reordering of academic curriculum, 66–70, 95–96
  stable goals and objectives for, 61–66
  teacher knowledge of, 137–138
Grouping decisions, 25–26

Hall, N., 122
Hammill, D. D., 24
Hammond, R., 169
Hawkins, David, 159, 171–172
Hendrickson, J. M., 6, 9
Heshushius, L., 7, 176
Hewett, F. M., 1, 3, 6, 95, 138, 168, 180
Hidden curriculum, 162
Hobbs, N., 2
Horne, M., 180
Howard, J., 169

I, Thou, and It (Hawkins), 171–172
Ignoring behavior, 81–83, 105–106, 145–146
Individual Education Plan (IEP), 149–150, 179
Instructional groupings, 25–26

ABOUT THE AUTHOR

Joseph Cambone has been a teacher of troubled and troubling children in public schools, residential and day treatment centers, and psychiatric facilities. He is now an assistant professor of education in the Graduate School of Wheelock College in Boston, Massachusetts.